FARMERS, TEMPLES
AND TOMBS

Farmers, Temples and Tombs

Scotland in the Neolithic and Early Bronze Age

Gordon Barclay

Series editor: Gordon Barclay

CANONGATE BOOKS
with
HISTORIC  SCOTLAND

THE MAKING
OF SCOTLAND

Series editor:
Gordon Barclay

Other titles available:

WILD HARVESTERS:
The First People in Scotland

SETTLEMENT AND SACRIFICE:
The Later Prehistoric People
of Scotland

A GATHERING OF EAGLES:
Scenes from Roman Scotland

First published in Great Britain in 1998
by Canongate Books Ltd, 14 High
Street, Edinburgh EH1 1TE

British Library Cataloguing-in-Publication Data
A catalogue record for this book is available on request
from the British Library

ISBN 0 86241 780 5

Series Design:
James Hutcheson, Canongate Books

Printed and bound by
GraphyCems

Previous page
Excavation at Clava, near Inverness
HISTORIC SCOTLAND

Contents

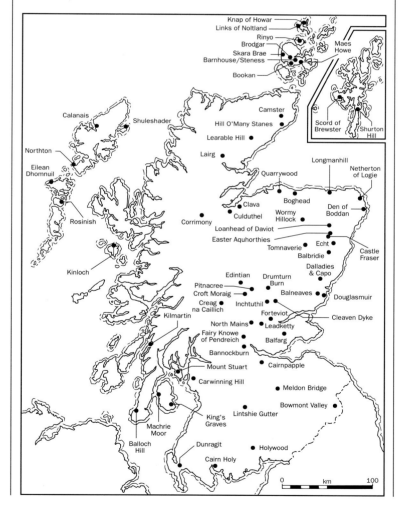

Location map
Sites mentioned
within text

Misconceptions of the Neolithic

Many people have the strangest ideas about what happened in this period of history, assuming that the ceremonial sites of the period were built by the druids, who turn up in history over 2000 years later.

Out of the Wildwood

This book describes the beginnings and development of the farming communities of Scotland until about 1500 BC, how they worked the land, how they lived, how they buried their dead and how they worshipped; the things they made and exchanged; and how they transformed the landscape.

There are many misconceptions about the period, and about the monuments that were built then. Modern 'pagans' claim some of the sites discussed here - but they mistakenly impose their search for alternative beliefs on the artefacts and the people of the past.

In the pages that follow I will be describing great monuments and simple settlements – farms, pots, metalwork. In books about the past we can sometimes lose touch with the fact that sites were built and used, farms run, and metalwork and pots made, by people; people with children and other responsibilities; people sometimes far-sighted and sensible, sometimes caring only for the short term and just as capable of making mistakes as any of us. They were indeed like us in many ways - certainly physically, although they will have had ideas about the world and the way it worked that might seem very alien to us. They cared for their ill and old, and buried the dead with great care; they designed and built great structures. Archaeology can only show us fleeting glimpses of the day-to-day lives of people, and we see them through the eyes of our modern culture. In the pages that follow think of real people. They were a little shorter than us on average. They suffered like us from the pain of injury and illness, without the resources of modern medicine, but with folk-medicine, perhaps of great sophistication. They were certainly at greater risk from death by accident and illness, had a life expectancy of 20 to 30 years less than ours, and would have had a far higher rate of child mortality. But forget any idea that they lived in a 'golden age' in harmony with their environment. They, like us, were capable of damaging their environment, and we have evidence of the disastrous consequences of their actions, for example soil erosion caused by deforestation, in prehistory.

It was in the Neolithic period that the process of creating the modern 'cultural' landscape really began. Before the first farmers began cutting the wood for agriculture, woodland covered most of the country below the tree-line (the height above which trees will not grow); Britain now has relatively little woodland compared to other European countries. The change from one state to the other has been the subject of what the ecologist Oliver Rackham has described as 'countryside myths' - the loss of woodland has been blamed on the Romans, the warfare of the Vikings (who certainly had little impact), the iron masters of the eighteenth century (who actually had more to gain from managing the woods, as they did in reality), and ship-building for the Napoleonic Wars. While all no doubt played a greater or lesser part in the history of Scottish woodlands, the loss of woodland has been caused almost entirely by one activity - the clearing of trees to provide farmland, both for growing crops and for pasture.

There is evidence of human management of the woodlands that existed before the beginning of farming - areas may have been burned or cleared to aid hunting. What is valued is protected and much woodland was preserved and managed throughout history to provide timber and other woodland products. But the clearance of the wildwood was more than half completed long before the Romans set foot upon this island - the first farmers described in this book began the process of turning a wild landscape into a domesticated one by ordering the land and cutting down the trees. This process of change has resulted in the landscape we see about us, from the sea shore to the high hills, which is far from 'natural'.

Many books on the prehistory of Scotland have perhaps over-emphasised areas where stone structures of the period survive – mainly in the uplands and the Northern Isles – and neglected areas that were of just as much importance in the past, and possibly more densely settled, in the lowlands of mainland Scotland. This book is about *all* of Scotland. I also refer to what was happening in the rest of Britain and in Ireland at this time. Even though prehistoric remains in the lowlands may not be as obvious at first sight as in the areas of stone building, they *are* there, in great profusion.

DATES

For over 40 years archaeologists have been able to use a scientific process called radiocarbon dating to tell the age of organic material (such as wood, charcoal, textiles). Radiocarbon dating does not provide real calendar dates; to provide these the raw determinations have to be calibrated using radiocarbon dates taken from materials of known age (for example wood from long-lived trees where counting tree-rings can give us an exact age). Throughout this book I have used dates based upon calibrated radiocarbon determinations – for example 'around 4000 BC'. For more information on radiocarbon dating see the 'Further Reading' list at the end of the book.

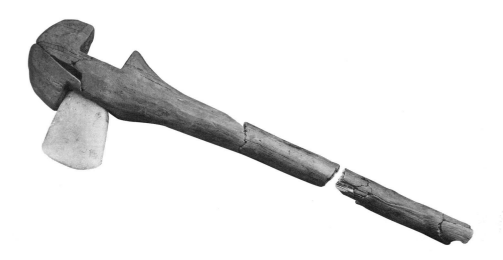

Shuleshader Axe

This Neolithic axe was found, complete with its handle – a unique discovery – in a bog on Lewis. This find shows the importance of wooden artefacts, which are rarely preserved.

NATIONAL MUSEUMS OF SCOTLAND

What is the Neolithic?

The Neolithic (the word means 'new stone age') is the period of the first farmers in Britain. Around 4000 BC, for the first time, people began to use domesticated animals and plants (both introduced from continental Europe) as food sources. New technology was also introduced – pottery and polished stone axes (although some of these were found earlier in Wales). Around the same time people began to build large tombs for burial.

What came before?

By around 8000 BC the last ice sheets of the most recent Ice Age had melted and the climate was warming rapidly. The ice in large glaciers can be more than 2km (over 1 mile) deep, accumulating on high, cooler ground and moving downwards and outwards to lower, warmer levels; in doing this they exert colossal stresses on the underlying land, grinding out deep valleys and wearing down hills. The ice sheets over Scotland comprised billions of tonnes of frozen water. As they melted, vast quantities of silts, sands and gravels created by the grinding effect of the glaciers on the underlying rock, were washed over the lower land, transforming the landscape into a general shape we would recognise today. However, it was a devastated landscape of gravel, sand, and lochs. There was no soil and at first nothing lived there; in some areas boulders would have been thickly strewn across the land.

A Glaciated Landscape
This scene is in Iceland. Scotland looked like this 10,000 years ago, and only hundreds of generations of natural processes and hard work can turn this into the landscape we know today.
NOEL FOJUT

Over the following hundreds and thousands of years the soils developed by natural processes (such as water action, frost, chemical reaction), reflecting the type of rock or glacial outwash on which they formed. Plants colonised the land – first herbs and shrubs, such as sedges, birch, dwarf willow, juniper and the like, then denser woodland, such as oak, hazel and elm over most of the lowlands, birch, hazel and oak in the north-east, and pine and birch in the Highlands. With the trees came animals – bears, wolves, wild cattle, wild pig, squirrels, otters, hedgehogs, voles and shrews. To the coasts, rivers and lochs came fish and to the skies, birds. And finally, with the animals and the fish, came the people who hunted and fished, and gathered the products of the forest – such as nuts and fungi: the 'hunter-gatherer-fishers'. The story of these people is told in detail in Bill Finlayson's companion book in this series *Wild Harvesters*, but we must describe them briefly here, because to understand the first farmers, we must try to understand their predecessors.

These 'hunter-gatherer-fishers' exploited the natural resources of the land – they hunted large and small animals, birds, freshwater and coastal fish, and gathered shellfish in great quantities. They built complex traps for

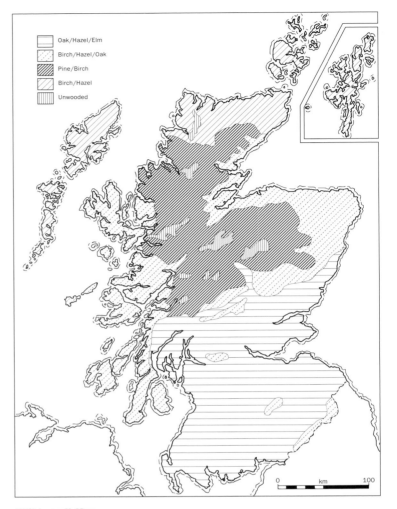

'Wildwood' Map
The makeup of the 'wildwood' after the last glaciation. *After Edwards and Whittington*

Legend:
- Oak/Hazel/Elm
- Birch/Hazel/Oak
- Pine/Birch
- Birch/Hazel
- Unwooded

fish, and skilfully fashioned tools of flint and other stones. Too often these people are still thought of as 'squat grunting savages', a misconception from the days when our ancestors preferred to believe that modern equivalents of such people, for example the native Australians, were 'lesser beings' in order to ease the theft of the natives' land by European colonists. These native peoples were not 'primitive', in the sense of stupid or simple: peoples who pursue a hunting and gathering way of life have complex social structures, ancient and sophisticated religious beliefs, traditions of occupation and use of landscapes, all preserved in oral history and traditions of story-telling. They make tools and art of great complexity. The limited evidence we have from archaeology suggests that our hunter-gatherer-fisher ancestors were just as sophisticated.

Clearing the Land

Before the first farmers, much of Scotland was covered by woodland. Around 3800 BC, however, there occurred the most widely recognised environmental event in this period - the sudden and substantial decline in the elm population of Britain and Ireland; the amount of elm pollen falling into bogs dropped by some 50 per cent. At one time this was thought to be a direct consequence of human intervention - such as the feeding of elm to animals or the felling or pollarding of trees. However, human activity alone cannot account for the vast scale of the decline and it is more likely that the reduction was caused by elm disease of the kind that has affected Britain in recent years. Pollen analysis of bogs has also recovered traces of cereal pollen some time before the elm decline, around 5000 to 4500 BC, probably indicating that farming of some kind was already going on.

What is farming?

Farming is both a system of food production, and a series of beliefs and attitudes. Reliable food production involves skilful management of animals and plants in varying conditions; the beliefs and attitudes include how people think about land and its ownership, perhaps in different ways from hunter–gatherer–fishers. Farming also necessitates different social and economic systems for the exchange of goods, customs and religious beliefs related to the cycle of the seasons. Archaeology can answer some of the questions about how farmers first tilled the fields of Britain, how they lived, something of what they believed, and how they organised their society.

There are some basic building blocks of a farming way of life and most of these were introduced into Scotland: they are *domesticated animals* - cattle (the local wild cattle were larger), sheep, goats and pigs; *domesticated plants for eating* – cereals like wheat and barley, and beans; and *domesticated plants for other uses* – for example, flax for making cloth. Not all of these are needed, as some farming societies, for example, may be based solely on the herding of cattle, with little or no planting and harvesting of crops.

The use of local, naturally occurring foods and other resources is found in every non-industrial farming system. In particular, local wild food sources are used – freshwater or sea fish, small and large game animals, nuts, herbs and fungi. The natural resources of the land are also exploited, such as in the mining of stone for tools.

Since people first came to Scotland they have been cutting,

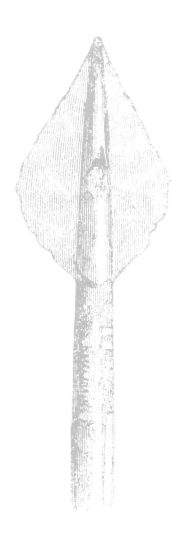

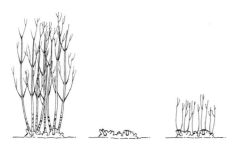

Coppiced Tree

How a coppiced tree is managed. When a tree, like hazel, is cut down, it will send up new shoots from the stump – these thin straight 'rods' can be used for making baskets and hurdles, hafting tools or making fences. The 'rods' can be cut every few years for a very long period – hundreds of years in some tree species. The rods begin to grow again straight away.

After Rackham

preserving and managing Scotland's forests. Farmers were then, as they have been throughout history, the main fellers of woodland, to clear land for agriculture. There is evidence that the hunter-gatherer-fishers were clearing hunting areas by fire, and they certainly used wood to make their tools and shelters. But they also learned very early to manage woods, to ensure consistent supplies of large forest-grown trees for building, and lighter wood for fences, firewood and wooden handles of tools, and so on. The lighter wood can only be guaranteed by active management of woodland, for example by coppicing. There is limited evidence in Scotland, but elsewhere in Britain we have evidence of Neolithic and Bronze Age people managing woodland for a number of different purposes – to make planks and beams, poles and pegs, bowls, baskets and other containers.

Where did farming come from?

The ultimate origins of the domesticated crops that formed the basis of farming in Britain lay in the lands bordering the eastern Mediterranean - the Levant, Turkey, the Balkans. Here the wild ancestors of modern cereal crops grew naturally in dense stands. Intensive use and management of these wild plants by hunter-gatherer-fishers led to the development of particularly useful and productive domesticated variants. Much the same processes governed the development of domesticated variants of sheep, cattle and pigs. As people managed these resources more and more intensively, a recognisable 'farming' system developed.

Farming as a way of life spread rapidly across central Europe – apparently by people moving to seek new land. By around 5000 BC the fertile soils of the major north European river valleys supported farming communities who lived in long timber houses, made pottery containers, cultivated wheat, barley, lentils and flax, and raised domestic cattle, pigs and sheep. In the westernmost areas, farmers may have been indigenous peoples who had adopted farming, rather than colonists. Somehow the actual domesticated animals and cereals, as well as the knowledge of how to manage them, and how to make pottery, were transported across the North Sea to the British Isles. However, we know very little about how farming was adopted by the hunter-gatherer-fisher communities of the north-west continental coast.

Local development or foreign import?

Precisely how farming came to replace hunting and gathering as the predominant way of life in north-west Europe and Britain is a matter of considerable argument. Nowhere in Britain have we yet discovered anything that looks like a farm or house-type transplanted from the continent to Britain. The best candidate for a structure built by incomers, although perhaps not by early generations, is at Balbridie near Aberdeen, which may be compared (but only in very general terms) to continental structures. However, very few sites have yet been excavated by archaeologists.

We do not fully understand how agriculture became the way of life of the majority of Britain's people. Was the existing population of hunter-gatherer-fishers replaced by an immigrant population from continental Europe? Did the local population adopt farming gradually, with little influence from abroad? The answer probably lies somewhere between – there were immigrants who brought the

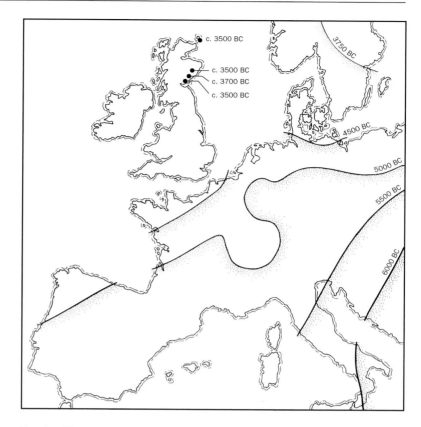

Farming Map
Map showing the approximate dates by which farming has spread across Europe.
After Bradley, Ammerman and Cavallo-Sforza, with the addition of radiocarbon dates from early Neolithic sites in eastern Scotland

animals, equipment and ideas, but the local population began to adopt some or all of the ways of life, at different rates and in different ways, in the various regions of Scotland. It has been suggested that there were three stages in the change.

Firstly, the idea of agriculture became apparent to hunter-gatherers, from contact with farmers, who had the necessary domestic animals and plants and the skills to use them. Then hunter-gatherer-fishers adopted some aspects of the farming way of life and so began the process of substitution of one economic system for another. And lastly, the change was consolidated and the economic system became wholly based on farming, with consequent changes to the social structure, making a 'return' to hunter-gathering impossible.

Recent studies show that hunter-gatherer-fishers across Europe may have been using plant resources quite intensively, managing them in such a way as to preserve and maximise the resource, in the centuries before farming became established.

A Neolithic Hall
In this reconstruction of the Balbridie building, everything above ground level is conjecture.
DAVID HOGG

Pots
Some of the pottery from Balbridie.
IAN RALSTON

Balbridie excavation

The early Neolithic building at
Balbridie, during excavation.

IAN RALSTON

Balbridie

So far nothing similar to the massive
building at Balbridie, Aberdeenshire,
has been excavated in Britain, either
in scale (it is 24 metres long and 10
metres broad) or style of construction,
although broadly comparable
cropmark sites are now known
(including one on the opposite bank of
the River Dee), but have not yet been
excavated. Radiocarbon dating puts
the building around 3900–3700 BC.
The excavator of Balbridie commented
that '. . . the farmers of Balbridie were
– in terms of their building and, it
would seem, of their strategy with
cereals – closer to continental
European practice than has normally
been identified in the British Isles.'
The building can be compared very
generally to some examples on the
continent, for example one at Flögeln,
near Cuxhaven in northern Germany.
The floor surface of the house has
been lost to modern ploughing so
there is no sign of a hearth. Considerable quantities of charred grain
(emmer wheat, bread wheat and
barley) were found in some of the
postholes. It is likely that the people
living in the building also herded cattle
and caught fish in the nearby river
Dee. We have no real idea if the
Balbridie building was a house in
which perhaps an 'extended family' of
three generations lived, or some sort
of communal structure in the middle
of a settlement of smaller houses, or
an isolated building with a mainly
ceremonial or religious function.
However, it is entirely possible that
the Balbridie building does represent
a settlement built by people from the
continent, or their close descendants.

Interestingly the pottery and
cereal grain was concentrated in the
western end of the structure, implying
that different parts of the building
were used in different ways or for
different purposes.

This might have made the change to agriculture – the even more intensive use of plant and animal resources – easier to adopt. Even when farming had been adopted as the main food source in Britain, hunting and fishing continued to play an important part in most people's diet.

The Regional Dimension

Unfortunately, explanations of the Neolithic period in Britain have generally relied perhaps too much, on the results of work done in areas where most sites have been excavated - southern England, Yorkshire and Orkney. While the results of much of the work done in these parts of the country may be relevant to other areas, it is becoming clear, as more work is done elsewhere, that there is considerable variation from one part of the country to another in how farming began, and how the farming societies lived, worked, worshipped and developed. So, we cannot interpret the timber settlements of the Neolithic in Aberdeenshire using the results of the excavations on the stone buildings at Skara Brae, nor use Stonehenge and Avebury as models with which to interpret the religious life of other parts of Britain and Ireland.

The uplands

In upland Scotland many features built of stone and soil survive, particularly burial mounds. Here traditional archaeological field survey can locate and describe sites, and early antiquarians and archaeologists discovered and excavated many of them. The remains of houses and fields are far more difficult to spot, because of the lack of any upstanding elements such as a bank or ditch, or cairn, and it is only recently that much work has been done on this aspect of life in the past. Sites that were made wholly out of timber (where only filled-in postholes will mark the site) will not normally be detected without excavation.

Cairn
The chambered cairn at Cairnholy, Dumfriesshire.
HISTORIC SCOTLAND

The lowlands

In the well-drained, easily-cultivated soils of the lowlands, where human settlement has always been densest, from the time of the hunter-gatherers to the present day, the remains of past peoples have very often been removed or flattened by later agriculture. Although many sites survive here surprisingly well, we rely to a great extent on aerial photography, which in the right conditions can reveal the remains of archaeological sites no longer visible on the surface. These sites would have been built not with stone, but with turf and timber. Over centuries and millennia they have fallen down and been ploughed flat.

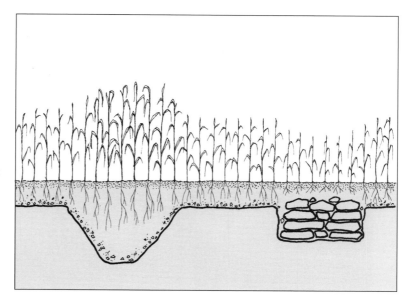

Cropmarks

How cropmarks are formed. In dry weather the cereal crop grows taller, and stays green, over the topsoil fills of a ditch, which holds water. The ditch shows up on aerial photographs as a green line of higher plants, against the ripe golden crop. Over the wall, in contrast, the crop has less water, and falters and whitens.
After Wilson

However, aerial photography will only detect sites where fairly substantial pits and postholes have been dug – it is features such as these that produce the marks, known as cropmarks, on aerial photographs. Structures built using shallow postholes, or erected wholly on the ground surface, cannot normally be detected from the air.

Serious archaeological aerial photography only began in Scotland in the mid 1970s, but the results have transformed our understanding not only of the Neolithic, but of prehistoric Scotland as a whole. We now know that thousands of sites not made of stone survive beneath the ploughed fields of lowland Scotland.

Little evidence has been found in southern England for Neolithic houses or arable farming. Many archaeologists working there feel that this evidence should have turned up by now if it existed. The conclusion they draw is that as no houses or fields have been found, few or none existed and that the Neolithic way of life was therefore mobile – for example people might have moved around with their herd of cattle, living in tents or other portable structures. Their view of the Neolithic may well be valid for southern Britain, but some of their arguments have been transferred wholesale to northern Britain, where they may be inappropriate. These archaeologists may be taking too little account of the evidence for houses that has appeared in other parts of the British Isles, and of the threats to the survival of the remains of these possibly slight timber buildings in intensively cultivated areas, where generations of farmers have ploughed and reshaped the land on which they stood.

Round Barrow
The Neolithic round barrow at Pitnacree.
HISTORIC SCOTLAND

Long Barrow
The barrow at Longmanhill. The burial mound seems to have been built in two stages – first, a round mound, then a long 'tail' added. The boundary between the two is marked by a dip.
HISTORIC SCOTLAND

The Early Neolithic

Our modern world separates daily life from religion or ritual to an extent that would be incomprehensible to a farmer in the Neolithic period. In most non-industrial societies all aspects of life, from the processes of farming to the choice of a marriage partner, from the treatment of illness and death to the relationships between and within families, are bound together by custom, mutual obligations, ritual and religion to a far greater extent

Long Cairn
A ceremony in the forecourt of a long cairn.
HISTORIC SCOTLAND

than in our own society. For convenience, we can consider ritual and religion in two ways. First, the normal everyday observances that structure daily life (such as saying grace before a meal), and the 'set-piece' religious or ritual occasion, when special places may be used and larger than normal gatherings of people come together (such as a wedding or a funeral).

Our understanding of Neolithic society in the British Isles is based largely on interpretations of the many burial and ceremonial structures that survive, and the changes over time in the way these places were used. We have far less information about the day-to-day life of these people, and of course no written evidence.

Tombs of the ancestors

The most prominent and widespread remnants of the first farmers are their burial mounds, built out of timber, turf stripped from the surrounding areas, soil and subsoil dug from ditches immediately beside the mounds, and stone cleared from fields. Over most of Britain the burial mounds of soil and stone are long, but in some places (Yorkshire and Perthshire/Angus for example) they are more often round. In much of lowland Britain (in eastern and south-western Scotland, the east and south-west of England) the mounds, whether long or round, tend to cover broadly similar complex timber mortuary structures. In other areas (in Scotland, the west, the Northern Isles, and once again the south-west), a perplexing range of stone-chambered tombs was built, reflecting practice in different areas and at different times. The major difference between the timber and stone mortuary structures is that the stone chambers could be re-entered, perhaps

Mortuary Structure
A reconstruction of how a linear zone mortuary structure might have looked in use.
DAVID HOGG

Burial Chamber
The stone burial chamber of a tomb as drawn in the 19th century.

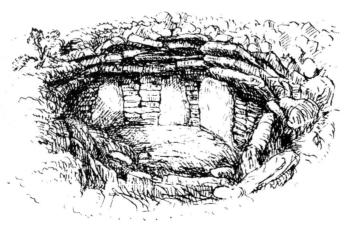

repeatedly, to bury more bone; in contrast, the wooden chambers were probably used for repeated interment of bone only while they were free-standing structures: they seem only to have been covered with mounds at the end of their use. Much ink has been spilt over the meaning of the different shapes of the stone chambers, but it has hardly advanced our understanding of the nature and use of the tombs.

Excavation of burial sites usually demonstrates one thing in common – the burial of numbers of bodies together. Often the bodies have either been defleshed before they were buried or the bones have been re-arranged later; for example, the long bones of a number of individuals being placed together in one part of a tomb, with skulls in another part. This has been interpreted as indicating that in death, people were not represented as individuals, but as part of the communal mass of 'ancestors' – taken further, this has been thought to show that the society that built these tombs was one in which individual differences in status were played down. This is in contrast to the late Neolithic, when there is evidence that this attitude changed.

Defleshing bodies prior to final burial has been practised widely. In many societies studied around the world in the recent past, death is seen as more complex than the difference between the human machine working, and then not working. Some peoples consider that there is an intermediate phase, lasting as long as the body still has flesh on it, where the spirit of the dead person is still in transition from life to death – at this time the spirit is often seen as dangerous to the living, particularly to the spouse or close relatives. Defleshing therefore may be hastened by exposing the body to animals or to birds – a process known as 'excarnation', or by putting it in a temporary grave for some months. At the end of this process the unfleshed body is usually given a final burial.

In Britain we have some evidence of excarnation. At Hambledon Hill in Dorset, part of the Neolithic enclosure complex seems to have been given over to excarnation; in one case the pelvis and upper leg bones of a man ended up in a ditch, after being gnawed and dragged round by dogs. Exposure to birds was perhaps more efficient, in that the main portions of the body were more likely to remain where one left them, although small parts such as finger and toe bones might be removed. However, to ensure that the body is not disturbed by larger creatures, a more elaborate structure is needed to protect the corpse. A possible exposure site is known at Balfarg in Fife, where two small timber enclosures had surrounded a sequence of two- and four-post structures, interpreted as platforms for exposing human remains.

Rectangular ditched enclosures identified first in southern England have been interpreted as being related to these burial traditions because they are similar to long barrows in size, shape and date. They are usually called 'long mortuary enclosures'. One such site excavated at Inchtuthil in Perthshire measured 50 metres by 10 metres and dates to about 3900 BC. A fence of posts and hurdles had been set up in the ditch, and at some time later had been set on fire. While it was still burning, it had been pushed over and gravel and soil dumped on top of it. Ploughing, however, had removed all trace of what had happened inside the enclosure, or any covering mound, and we cannot tell if the site was actually used in the disposal of the dead.

Avenues of power: cursus monuments and bank barrows

Although the burial mounds of the early Neolithic were substantial earthworks, they appear relatively insignificant in relation to two other types of monument being built in the early Neolithic - cursus monuments and bank barrows. Both kinds of monument appear to be related to the tradition of the long barrows, but seem designed to make a far greater 'statement' in the landscape. There are few reliable radiocarbon dates for either cursus monuments or bank barrows, but it seems likely that their construction started later in the early Neolithic.

Cursus monuments were so named in the eighteenth century by early archaeologists because they looked liked Roman chariot-racing tracks (*cursus* in Latin). Most cursus monuments in England, where they were first discovered, are long, rectangular ditched enclosures, the longest being the Dorset cursus, 10km and 100m wide. In most, the soil dug from the ditch was piled up on the inner edge of the ditch.

All but one of the 30 or so Scottish cursus monuments appear as cropmarks, defined either by ditches, as at Holywood (Dumfriesshire), or - a Scottish variation - by parallel lines of pits, as at Balneaves, in Angus. At Bannockburn, Stirlingshire, two sites defined by pits were excavated; one consisted of simple pits, in the other the pits had held posts. Although all these sites were

Exposure Platform
A North American Indian platform for the exposure of the dead.
PETER YEOMAN

Cursus Monument
An aerial photograph of one of the cursus monuments at Holywood.
RCAHMS

clearly related to the same tradition, it is difficult to suggest that they all had the same purpose.

Bank barrows are also very long, up to 2km. They appear to be grossly exaggerated versions of normal long barrows. There is clear evidence that cursus monuments and bank barrows are related – not least because in Scotland we have one monument that appears to be both cursus and bank barrow – the Cleaven Dyke.

Other aspects of the religious lives of the early Neolithic people were represented by less obvious structures than burial mounds, cursus monuments and bank barrows. There is consistent evidence that some sort of ceremonial activity involved the placing of, most often, burnt and broken pottery, but also stone tools and possibly organic material, in pits; the material is not thrown in, as if it were rubbish, but placed carefully, for example, lining the edge of the pit, or sealed under a carefully laid layer of stone.

Distribution Map
The distribution of cursus monuments and bank barrows in Scotland.

0   km   100

Douglasmuir Cursus
The cursus-type enclosure at Douglasmuir under excavation; the pits held massive oak posts. It was almost certainly built in two phases, one compartment after the other.
HISTORIC SCOTLAND

Opposite
Cursus Under Excavation
One of the Holywood cursus monuments under excavation. The dig revealed that the ditch had been re-excavated after it had filled in, and a screen of postholes was placed across one of the entrance gaps. RCAHMS

Cleaven Dyke

How the Cleaven Dyke probably looked during construction, over 5000 years ago.
DAVID HOGG

The Cleaven Dyke

The one Scottish cursus monument which does not appear as a cropmark is the Cleaven Dyke, Perthshire, which runs for over 2km. The central portion (1.8 km long) survives as a visible earthwork - a 9m wide bank, standing 1-3m high, running midway between two ditches, 50m apart. The construction of the Dyke has been dated to around 3300 BC.

Detailed survey of the monument has shown that it was built in five main sections, separated by breaks in the bank and ditches, and subdivided within the sections into about 34 segments. The boundaries between segments are marked by dips in the height of the bank and by narrowing of the ditches at the ends of segments.

The building of the Dyke seems to have started at the north-west end, where the first part was an oval burial mound (like Pitnacree, page 18). Then a long 'tail' was added; this looks like a normal long barrow of the period and with its quarry ditches beside the bank. Finally, the Cleaven Dyke proper, with its widely spaced ditches and central bank was added.

The apparent large scale of the effort necessary to construct the Cleaven Dyke may be an illusion; it, and other cursus monuments, may have been built over a long period, in relatively short segments. The 34 segments of the Dyke may reflect the number of years of construction; in other words, within two generations. In some societies coming together over a long period to repeat some ritual activity (in this case the construction of a segment of the Dyke) may be more important than the monument eventually produced by many years' labour.

Cleaven Dyke

The north-western end of the Cleaven Dyke had a complex building history – first, an oval burial mound; second a long barrow the ditches of which cut the edge of the earlier oval mound; finally the Cleaven Dyke proper, with its widely-spaced ditches, which continued for almost 2 km.
DAVID HOGG

OVAL BARROW

LONG BARROW

CLEAVEN DYKE PROPER

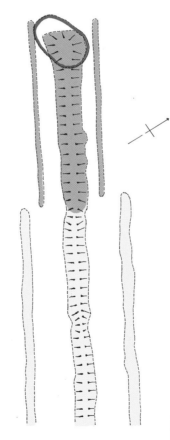

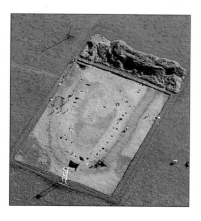

The farm

Where the evidence survives and has been investigated by archaeologists, it seems that the early Neolithic people in Scotland lived in small rectangular houses and indeed built their ceremonial structures in much the same shape. Excavations at Eilean Domnhuill, North Uist, have provided evidence of two roughly rectangular houses measuring 6.5m by 4m and 4m by 3m internally, and probably dating to around 3500 BC. They are similar to those found at Knap of Howar, Orkney, measuring 7.5m by 3m and 10m by 4.5m internally, where evidence of an economy based on arable agriculture in the form of cereal grains and querns and on a variety of wild resources, was also found.

These structures in North Uist and Orkney can be compared generally with surviving evidence in other parts of Britain and Ireland, for example the houses at Ballyglass in Ireland (measuring 7.4m by 6.4m) and the recently excavated house at Tankardstown in Co Limerick, both of which have produced dates around 4000 BC. The houses at Lismore Fields, Derbyshire, are of similar dimensions. Some of the houses mentioned recall aspects of Neolithic timber houses in continental Europe.

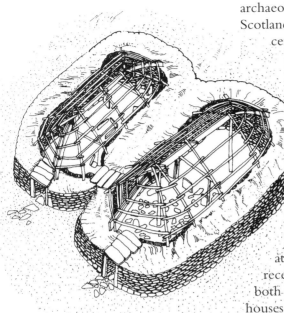

Knap of Howar

A reconstruction of the two houses at Knap of Howar, showing how the roofs were constructed.
HISTORIC SCOTLAND

Plans

Plans of some Neolithic structures from Britain and Ireland – some roofed, others not. 1 & 2 – possible mortuary structures at Balfarg, Fife; 3 – ceremonial structure at Littleour, Perthshire; 4 – house at Ballynagilly, N Ireland; 5 – the vast building at Balbridie, Aberdeenshire; 6 – two houses built end to end at Lismore Fields, Derbyshire.

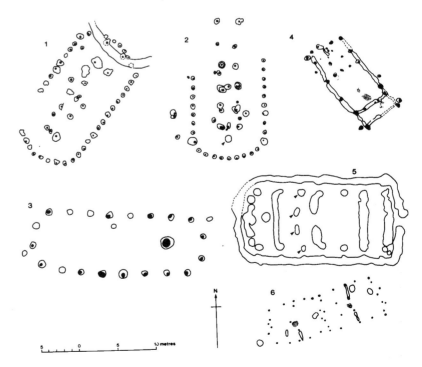

To date, the massive building at Balbridie, Aberdeenshire (page 15), has no excavated parallel in Britain, either for scale or construction.

In southern Britain there are many massive enclosures, dating from about 4000 BC to 3000 BC; these have been called causewayed camps, because the ditches and banks surrounding them are broken by many gaps. They seem to have served many purposes – settlement, defence and exposure of the dead. In Scotland, there is as yet no certain evidence for large-scale Neolithic enclosures to compare with these southern British sites, although an example has recently been found in Northern Ireland. There are hints of similar enclosures at Balloch Hill, Argyll and Bute (associated with Neolithic pottery), and at Carwinning Hill, Ayrshire, where causewayed ditches were recorded under later hillforts. The very limited excavation of a possible domestic enclosure at Kinloch Farm, Fife, has suggested there may also be a tradition of enclosed Neolithic settlement in eastern Scotland yet to be explored. Aerial photography has revealed possible causewayed sites, such as Leadketty, Perthshire; field walking here has produced flint tools of types used in the Neolithic.

As yet there is only limited evidence in northern Britain of the warfare seen on sites in the middle part of the Neolithic in southern and south-western England, where large fortified enclosures were attacked and burned. In one striking case in Dorset, archaeologists found in the ditch in front of the fort wall, the skeleton of young man who had been shot in the back with an arrow, while running holding a child.

The excavation of the Neolithic settlement at Knap of Howar has provided a useful picture of the nature of settlement and range of resources being exploited around 3500 to 3000 BC. There is evidence of cereal cultivation (grinding stones and cereal grains and pollen), and of cattle and sheep or goat. There is also evidence for some pig keeping, limited use of wild animals for wood (deer, seal, whale, otter), and more intensive exploitation of sea birds, fish and shellfish. At Knap of Howar there is also evidence of the collection of seaweed, perhaps as manure or food (for animals or humans), or for use as thatch (as was common in Orkney until recent times).

Leadketty
Aerial photograph of the massive enclosure at Leadketty, near Perth; the considerable number of breaks in the ditch suggests a relationship with the causewayed camp of England. There is another, undated enclosure, to the left. Flint tools found in the topsoil are of Neolithic date.
RCAHMS

A model that might be useful in the interpretation of the available information is crofting, which also used intensively a wide range of wild and domesticated resources. This model of a small-scale, intensive, subsistence economy which made use of a wide range of resources may be more helpful than previous comparisons made with later large-scale prehistoric agricultural systems in southern England. More recent farming communities have managed very well using hoes and spades for cultivation – it has been written of more recent spade cultivation in Scotland: 'Twelve men using *caschroms* [foot spades] could till an acre a day, and a season's work with one from Christmas till late April or May could till enough ground to feed a family of seven or eight . . . for a year'.

There is evidence for enclosures or fields in the early Neolithic – at Shurton Hill on Shetland, for example, a stone dyke seems to have been built around pasture land soon after c. 3600 BC. What was being grown in these fields and plots? Direct evidence for cultivated cereals is limited for both the early and late Neolithic. Evidence for both barley and wheat was recovered from the settlement at Knap of Howar, Orkney. At Balfarg, Fife a carbonised barley grain was found incorporated within an early Neolithic pottery sherd; this was radiocarbon dated to around 3600 BC. At Boghead, Moray, around 4000 BC barley made up 88 per cent of the cereal grains, and emmer wheat 11 per cent. The material from the timber building at Balbridie, broadly contemporary with Boghead, has added considerably to our knowledge. Emmer wheat made up a large component (almost 80 per cent) of the cereals found, barley 18 per cent and bread wheat 2 per cent. Other, non-food, plants were also used, for example cultivated flax at Balbridie. Our Neolithic ancestors therefore probably worked for part of the year in productive plots, cultivated using hoes and spades, possibly with ards to cut up the ground surface; the cultivated areas were perhaps of considerable extent; the organisation, size and boundary structures of such plots or fields might vary widely, from permanent arrangements to areas re-defined frequently by shifting hurdles or even slighter demarcations, depending on local practice and land tenure arrangements. There is evidence for managed pasture under the long barrow at Dalladies, Angus, and under the Cleaven Dyke, Perthshire.

Although there is no direct evidence for 'transhumance' – the process of moving cattle, sheep or goats to high pastures in the summer – in the Neolithic, the practice has a very long history in Europe. The recent Scottish tradition of transhumance, the occupation of the shielings in the

Cup-and-ring Markings
Complex cup-and-ring markings, from Aberdeenshire, discovered during the construction of farm buildings.
ANN MILES: HISTORIC SCOTLAND

summer, only finally died out within living memory. However, it has been suggested that the distribution of cup-and-ring marks is related to transhumance. Recent work on the location of cup and ring marks in Perthshire and Dumfries and Galloway suggests that the more complex patterns are grouped in upland areas, around basins or waterholes, or on isolated hilltops and on routes to upland pastures, although for no purpose that we can at present determine. Cup and ring marks are found first in the early Neolithic. Most, on standing stones, stone circles, in burial cists and on rock outcrops, were probably made in the late Neolithic and Bronze Age.

Axes and pots

During the Neolithic, resources were exploited, sometimes on a considerable scale, for the manufacture of tools and other items. There are examples in Scotland of the production of both stone axes and tools flaked from suitable stone, such as flint and chert. Four distinct groups of Scottish axehead rock have so far been identified by analysis of axes in museums, but to date only the exact location of one quarry has been found in Scotland, at Creag na Caillich in Perthshire, where quarrying went on in the late Neolithic.

The processes of quarrying and distribution raise many questions about the function, or range of functions, of the axes. The process of manufacture was once seen as a simple, almost industrial, process; only in recent years have we begun to appreciate its true complexity. For example, both of the quarries which have recently been examined in detail (Creag na Caillich and Langdale, Cumbria) are situated in striking locations with commanding views over the valleys below. The rock was quarried from the least accessible parts of isolated outcrops, not from the most easily available, suggesting that the choice of quarrying site was not wholly pragmatic, perhaps implying that the extraction areas were the preserve of privileged people.

Stone axes of this period range greatly in size and in quality of finish. Many are too small to have had a function as a cutting or digging implement, or are made of special materials (such as jadeite, the axes being imported into Scotland), are very finely finished and are either unsuitable for actual work or show no signs of having been used. Axe-shaped stones therefore may be functional or symbolic. It is in the latter role that axes may have been distributed over considerable distances, perhaps used in formal exchanges between individuals or groups.

Polished Axe
This highly polished, unused axe seems almost certain to have been purely symbolic.
NATIONAL MUSEUMS OF SCOTLAND

Creag na Caillich
The axe quarrying site at Creag na Caillich seems to have been chosen more for its prominence than for its ease of access.
NATIONAL MUSEUMS OF SCOTLAND

Flint Axe
The flint axe seems to have been of practical use.
NATIONAL MUSEUMS OF SCOTLAND

Pottery is one of the characteristic features of the Neolithic in Britain. Containers in earlier periods may have made of bark, skin or basketry. It may be that pottery has more than a simple pragmatic meaning – the transformation of a simple natural substance (clay), through skilled manipulation and fire, into a shaped, often decorated, hard, smooth and clearly non-natural pot, would have been a striking achievement to people not previously acquainted with it.

Throughout the Neolithic and Bronze Age people in different parts of Britain made pottery that varied in style and decoration, expressing their own local traditions. In the early Neolithic all pottery was round-bottomed, but varied greatly in shape and decoration.

Pots
A range of earlier Neolithic pots from different regional traditions.
DAVID HOGG

The Late Neolithic

There are many reasons to believe that there were significant changes in society over most of Britain starting around 3300 BC in Scotland. There was already evidence of increasing diversity from place to place in burial and religious practice, and as the changes progressed, even greater regional diversity can be detected. The construction of the cursus monuments (which may begin later in the early Neolithic, although this is not clear), indicates a change away from the society that built the communal burial mounds, the construction of which ended in most parts of Scotland around 2500 BC.

In most areas late Neolithic burials (where limited evidence survives) are more likely to be of individuals rather than of a mass of anonymous bone from several people; it may be that it was now possible for the status of prominent individuals to be reflected in the way they were buried; for example, occupying a tomb designed solely for them. At much the same time a completely new type of ceremonial site – the henge – was built.

Henges

We do not know what went on in enclosures of the kind known as henges, but they are generally accepted to be places in which religious ceremonies took place. They normally comprise a ditch with external bank, the purpose of which may have been to screen the interior from view (suggesting that only a select few took part in what went on in the interior); there are usually one or two entrances and often there are settings of timber or stone uprights. Enclosures that can be interpreted as being henges or

Cairnpapple Henge
How the henge monument at Cairnpapple might have looked when it was being built.
DAVID HOGG: HISTORIC SCOTLAND

North Mains Henge

The classic henge monument at North Mains, Perthshire, under excavation.
HISTORIC SCOTLAND

related to the henge tradition vary in diameter from less than 10 metres to almost 400 metres in diameter (the largest being found only in southern England); the smallest (below 20 metres) are called hengiform enclosures. Stonehenge, although providing the origin of the name, can now be seen probably to be more a development of the southern British causewayed camp tradition.

More work was required to construct a substantial henge than an early Neolithic burial mound, but less than for a cursus monument like the Cleaven Dyke. However, the construction of the Dyke, and possibly other cursus monuments, was undertaken over a prolonged period; the henges were presumably built in a single operation. The amount of labour and the organisation necessary to construct the medium and large henges has been used to support the view that in the late Neolithic a more hierarchical society was developing, indicated by the appearance of single burials (possibly of 'chiefs') already mentioned. Such a society, where larger numbers of people were grouped together under the sway of an individual or family, might have a need for large-scale gatherings of the kind implied by the large scale of henge enclosures. However, many of the Scottish henges are small, and would have required less effort than the construction of one of the earlier burial mounds.

The point at which the organisation of religious life around burial mounds (characteristic of the early Neolithic) began to give way to the late Neolithic ceremonial enclosures - the henges - may have been detected by archaeologists at two sites in Scotland, at Maes Howe in Orkney and at Balfarg in Fife. At Maes Howe, the tomb (see page 40), part of a late local survival of the communal burial tradition, was encircled by a ditch and bank which has been compared to a henge; a further possible example has been recognised recently by Richard Bradley, at the tomb of Reay of Bookan, Orkney. Two 'true' henges were constructed nearby, at Stenness and the Ring of Brodgar. At Balfarg, Fife, a structure possibly used in the exposure of bodies

prior to communal burial in the early Neolithic tradition was, at the end of its use, covered by a low mound of earth and surrounded by a henge. Both mound and ditch contained Grooved Ware pottery; the ditch deposits were dated to around 3100 BC. Perhaps such sites had to be altered to underline the change in ceremonial practice then underway – the same sort of thing happened when the church 'Christianised' henges and stone circles by building churches within them or enclosing them in churchyards or using them as cemeteries.

Wormy Hillock Henge
One of the smallest henges – the site at Wormy Hillock, Aberdeenshire.
HISTORIC SCOTLAND

Grooved Ware

Another strand of evidence in interpreting the late Neolithic period comes from a completely new type of pottery – Grooved Ware, which has often elaborate decoration in the form of scored grooves or applied ridges. In much of Britain it is found mainly in the new ceremonial sites, but in Orkney it is found also in the settlements of the period, although often for special uses (for example, as at Barnhouse, pages 37 – 39). Grooved Ware is found in Orkney, Tayside and Fife, and south-west Scotland; in England it is found in Wessex, East Anglia and Yorkshire. The gaps in the distribution (for example there is one isolated findspot at Raigmore in Inverness) may be the result either of real original differences in distribution, or of the amounts varying of archaeological work undertaken in different areas of Britain.

There are also other styles of late Neolithic pottery, heavily decorated, but we know even less about how and where they were used than we do about Grooved Ware.

At Balfarg Riding School one of the larger Grooved Ware vessels found in a henge contained a substance based on black henbane (a member of the hemlock family), possibly used as an hallucinogen. Recent work has suggested that the some of the decorative patterns used on Grooved Ware may have originated in patterns seen by people in trance states brought on by using hallucinogens.

The radiocarbon dating evidence for the introduction of henges and of Grooved Ware consistently points to their use earlier in northern Britain than elsewhere, and it may be that whatever initiated these changes in society also began here.

Regional variation – late Neolithic stone circles

While henges are the typical large public monuments of the late Neolithic, a very different type of site is characteristic of north-eastern Scotland - the recumbent stone circle.

Ian Shepherd has argued that the construction of these circles

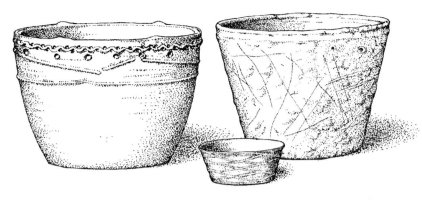

Pottery
Pottery of the Grooved Ware tradition. DAVID HOGG

began in the late Neolithic, as early as 3000 BC. There are about 100 of these known in the relatively small area of the modern local authority area of Aberdeenshire. These sites comprise a ring of stones, around 20 metres in diameter with, in the south, or south-western arc, a large (sometimes very large) stone lying on its side (the 'recumbent' stone). This stone is almost always flanked by the two tallest stones in the circle, the height of the rest reducing towards the part of the circle furthest from the recumbent stone. In the 1970s it was suggested that the axis of the circle, looking over the recumbent stone, was aligned on points where the moon rose and set at its 'standstills' (the moon sets at different points along the horizon, depending on the place in its cycle – where the setting point stops moving in one direction, and changes to the other, is the 'standstill'). Since then careful study of the sites on the ground has suggested that it was the midsummer full moon in the sky that was important; therefore, rather than observation of the moon, we should perhaps consider that the moon, between the uprights and over the recumbent, was illuminating the circle. In the restricted area in which these circles occur there are very few henge monuments - only three, and all of them very small and unusual (see the map of the distribution of henges and recumbent stone circles on the next page). This means that, whilst in other parts of Scotland (and in much of mainland Britain) the henges – indications of communal construction and ritual - were being built, in the north-east the ceremonial monuments were completely different. Not only are they relatively small, but there are many of them; often two or three circles are in close proximity. Does this indicate that in this area society had not changed as it had elsewhere, and was still operating on the basis

Netherton
The recumbent stone circle at Netherton of Logie, as drawn by Fred Coles in the early years of the 20th century.

Castle Fraser Stone Circle
The recumbent stone circle at Castle
Fraser, Aberdeenshire.
HISTORIC SCOTLAND

The Midsummer Full Moon
A recumbent stone circle as it might been
used; the alignment of the sites suggests
that the time of the midsummer full moon
was significant in their design and use.
DAVID HOGG

of small groups of families rather than 'tribes' or 'chiefdoms'? This situation provides perhaps the clearest example of differences between regions, at least in traditions of monument building and ritual practice, in this period. It is interesting to note that no Grooved Ware, the pottery type found most often in henges, has yet been found in the north-east. The contrast in henge distribution between the north-east and Angus and Perthshire is particularly striking.

This impression of regional individuality given by the recumbent stone circles is further strengthened by the distribution of a distinctive type of find – the carved stone balls – which is also heavily concentrated within the same area.

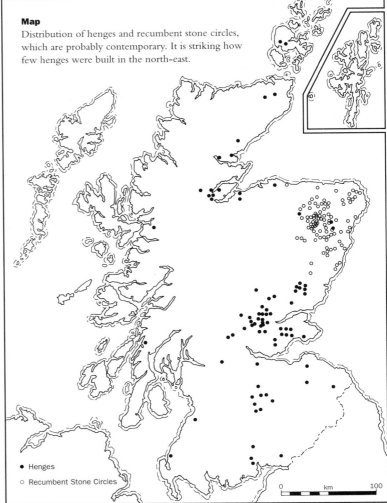

Map

Distribution of henges and recumbent stone circles, which are probably contemporary. It is striking how few henges were built in the north-east.

● Henges

○ Recumbent Stone Circles

0   km   100

In Arran, also in the late Neolithic, some of the impressive stone circles on Machrie Moor have been shown to have been built over the remains of earlier circles of upright timbers, associated with Grooved Ware pottery. At much the same time the impressive stone alignments at Calanais were being built, indicating another region's approach to the construction of ceremonial structures in the late Neolithic; here there was also an interest in the movements of the moon on the horizon. It is interesting to note that henge monuments have not yet been discovered in either Arran or the Western Isles.

Stone Ball

One of the enigmatic carved stone balls, most of which are from Aberdeenshire.
NATIONAL MUSEUMS OF SCOTLAND

Barnhouse Settlement

The village at Barnhouse, on Orkney, lies close to the two Orkney henge monuments - the Stones of Stenness and the Ring of Brodgar - within sight of Maes Howe. The settlement contains at least nine rounded late Neolithic houses, all with stone-built beds and dressers, of a kind generally familiar from the well-known settlement at Skara Brae, where, however, the houses are squarer and the stone-built fittings are not set in niches in the wall; the excavator of Barnhouse believes that the Skara Brae houses are later. At Barnhouse the walls only survive to a few centimetres high (although they have now been partly reconstructed). The houses all had stone-built drains. The walls at Barnhouse were probably built of turf and stone but it is not clear how the houses were roofed; the walls are thick enough to have supported a significant roof structure. In the reconstruction painting overleaf, the roofs are shown as being built on a wooden framework set at an angle of 40 to 45 degrees, covered with a thick thatch, probably of seaweed. In a wet and windy climate a flat or lower pitched roof would have been entirely impractical and would actually have been more difficult to build and maintain. The techniques assumed for the reconstruction survived in common use in north and north-western Scotland in simple farm and croft houses until relatively recently. There were signs that houses had been rebuilt on the same site a number of times. There was an open area at the core of the settlement, in which people had worked, making pottery, knapping flint and preparing hides for clothing.

One of the most exciting aspects of the Barnhouse excavation was that a fairly large part of the settlement could be investigated, showing that there were other types of structure in the village (this had also been noted at Skara Brae). In the south-west part of the village, there was a building ('house 2') that was very much larger than a normal house; it had two chambers instead of one, each with a central hearth. Like the smaller buildings it had bed recesses and a place for a recessed dresser. Interestingly, access to the inner chamber could only be obtained by going right round the hearth in the outer chamber. The excavator of Barnhouse, Colin Richards, has written compellingly about the parallels to be drawn between the layout of the late Neolithic houses of Orkney and other, more recent, societies in the way houses are laid out and used. Certain areas may be given over to different people - male or female, old or young, parent or child. Also, the way that houses are set out may reflect broader beliefs about the relationship of people to their world.

Opposite the entrance to the largest house is an even more impressive structure, which probably dates from soon after the abandonment of the rest of the settlement. The structure consists of a wall that encloses an area, over 20 metres across, which contains a large squarish building, more similar to the houses at Skara Brae than to the rest of the Barnhouse buildings. To enter it one would have had to walk over a hearth (one hopes without a fire lit on it!) - once again stressing the apparent symbolism of the hearth already seen in the two-chamber building. In the centre of the enclosure building was another hearth, behind which was the dresser commonly found in the normal houses; here, however, it was not in a recess, and looks more like a Skara Brae layout. All in all this was a strange building, especially when one considers how similar it (and some of the features of the other houses) is in layout to the Maes Howe type of tombs, and to the layout of the Stenness henge (which has a large paved area - intended to resemble a hearth? - at its centre).

Within the enclosure, a Grooved Ware pot containing traces of barley was found set in the ground up to the neck. We can only guess at the significance of this deposit.

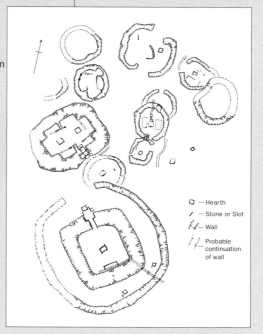

Barnhouse Plan

Plan of the settlement at Barnhouse; the large structure at the bottom was probably built after the rest of the settlement had been abandoned.
After Richards

Key:
⬠ — Hearth
╱ — Stone or Slot
〰 — Wall
〰 — Probable continuation of wall

Thatch

Turf

Turf

Hearth

Door

Drain

Barnhouse Settlement

How the Barnhouse settlement may have looked. The reconstruction of the roofs – with a wooden frame at 40–45 degrees, covered by a deep thatch of seaweed – is based on more recent buildings in the northern isles. A flat roof would have needed more substantial timbers, and would have been very unstable in a windy environment.

Inset illustration *(left)* is a cutaway drawing showing how the roof would have been built.

DAVID HOGG

Barnhouse Excavation

The settlement at Barnhouse under excavation.

COLIN RICHARDS

Stone Balls
Three carved stone balls from
Aberdeenshire.
NATIONAL MUSEUMS OF SCOTLAND

Calanais
Calanais - the most spectacular stone
setting in Scotland, as recorded in this
19th century antiquarian print.

Regional variation – Maes Howe and the late tombs of Orkney

In Orkney a series of massive, complex chambered tombs was built by the people who used Grooved Ware. Of these, Maes Howe is the best known and most impressive - it is one of the greatest architectural achievements of this period in Britain. Why the use of massive communal burial structures continued into the late Neolithic in this part of Scotland, when they were no longer being built in the rest of Scotland, is unknown - it hints at significantly different social structures at the time here, as do the recumbent stone circles in north-east Scotland.

The Maes Howe type tombs are not simple heaps of stones - the visitor can see easily that the chambers and cairns of this group are beautifully and impressively constructed. The tall steep-sided 'core cairns' around the chamber, which are a

Maes Howe Chamber
How the chamber of Maes Howe may
have looked in use.
HISTORIC SCOTLAND

necessary part of the chamber, to support the stepped 'corbelling' roof, are very stable structures built of densely packed, horizontally-laid slabs, faced with good quality masonry.

The late Neolithic village

For archaeologists, Orkney provides the best settlement evidence for the late Neolithic, in particular from the excavated sites at Rinyo, Skara Brae, Links of Noltland and Barnhouse. The norm, different from what we know of the early Neolithic, seems to have relatively large-scale, communally-based settlement, occupied for long periods. In the earlier part of the period the houses were more free-standing (as at Barnhouse) - in the later village at Skara Brae the houses are more closely spaced, or even joined). Their inhabitants had a rich material culture and incorporated both mixed agriculture and intensive exploitation of wild resources, such as freshwater and sea fish. It appears that in Orkney and the Western Isles less easily cultivated, but more productive, clayey soils were exploited in the late Neolithic, following earlier exploitation of more easily cultivated land (which was however prone to drought in dry summers).

Maes Howe
Maes Howe as depicted in the 19th century

Maes Howe Plan
Maes Howe - plan & section of the chamber prepared for the Inventory of Monuments of Orkney in 1929.
RCAHMS

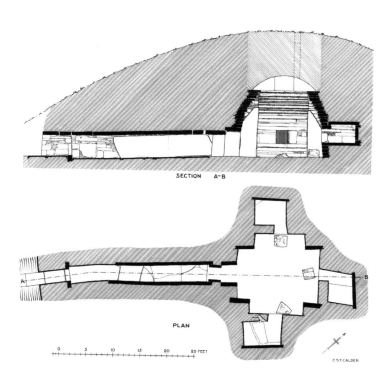

Boddam Den

Boddam Den, Aberdeenshire – how the late Neolithic flint quarries may have appeared in use.

DAVID HOGG

Calanais

The stone setting is only one phase in a complex sequence of use over many centuries

HISTORIC SCOTLAND

There may be a direct relationship between the development of Maes Howe type tombs and Grooved Ware and the economic and social innovations (including the development of larger scale settlements of the Skara Brae type) which allowed the communal effort necessary to exploit more difficult land.

Evidence of the use of 'ards' has been found at the Links of Noltland, Orkney; ards are simple cultivation implements, which were probably used to break up ground before cultivation using hoes and spades. At North Mains, Perthshire, a massive round barrow of the earlier part of the Bronze Age (before about 2500 BC) covered a surface that had been cultivated using narrow spade-dug ridges. Spade-dug ridges do a number of things - they improve soil drainage, they increase the depth of soil available for cultivation (on the ridges), and they increase soil warmth, all of which aid successful cultivation.

In Shetland there is evidence of land having been cleared and divided by walls between 3200 and 2800 BC. In Ireland there is evidence for very extensive and complex systems of fields, covering many square kilometres, by around 2800 BC. In some agricultural societies where land is held communally, cultivation plots may be marked in far less permanent ways, perhaps annually; for example, there is evidence of plots being divided by light fences in the late Neolithic on Arran, and by simple lines of hand-sized stones in the Bronze Age in Sutherland.

The balance of crops grown in the late Neolithic differed from those in earlier times - at Skara Brae, emmer wheat, the main crop at first, had declined to less than 10 per cent of the crop later in the Neolithic, and the decline continued into the earlier Bronze Age, in favour of barley. The actual size of emmer grains decreased at the same time, a sign of poor adaptation to the northern climate. Hulled barley, not represented in the early Neolithic at Boghead, Fochabers, was found in the late Neolithic at Skara Brae. A considerable use of wild resources is indicated at Northton, Harris, where 14 types of wild animals were found and at Noltland, Orkney, where 15 wild deer skeletons were recovered.

The more scattered late Neolithic settlement at Scord of Brouster in Shetland perhaps demonstrates that the sort of 'village' seen in Orkney was not necessarily the normal form of settlement throughout Scotland at this time.

Elsewhere in Britain the accidents of preservation have revealed only limited evidence of settlements, for example the two wooden buildings found under later burial mounds at Trelystan, Powys; the ground plans of these buildings are similar to those at Skara Brae, although they are lightly built of wood. While similar structures may remain to be found in lowland areas, it is probable that they will only survive, and be discovered, by chance.

At Meldon Bridge, Peeblesshire, is the only excavated example of a small, widely dispersed group of very large enclosures defined by massive posts, the postholes of which are clearly visible on aerial photographs. The sites are found as far apart as Forteviot in Perthshire and Dunragit, Dumfries and Galloway. The common characteristic is a narrow entrance passage formed of posts running out from the wall of the enclosure. At Meldon Bridge the timber fence cut off a promontory formed by the River Tweed and the Meldon Water, enclosing an area 10 hectares in extent. In the interior were found pits and postholes, possibly including traces of structures, associated with another type of late Neolithic pottery - 'impressed ware' - found over much of eastern Scotland. The enclosure had later been used for burial in the Bronze Age.

Two Pots

Two pots of the late Neolithic 'impressed ware' tradition.
DAVID HOGG

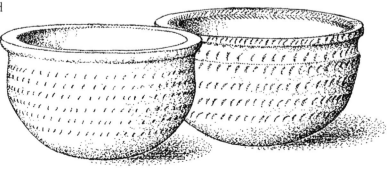

Equipment

Before metalworking was known, tools would have been made of wood and stone. Throughout the Neolithic wood was fairly easily obtainable over most of Scotland, but stone suitable for making sharp and strong tools is found only in certain areas.

Flint was the most commonly used stone for making tools – when struck it produces sharp edged flakes which can be used for cutting or scraping; larger pieces can be flaked and then ground into knives or axes. Clear evidence of large-scale late Neolithic flint extraction has been recovered from the Buchan gravels in Aberdeenshire; the largest known quarrying site is at the Den of Boddam, near Peterhead. Here both sides of a small valley had been ravaged by hundreds of intersecting quarry pits dug over several centuries to extract flint from the gravels. Radiocarbon dating places this activity in one part of the site between 3500 and 2000 BC. We do not know who dug the flint or how it was traded or distributed.

At Creag na Caillich in Perthshire, quarrying of stone for the manufacture of axes was being carried on around 2900 BC to 2300 BC. Axes made of stone from this site were widely distributed – one axe has been found as far away as Buckinghamshire.

Balfarg

The ceremonial complex at Balfarg, on the northern outskirts of Glenrothes New Town in Fife, is one of the most extensively investigated complexes of its kind in Britain. It was in use for over 1500 years, during which time it underwent many significant alterations, reflecting changes in practice and belief. The first recorded activity on the site was the digging of shallow pits, between 4200 and 3400 BC. In one of these pits, slabs of broken and burnt pottery were laid carefully round the edge; the pit was then filled and sealed near the top by a layer of stones. This kind of ritualised activity is a feature of much early Neolithic ceremonial activity.

Then two rectangular timber structures were built, probably one after the other, between 3700 and 3300 BC. These seem to have been fenced-off areas within which there were two- and four-post structures, possibly used for the exposure of the dead, prior to final burial. They are comparable with examples from other parts of the world.

One of the structures was certainly, and the other was probably, covered with low mounds of soil; the mounds contained Grooved Ware pottery, containing traces of black henbane, a plant used as a hallucinogen. The earlier structure had a ring cairn (a band of stone surrounding an empty central area) built over one end. The later of the two structures had a henge built round it. This could represent the conversion of a site associated with the earlier practice of communal burial to one associated with late Neolithic ceremonial activity.

Another henge was built a few hundred metres away; more Grooved Ware was found broken and burnt inside it. The henge enclosed a series of timber rings, which were eventually replaced by a stone circle.

At about the same time another stone circle was built to the east, at Balbirnie. In turn it was buried under a stone cairn.

Both henges, the Balbirnie stone circle, and the Balfarg ring cairn were later used for burials associated with Beakers and Food Vessels. One of the slabs of a cist at Balbirnie was decorated with cup and ring markings. Finally, many small deposits of cremated human bone were made on the Balbirnie stone circle and the ring cairn.

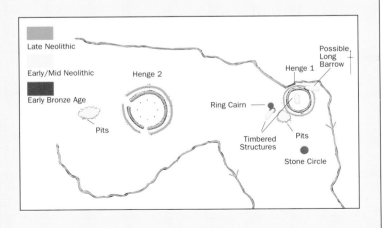

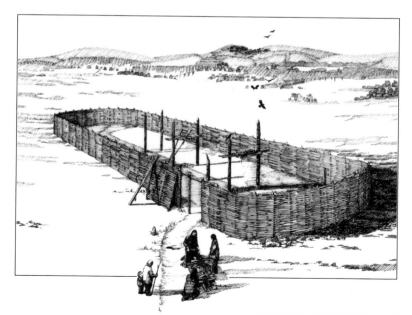

Ring Cairn – Balfarg

The ring cairn at Balfarg, built over the end of one the timber structures.

HISTORIC SCOTLAND

Balbirnie Stone Circle

Balbirnie stone circle, under excavation in 1970.

GRAHAM RITCHIE: HISTORIC SCOTLAND

Balfarg Structures

A possible reconstruction of one of the structures at Balfarg, as an enclosure and platforms for the exposure of the dead. See the North American Indian platform on page 21.

DAVID HOGG

Balfarg (opposite)

A simplified plan of the significant features of the ceremonial complex at Balfarg.

DAVID HOGG

Other stones suitable for flaking into implements - Arran pitchstone, Rhum bloodstone, chert and quartz - were also exploited, but the processes of their distribution are even less well understood.

As in the early Neolithic, goods were also exchanged between neighbouring groups - the most striking possibility being the carved stone balls already mentioned. The balls seem to have no intrinsic purpose, perhaps strengthening their interpretation as purely symbolic items.

Twenty years ago, Euan MacKie, drawing on the work of Alexander Thom (see p57), and on his own experience in the study of Mayan civilisation, argued that Britain in the late Neolithic was a theocracy, in which an elite of 'wise men, magicians, astronomers, priests, poets, jurists and engineers with all their families, retainers and attendant craftsmen and technicians' lived in major ceremonial complexes and in other special sites (such as all the known Skara Brae type settlements on Orkney). Fed by the efforts of a peasantry living in primitive conditions, this elite were supposed to undertake precise astronomical observation and set out their complex ceremonial sites using advanced geometry and a standard unit of measurement. His views have been dismissed by other archaeologists, who believe that the evidence shows a sophisticated and capable Neolithic farming society, not MacKie's society largely of primitive peasants run by a sophisticated elite.

Consolidating the hold: people and their environment

It is from the late Neolithic that we begin to see clear evidence of widespread and long-lasting clearance of woodland from the landscape (except Orkney and the other islands, which were not heavily wooded at any time), accompanied in some cases by significant soil erosion from the cleared land; for example, in the Bowmont Valley, Borders, the removal of trees for agriculture around 2000 BC seems to have resulted in catastrophic soil erosion. Many people would like to think that people in the past lived in a desirable equilibrium with their environment; however, examples of environmental damage caused by people in the past show that this is wishful thinking. In the late Neolithic results of pollen analysis were interpreted as showing a decline in the amount of land farmed, and a regeneration of woodland. However, it can as easily be explained by changes in the pattern of human settlement.

The Bronze Age

We must now deal with the change, real or otherwise, from 'the Neolithic' to 'the Bronze Age'. The first part of our journey into the past has been concerned with the establishment of a new way of life – farming, and the society that developed with and after that change. For much of the Neolithic and in most of the country certain unifying traditions could be detected, more strongly in the early Neolithic and weakening in the late Neolithic – the forms of burial in the early Neolithic, cursus monuments in the mid part of the period, and henges in the late Neolithic. In the Bronze Age the differences between regions become far more pronounced: although there may still be unifying traditions, and the way these are interpreted, for example in building of religious monuments and the way people were buried, becomes far more varied.

Until 30 years ago, virtually all changes within British prehistory were explained by 'invasions' of one people replacing another, rather than by changes within society. The Bronze Age was therefore seen as being the product of an 'invasion' by a separate group of people who used a special type of pot – the 'Beaker people'. But few would hold to such a view now.

'Magic Metal'
– the transformation of substances

It is perhaps difficult for us to understand just how amazing the process of working bronze would have seemed to people who had never seen it before. Copper ore would be transformed by heat into a shining pool of bright metal, and then by the smith's art and the addition of tin, into bright, shiny, hard and durable tools and ornaments. Throughout history metalsmiths have been seen as people apart, dangerous or powerful individuals; their power to transform substances must lie at the heart of this. Perhaps the occurrence of evidence of metalworking within many abandoned stone circles and henges, long after these sites had fallen out of use, indicates the religious awe which surrounded metalworking. Copper ores are widely available in Scotland, for example in Angus and Perthshire. No Bronze Age mines are yet known in Scotland, but at the Great Orme mine at Llandudno in Wales, a major complex of Bronze Age shafts and passages, has been investigated by archaeologists, and other mines are known in Ireland. Tin, the other important ingredient of bronze, is

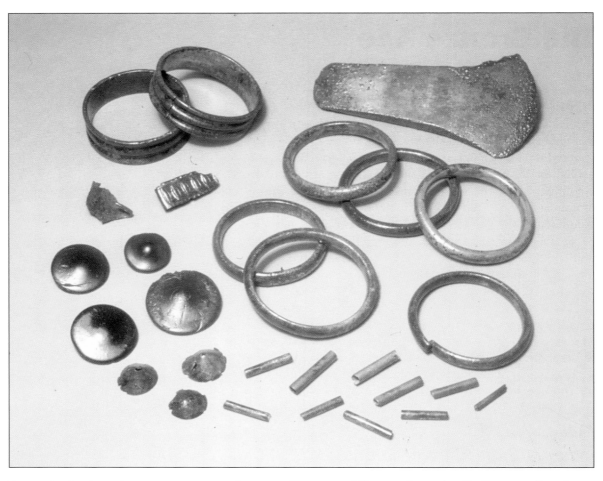

Bronze Age Equipment
A selection of early Bronze Age equipment.
NATIONAL MUSEUMS OF SCOTLAND

much rarer – Devon and Cornwall are the likeliest suppliers for the whole of Britain, although some tin may have come from mainland Europe.

The smelting of ore to produce copper requires very high temperatures – 1083 degrees Celsius. The ore is broken up into small fragments and placed in a small bowl furnace; charcoal is used as the fuel to heat it, blown to great heat by bellows. The molten metal collects in the bottom of the bowl. When it cools it can be re-melted in a crucible and then poured into moulds. Moulds and mould fragments are quite frequent finds on Bronze Age settlement sites in Britain as a whole. The finished tools could then be 'tinned' to give a shiny silvery finish, and polished, or ornamented by using gouges or punches,

Bronze Age people also worked gold into jewellery of great beauty. The gold, and most of the finished objects, probably came from Ireland, although there are naturally occurring gold deposits in Scotland, for example, in the Helmsdale River in Sutherland.

The creation of the metal tools and other equipment, particularly the larger, more decorative items, and the goldwork, was probably controlled by a limited number of people. We have seen that in the late Neolithic period changing burial practices, and the development of major ceremonial sites (the henges), perhaps indicated that individuals or families of higher status were increasingly playing a part in the organisation and control of society. It was perhaps these same groups who controlled the production and distribution of metalwork and other prestige goods. A society which uses artefacts as outward symbols of status and rank is likely to be competitive, because such symbols are open to imitation; effective maintenance of authority depends on control of manufacture and circulation of high-status objects.

'Powerful Pots'

Through the 19th century and for much of the 20th, the most commonly discovered features of the early Bronze Age were the burials – stone-lined graves (cists) containing one or, less often, more bodies, usually accompanied by a finely made pot, of the types called Beakers and Food Vessels (although both probably contained much the same sort of substances), or urns containing cremated bone. These pots were normally finely made and

Lunula
A gold lunula, or collar.
NATIONAL MUSEUMS OF SCOTLAND

Lunula Detail
A detail of a lunula, showing the extraordinary workmanship.
NATIONAL MUSEUMS OF SCOTLAND

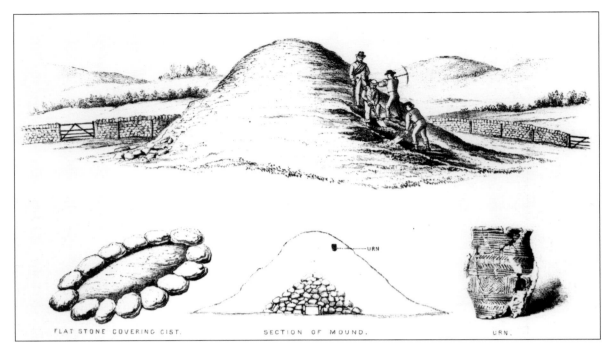

The Fairy Knowe of Pendreich A typical 19th century 'excavation' of a Bronze Age burial mound – the Fairy Knowe of Pendreich, 1867.

Bronze Age Cist Burial
A typical early Bronze Age cist burial; a woman aged about 25 at death, buried within the henge at North Mains, in around 2000 BC.
HISTORIC SCOTLAND

elaborately decorated. In most of Scotland they are found in burials, although they are also found on ceremonial or religious sites. In the Western Isles however, they turn up on settlement sites of the period – it may just be that we have not yet found these settlements in other parts of Scotland.

Although we have seen that in the late Neolithic period single burial was becoming common, the single burials we find still seem to be of special individuals – it is with the appearance of Beakers (at approximately the same time as the working of metal)

Bronze Age Pots A range of early Bronze Age pots from burials. Beakers, Food Vessels, an 'enlarged Food Vessel' and a collared urn. DAVID HOGG

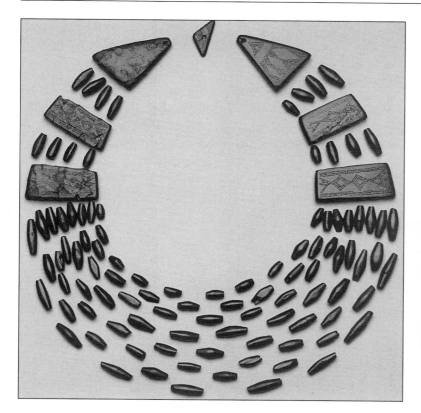

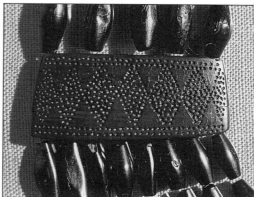

and, later, Food Vessels that we have a more consistent form of
burial that seems to provide for larger numbers of the population.
At one time it was thought that there was a simple sequence -
burials of bodies with Beakers, then with Food Vessels, and then
a change of burial practice to cremation, with the burnt bone
being placed in special urns. However, more recent excavation
and radiocarbon dating confirms not only that Beakers, Food
Vessels and urns may occur on the same site, possibly at much the
same time (because Beakers went on being used for a very long
time), but that other burial types are found there too - bodies in
unlined pits, with or without pottery vessels, cremations in small
pits, on occasion in cists with Beakers and so on. It has also
become clear that many cemetery sites were covered by mounds,
which have since been ploughed away. It may be that the type of
burial a person received was more to do with who they were, or
when they died, than with simple changes in tradition over a
long period. At one cemetery in Fife a body had even been
buried in a coracle which had been placed in a pit.

Recent work on analysing the pollen in the soils in the
bottom of cists has shown that bodies may have been
accompanied by flowers. However, many Beakers and Food
Vessels have 'tide-marks' of crusty organic material showing the

Culduthel Grave Goods
The finds from the grave at Culduthel,
Inverness-shire. The body was
accompanied not only by the pot but by
an archer's wristguard and eight flint
arrowheads.
NATIONAL MUSEUMS OF SCOTLAND

original height of a liquid or semi-liquid material within them, possibly food or drink. Unfortunately, it is difficult to tell what pollen belongs to the flowers in the cist, and what relates to the material in the pots.

One of the other characteristic finds of the period, in particular in Beaker graves, is archery equipment - arrowheads and wrist guards - much of which is finely crafted. Although equipment made of flint, other stones, and metal may survive, the wooden parts of equipment of all kinds does not, except in rare circumstances - it is to this form of preservation that we owe what knowledge we have of the shafts of arrows or even of bows themselves. The only bow we have from the period we are considering in this book is from the early Neolithic, at Rotten Bottom in Dumfriesshire. That archery had more than ordinary significance is shown by two examples where arrows may have been used for the ritual killing of people who were then buried on sacred sites - one case at Stonehenge, and the other within a timber circle (accompanied by a Food Vessel) at Sarn-y-bryn-Caled, in Wales.

It is clear, however, that the relatively small-scale cists and cremations of individuals do not represent the whole spectrum of burial throughout the period. At North Mains in Tayside, a vast round mound 40 metres across and 5 metres high, proved on excavation to have a long and complex history.

First, the mound was set out on the ground using complex patterns of light wooden fences. There was a circular area in the middle, and fences radiating out forming a series of bays, like the slices of a cake. Then, the radial bays were filled with material dug from around the site, to create a ring bank with the central fenced area still open, and accessible from one side. One or more burials were placed in this area, and it was filled in. After this the mound was finished off to a more bowl-like shape, and a huge fire was lit on the top. Finally, the mound was smoothed off using turf, and a layer of stone was laid over the whole surface.

North Mains 1
The first phase of construction at North Mains saw the erection of a central timber enclosure, and many radial fences. Within the segments soil from the ditch was piled.
HISTORIC SCOTLAND: DAVID HOGG

Burials in cists were dug, at about the same time or later, into the surface.

Recent excavation and radiocarbon dating on the Clava cairns (named after one group of cairns at Balnuaran of Clava), near Inverness, seem to show that the cairns and their surrounding stone circles are broadly contemporary with North Mains, not several hundred years earlier, as was originally thought. The only surviving evidence of burial at a Clava Cairn (at Corrimony near Drumnadrochit) is a stain showing the position of the body of a single individual. It may be that all these massive round mounds of the early Bronze Age are indeed the burials of prominent individuals.

North Mains 2
At the end of the first phase of construction the mound at North Mains consisted of a stone and earthen bank surrounding an open central area, accessed by a passage. One or more bodies were buried in the central area, before 2000 BC.
HISTORIC SCOTLAND: DAVID HOGG

Clava Cairns
One of the Clava cairns as it appeared in 1860.

Body Stain
The body stain in the chamber of the Clava-type cairn at Corrimony seems to be of a single individual.
STUART PIGGOTT

Clava Cairn The north-east cairn at Clava, under excavation in 1996. HISTORIC SCOTLAND

Stone circles

Stone circles are almost the definitive monument type of the Bronze Age. Many circles (for example, those within henge monuments and the Recumbent Stone Circles of north-east Scotland) can now be seen to date to the late Neolithic, but the majority of circles belong to the following thousand years, for they continued to be built until quite late in the Bronze Age. Modern excavations show that many stone circles were built on the sites of pre-existing circles of timber posts. We do not really know what went on the circles, although we speculate that they were used for communal ceremonies; what is very common, however, is that the circles were used for human burial late in their use, implying that they were sacred sites.

Astronomy and geometry

In the late 1960s a professional engineer, Alexander Thom, published surveys and interpretations of stone circles which he believed proved that the builders of the circles used complex geometry in setting them out, and used the circles for very detailed astronomical observation. At first his views and conclusions were dismissed entirely by the archaeological profession. However, more scientific survey and analysis of the results has confirmed that prehistoric people in Britain *were* interested in astronomical events and built their religious sites to align on them, but that they were not undertaking the precise observations suggested by Thom. The alignments used relate to major events in the annual movements of the sun and moon along the horizon, and the alignments are accurate only to within one or two degrees.

Thom's assertions that the stone circles were laid out using complex geometry, and a standard unit of measurement (the 'megalithic yard') have also been examined and found wanting. Studies of the geometry of stone circles rely on the application of very precise methods of analysis to monuments, often incomplete or altered during use, constructed of rough and irregular stones.

The fact is that geometry can be used to *describe* any shape that already exists, including any stone 'circle'. There is no proof whatsoever that complex geometrical processes were actually used to set out the shapes on the ground. Indeed, when exact geometrical shapes are applied to such sites, many of the stones

Edintian Stones
The 'four-poster' stone circle at Edintian in Perthshire, as drawn by Fred Coles in the early years of the 20th century.

Learable Hill Stones
The simple stone rows at Learable Hill, Sutherland. These are very simple, compared to some of the far more complex settings of Caithness. What any of the rows were for is a mystery.
HISTORIC SCOTLAND

Echt Stones
The stone circle and later kerb cairns at Echt, Aberdeenshire.
HISTORIC SCOTLAND

will not lie on the theoretical line. It is more widely accepted that stone circles (many of which are not exactly circular) were laid out using simple methods, many by eye.

Settlements and environment

While the settlements of the Neolithic period are relatively rare, we know of far more settlements of the Bronze Age in Britain in general, particularly of the later Bronze Age. This is mainly because of the accidents of survival of sites. During the Bronze Age people were settling the uplands, perhaps because increasing population had resulted in a shortage of land in the lowlands. Because these areas have not been used intensively for agriculture in the two to three thousand years since, many settlement sites and indeed field systems survive. Other sites survive in sand dunes, as in the Western Isles. However, sites in the uplands and islands do not tell us what was happening in the lowlands, where sites have been ploughed flat and may appear, if at all, only as cropmarks.

Unfortunately, few settlement sites of the Bronze Age have been excavated to modern standards and the amount of hard evidence remains limited. Therefore, while there are many house sites and associated field systems visible in much of upland Scotland, we cannot tell how many of them originated in the period we are discussing, up to 1500 BC; it is likely that most of the sites we can see on the hills are of a later period, covered in Richard Hingley's book in this series: *Settlement and Sacrifice*. On Arran, however, a hut circle was radiocarbon dated to around 1900 BC. Near Lairg, Sutherland, a long sequence of settlement from the early Neolithic (pits and pottery associated with agricultural soils) to quite recent settlement was recovered by excavation. It included phases of intensive agriculture in the late Neolithic. The first houses to be found within the excavated areas (but presumably not the first in the vicinity) were round houses, dated to between 1750 and 1500 BC. In and around these substantial timber buildings were found pots, charred cereals, quern stones for grinding corn, and the stone tips of ploughs.

In the hills of southern Scotland we can see that a type of settlement more common in the late Bronze Age had its origins in the centuries before 1500 BC. These 'unenclosed platform settlements' appear as strings of circular platforms cut into the hillsides of the Borders and Clydesdale. The platforms were built to allow the construction of round houses. At Lintshie Gutter such houses were dated to around 2000 BC, the earliest dates yet obtained for round houses. There is evidence that the occupants grew cereals and tended flocks of sheep and herds of cattle.

Significant evidence for settlements of this period has been found in the Western Isles where two contrasting sites were excavated. At Rosinish, clear evidence for cereal cultivation was found – in the form of charred barley and oats,

Houses, Fields and Cairns
An aerial photograph of an upland landscape – houses, fields and cairns – in Perthshire.
RCAHMS

and the marks of ard-ploughing. However, there was only a small lightly built house. At Northton, in contrast, there were two more substantial houses, but no trace of arable farming. However, there was clear evidence for the use of domesticated animals (cattle and sheep) and hunting and fishing – the people had gathered and caught shellfish, seabirds, deer, lobster, crab, seal, and whale.

In the Northern Isles substantial buildings were erected on sites which had been occupied since the Neolithic, as at Scord of Brouster.

A time of change

The period after that which we have been considering – the later Bronze Age – was a time of considerable change. It has been argued that this change was driven by a rapid and severe deterioration in the climate, which made mixed farming in the uplands impossible, forcing people to abandon their land. There have been claims that this was associated with major volcanic eruptions, but this is still a matter of debate. The period sees a considerable increase in the amount of bronze weaponry, and the establishment in many parts of Scotland of enclosed and, later, fortified settlements; both developments may relate to the

Bronze Age Round House

The reconstruction of an early Bronze Age round house.

HISTORIC SCOTLAND

shortage of land and people's efforts to take it by force or defend it. It is perhaps in this period that we can see the trend of the previous 3000 years reach a new stage of development - from an early Neolithic society in which overt expression of status was avoided in life and death, through the more hierarchical society of the late Neolithic, and finally to the fully-fledged tribal chiefdoms of the Iron Age.

As we move into the later Bronze Age, the construction of purpose-built monuments such as stone circles for special ceremonial purposes seems to decline, and the disposal of the dead becomes archaeologically less detectable – virtually no more cists or urns, no more cairns or burial mounds for over 1500 years. Perhaps here we see the beginnings of the later concerns with natural features - bodies of water and groves of trees – as places of worship.

Conclusions

The Neolithic and early Bronze Age, a period of over 2500 years, saw remarkable changes. Farming was established as the way of life of the great majority of the inhabitants of Britain, and we can see that these farming societies were capable of major works of design and construction, from great monuments to fine tools. Through their monuments, burials, settlements and possessions we can glimpse the richness and complexity of their daily lives and their religious beliefs. We can see also that these farmers were the ones who began the process of deforesting and smoothing the land – the people who began the processes that have led to our modern landscape.

Following page:
The Stones of Stenness
GORDON BARCLAY

How Do I Find Out More?

The remains of the Neolithic and early Bronze Age are scattered all over Scotland. Some areas have more that is both excavated and interpreted, but most areas have something worth seeing. The list is ordered by area, alphabetically. I have used a combination of the old region and the new local authority names – and have tried to give a broad geographical coverage, concentrating on monuments that are open to the public by Historic Scotland (marked HS) or by other bodies (marked P). Where there are no initials the site is on private land and the permission of the owner will be required. Ordnance Survey grid references are provided.

Aberdeenshire

Capo – (P) this enormous, well-preserved early Neolithic long barrow was not recognised until the 1970s. It stands in a large clearing in a Forestry Commission forest. NO 633 664.

Loanhead, Easter Aquhorthies, Tomnaverie – (HS) three recumbent stone circles. Loanhead and Easter Aquhorthies are particularly well preserved, while Tomnaverie has spectacular views over the Howe of Cromar. NJ 747 288; NJ 732 207; NJ 486 034.

Standing stones of Cullerlie – (HS) a complex Bronze Age stone circle with eight kerb cairns built within it. NJ 786 042.

Argyll

The Kilmartin Glen contains a remarkable series of burial and ceremonial sites (all HS):

Cup and Ring marked rocks – Achnabreck (NR 856 906), Ballygowan (NR 816 978), Baluachraig (NR 831 969), Cairnbaan (NR 838 910), Kilmichael Glassary (NR 857 934) – well preserved groups of marks.

Bronze Age and Neolithic Cairns – Dunchraigaig (NR 833 968), Glebe (NR 832 989), Nether Largie (3 cairns) (NR 830 983; NR 831 985; NR 828 979), Ri Cruin (NR 825 971).

Temple Wood stone and timber circles – NR 826 978.

Arran

Torrylin cairn – (HS) an early Neolithic long cairn. NR 955 210.

Machrie Moor – (HS) a spectacular group of five stone circles in a fine moorland setting. NR 910 324.

Auchagallon stone circle – (HS) a Bronze Age burial cairn surrounded by a circle of 15 standing stones. NR 893 346.

Caithness and Sutherland

The Grey Cairns of Camster – (HS) – two early Neolithic burial cairns – one long, one round – with spectacular chambers, now largely reconstructed after excavation. ND 260 441.

Cnoc Freceadain – (HS) two unexcavated long burial cairns with horned facades. ND 013 654.

Hill o' Many Stanes – (HS) one of the most complex of these enigmatic Neolithic or Bronze Age sites – multiple rows of small stones fanning out across the hillside. ND 295 384.

Dumfries and Galloway

Cairn Holy – (HS) two early Neolithic chambered cairns, one with a spectacular facade. NX 518 540

Drumtroddan cup and ring markings – (HS) three groups of well-defined marks. NX 362 447.

Fife

Balfarg – (P) elements of the early Neolithic to Bronze Age ceremonial complex, including a timber mortuary structure. The Balfarg henge and the Balbirnie stone circle have been laid out for visitors after excavation. NO 281 031.

Inverness-shire

Balnuaran of Clava – (HS) two Clava type passage graves and a ring cairn, each surrounded by a stone circle, and a kerb cairn, all of the Bronze Age. Examples of an unusual regionally restricted group of cairns. NH 752 439.

Corrimony cairn – (HS) a Clava cairn near Drumnadrochit, reconstructed after excavation. NH 383 303.

Lothians

Cairnpapple – (HS) – a complex site, with a henge, subsequently built over twice by burial cairns. The henge and outside of the cairns are accessible at all times. The site displays and the interior of the reconstructed cairn are open in summer. NS 987 717.

Moray

Quarry Wood henge – (P) a well-preserved henge monument of an unusual type. The ditch and external bank surrounding the enclosure are very narrow. The site lies in a clearing in a Forestry Commission Community Woodland. NJ 185 630.

Orkney

Orkney is the area in Scotland with the greatest number of visible Neolithic monuments; the few listed are a small selection.

Knap of Howar – (HS) a pair of stone-built houses of the early Neolithic, with cupboards. HY 483 519.

Maes Howe – (HS) this chambered tomb is the most striking example of Neolithic architecture in the UK. A large mound, surrounded by what may be a slightly later henge monument, covering a large stone chamber, reached by a long low passage HY 318 128.

Skara Brae – (HS) – spectacularly preserved late Neolithic village, with houses surviving to their full wall height and containing stone-built furniture. HY 231 188.

Barnhouse – (P) – the recently excavated

late Neolithic village lying close to Stenness, Brodgar and Maes Howe has been laid out for visitors by the Orkney Council. HY 306 124.

The Stones of Stenness and the Ring of Brodgar - (HS) - these two spectacular henges and stone circles overlook the Loch of Harry, close to Maes Howe and Barnhouse. HY 306 126 & HY 294 134.

Perthshire and Angus

Cleaven Dyke - the best preserved cursus monument/bank barrow in Britain. It survives for a length of 1.8km in woodland, crossing the main Perth to Blairgowrie road. The monument is owned by Meikleour estates, from whom permission to visit should be sought. NO 150 410 – NO 177 396.

Pitnacree - this early Neolithic round barrow can be seen easily from the roadside. NN 928 533

Carse, Dull - this 'four-poster' stone circle, although not open to the public can be appreciated from the roadside. When excavated in the 1970s a cremation in an urn was found within the setting. NN 802 487.

Croft Moraig - A complex double stone circle built on the site of an earlier wooden structure. NN 797 476.

Shetland

Staneydale 'Temple' - (HS) a large Neolithic building of stone. Heel-shaped on the outside, like the contemporary tombs on Shetland, with a large oval chamber within. The remains of a smaller building of the same period can be seen behind the path to the 'Temple', with contemporary field boundaries around it. HY 285 502.

Western Isles

Calanais (Callanish) - (HS) a spectacular complex setting of standing stones in an impressive situation. Excellent visitor centre run by local trust. NB 213 330.

Museums

Most local authority museums will have some Neolithic and Bronze Age material on display. However, some museums have particularly good collections of material from this period:

The National Museums of Scotland – the new Museum of Scotland is opening in Edinburgh in November 1998.

The Anthropological Museum, Marischal College, University of Aberdeen.

Tankerness House Museum, Kirkwall, Orkney.

Further Reading

Scotland: environment and archaeology 8000 BC to AD 1000, edited by Kevin Edwards & Ian Ralston (Wiley 1997). *Europe in the Neolithic,* Alistair Whittle (Cambridge University Press 1996). *Wild Harvesters: The First People in Scotland,* Bill Finlayson (Canongate 1998). *Settlement and Sacrifice: The Later Prehistoric People of Scotland,* Richard Hingley (Canongate 1998). *Neolithic & Bronze Age Scotland,* Patrick Ashmore (Batsford 1996). The *Exploring Scotland's Heritage* series (The Stationery Office), covers the whole of Scotland's prehistoric and more recent heritage in 9 regional volumes. *Altering the Earth,* Richard Bradley (Society of Antiquaries of Scotland 1993). *Archaeoastronomy,* Clive Ruggles (Yale 1998).

Acknowledgements

I am very grateful to the friends and colleagues who commented on drafts of this book – David Breeze, Richard Bradley, Elizabeth Goring, Alison Sheridan, and to Jackie Henrie for her editorial input. Thanks are due to the following individuals and organisations for their permission to reproduce their copyright illustrations: Historic Scotland; The Royal Commission on the Ancient and Historical Monuments of Scotland, National Museums of Scotland, Noel Fojut, Ian Ralston and Colin Richards. The illustrations on pages 11, 20, 33, 52, 56 and 57 appeared first in the pages of the *Proceedings of the Society of Antiquaries of Scotland.* The maps were prepared by Sylvia Stevenson and Rob Burns. The excavators of Balbridie (Ian Ralston), Barnhouse (Colin Richards) and Den of Boddam (Alan Saville) provided valuable input into the creation of the reconstruction paintings – the results, however, are my (and the artist David Hogg's) interpretation.

HISTORIC SCOTLAND safeguards Scotland's built heritage, including its archaeology, and promotes its understanding and enjoyment on behalf of the Secretary of State for Scotland. It undertakes a programme of 'rescue archaeology', from which many of the results are published in this book series.

Scotland has a wealth of ancient monuments and historic buildings, ranging from prehistoric tombs and settlements to remains from the Second World War, and HISTORIC SCOTLAND gives legal protection to the most important, guarding them against damaging changes or destruction. HISTORIC SCOTLAND gives grants and advice to the owners and occupiers of these sites and buildings.

HISTORIC SCOTLAND has a membership scheme which allows access to properties in its care, as well as other benefits. For information, contact: 0131 668 8999.

WILD HARVESTERS

Wild
Harvesters

The first people
in Scotland

Bill Finlayson

Series editor: Gordon Barclay

CANONGATE BOOKS
with
HISTORIC SCOTLAND

THE MAKING
OF SCOTLAND

Series editor:
Gordon Barclay

Other titles available:

FARMERS, TEMPLES AND TOMBS:
Scotland in the Neolithic
and Early Bronze Age

SETTLEMENT AND SACRIFICE:
The Later Prehistoric People
of Scotland

A GATHERING OF EAGLES:
Scenes from Roman Scotland

First published in Great Britain in 1998
by Canongate Books Ltd, 14 High
Street, Edinburgh EH1 1TE

British Library Cataloguing-in-Publication Data
A catalogue record for this book is available on request
from the British Library

ISBN 0 86241 779 1

Series Design:
James Hutcheson, Canongate Books

Design:
Stephen Chester

Printed and bound by
GraphyCems

Previous page
The rocky west coast of
Scotland, an area inhabited
by Scotland's first settlers.

Contents

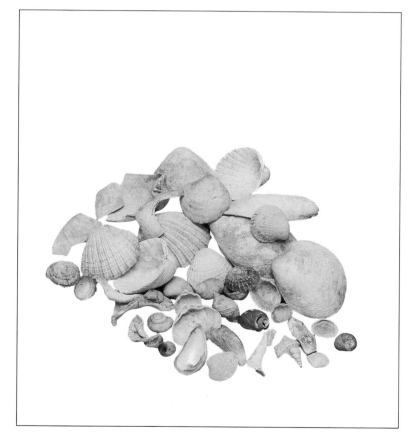

Mesolithic Midden
Shell remains found in
a midden dating to the
Mesolithic period.

After the Ice Age

This book is an introduction to the first people to live in Scotland. Relatively little is known about them – indeed it is only in the last 50 years or so that we have discovered their existence. They left none of the great monuments that later cultures built, the tombs, stone circles, hill forts and so on that are recognised as archaeological sites and can still be visited today. The period they lived in is covered by this book and is called the Mesolithic.

People first moved into the country after the end of the last Ice Age, about 10,000 years ago. They lived before the development of farming and had to get their food from the wild – fish, nuts, berries, and wild animals both large and small. They had no villages or even proper houses and had to be fairly mobile to take advantage of the different resources they needed, moving from place to place at different times of year. This way of life is known as hunter-gathering: hunting wild animals and gathering plant foods. Today this way of life only survives in a few, generally marginal, environments, such as the Australian outback and the Kalahari desert. Even in these places there are few, if any, who still survive entirely on natural resources. This makes it particularly difficult for us to study or imagine how the first people in Scotland lived, as their way of life was so different from ours. Also, as they built no houses, no temples and no forts, there seems at first little left from their life with which to study them today.

Scottish Pine Forest (*opposite*)
Ten thousand years of human occupation and changing land use have left few areas that resemble what the first people to arrive will have seen.
CAROLINE WICKHAM-JONES

Hunter-gatherers
Contemporary hunter-gatherers in southern Africa give us some understanding of how Mesolithic societies may have lived.
ALAN BARNARD

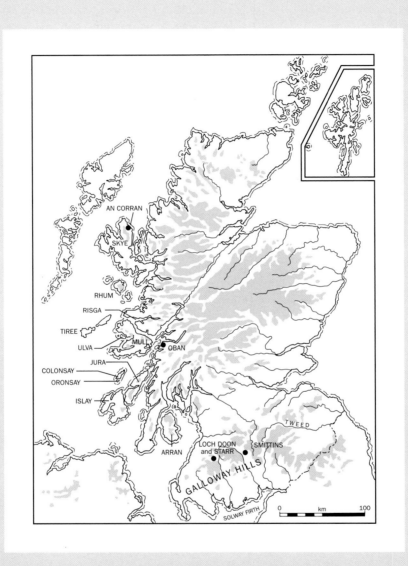

AN CORRAN

SKYE

RHUM

RISGA

TIREE

ULVA

MULL

OBAN

JURA

COLONSAY

ORONSAY

ISLAY

TWEED

ARRAN

LOCH DOON
and STARR

SMITTINS

GALLOWAY HILLS

SOLWAY FIRTH

0   km   100

Because of these difficulties we have to use a wide range of methods to learn about them. Of course we use the techniques of archaeology: the excavation of the camp sites these people lived in and the study of their stone, bone and antler tools, but we also have to use the techniques of botany and zoology to study the materials left in their rubbish heaps or middens to understand what they ate, how big or old it was when they caught it, and during which season they lived at each site. Furthermore, we have to use anthropology – the study of modern peoples – to gain some insight into the hunter-gatherer mind and way of life. In addition, we must interpret our results in the light of what other archaeologists have found out in other parts of Europe, because, while Scotland is particularly rich in some types of evidence, especially shell waste middens, it is poor in others, such as burials. The study of hunter-gatherers depends very much on combining these different strands of evidence.

Part of the fascination of studying these early people is in the search to understand them, in the development of the methods and theories which allow us to approach them. Another challenge results from how very different their lives were from ours. It is difficult to understand the way people survived, had families, and what they thought of the world, at such a distance from our own times. However, these people are our ancestors – the first to live in Scotland. A little bit of them will have come down to shape the way Scotland and indeed the Scots have developed. There have been changes since then and many new people have arrived, but from these earliest colonists onwards, through their interaction with the environment, the people living in Scotland have developed their own distinctive way of doing things.

In this book, I will try to show what we know of these hunter-gatherers and how we know it. I will explain how these people, despite living from 10,000 to 6000 years ago, with no farms and no houses, were in many ways like us. Physically they were modern humans, the same as we are. Their brains were the same as ours. We can never hope to know how they spoke, but we do know that they will have spoken a language rich in the words they needed to describe their environment. Indeed, through their way of life, they will have had a hugely rich understanding of this environment. People are superb at adapting to their conditions and while our modern conditions require that we know how to survive in cities, how to drive cars, use computers and so on, their's required that they knew how to survive in the natural environment, and they succeeded for thousands of years. They were not primitive savages grubbing out an existence close to the subsistence margin, but had a very

Location Map *(opposite)*
Map showing principal areas mentioned in text.

Kalahari San
Women digging up tubers. Plant foods
have always been important to hunter-
gatherers. In most societies we know
the bulk of plant foods are collected
by women.
ALAN BARNARD

successful economy. Also,
as modern people, living
together and meeting other
groups, having families,
arguing, grieving, rejoicing
and doing all the things that
make up a human society,
they will have had a rich
culture. However, much of
the material evidence for this,
the symbols that showed what
group they belonged to, how
important they were and so
on, would have been made
of perishable materials and
so have been lost to us.

Because of the mobile
lifestyle employed by most
hunter-gatherers, I will not
describe the archaeological
sites as isolated entities, but
rather will describe a
patchwork made up of a
number of sites, showing
how people used the different
parts of their environment to
provide different resources. I will look at how they did not just
wander the landscape collecting and hunting, but at how they
would have had carefully established strategies, how they would
have used their knowledge of the weather to predict when it was
time to move, how they would have sent out task teams to
specific areas, and, perhaps most significantly, how they would
have modified their environment. I will use evidence from
pollen studies to show the establishment of clearings in woods,
along with evidence from Colonsay for huge hazelnut harvests
that probably required large gatherings of people, and how to
encourage such a harvest they may have had to burn clearings,
and prune the trees. I will examine how such an investment in
a resource implies a concept of ownership, not necessarily the
same as ours, but a resource identified with a people, even if
they did not live beside the resource all the time, but only came
to it when it was ripe. As a way of giving life to these different
theories, one of the techniques used in this book is to use an
imaginative reconstruction, following a group of hunter-
gatherers as they make use of different resources at different sites
through the year.

Stone Age Stereotypes

'Man the hunter' is a dominant image from pre-farming societies, with wild hairy men chasing big dangerous animals. While we should not deny that hunting would have been an important activity, we must understand its place in the overall economy and society. Hunting for large animals is often a relatively high risk means of getting food compared to more predictable resources such as fish, shellfish, nuts and fruit. It can, however, be an important part of the diet as well as providing additional non-food materials, such as skins, furs, sinew and bones for tool manufacture.

Today we tend to think of hunting as either involving large groups of people, perhaps most typically in Scotland in grouse shooting, or as a solo activity, where a man stalks and hunts alone, or with a small group of friends, equipped with a

North-eastern Asian Hunters
There are very few hunter-gatherer societies today so old records provide a useful source of information.
COURTESY OF CAROLINE WICKHAM-JONES

powerful rifle for deer or the latest in high-tech fishing tackle for salmon. All these types of hunting have a social element to them, and bringing home food is only part of the activity. Our association with men as the hunters comes as much from this modern view of hunting as it does from our knowledge of hunter-gatherer societies or the past. Hunting amongst hunter-gatherers is a rather different activity. Hunting does not just provide food. It is also not so much about the thrill of the chase, or the moment of the kill, although these will inevitably have played their part and success in hunting may have been important to a man's status. Hunting is about catching a resource as economically as possible, whether that is done by traps, nets, fishing lines, spears or bows and arrows. It is also about butchering a carcass and taking the useful parts away for processing. Big animals may well have more meat on them than is wanted, and consequently much of the meat has to be processed, by drying or smoking soon after the kill, before it goes bad, perhaps even before the journey home. Often, while big animal hunting may be done by the men in a group, much hunting of smaller prey is done by the women, as is much of the processing of the carcass. It is also important to remember the importance of fishing, especially in a country like Scotland, where both coastal waters and rivers will have been rich with fish (in fact, the more accurate term for the people we are studying should be hunter-gatherer-fishers).

Much of our modern understanding of hunter-gatherers comes from studies of modern or recent hunter-gatherers, people like the San in southern Africa, most of whom live in or around the Kalahari desert, the Eskimos and other northern peoples, who live around the Arctic, or aboriginals from Australia. However, there are a few very serious problems with using these as analogies for the Mesolithic in Scotland. The first is that they are modern societies, and just because they live a hunter-gatherer lifestyle, we should not forget that 6–10,000 years separates them from our hunter-gatherers. The second is that all modern studies of these peoples see them as they are now, living in contact with the modern world, not as they were before contact. Indeed, many modern hunter-gatherers have at times lived at least partially by farming, or have had a close relationship with farmers with whom they trade. The third, and perhaps the most significant divergence, is that modern hunter-gatherers tend to live in marginal environments such as deserts or arctic wastes, where farming is impossible. Our hunter-gatherers lived in a rich temperate environment, full of resources, so full indeed that we can suggest a number of different economic strategies they could have adopted. Therefore, although the information we can gain

from hunter-gatherer anthropology may be useful, we have to be careful how we use it. More than that, if we are interested in the past, we have to examine the past to see how human society has developed and changed. We must not just take modern examples and put them back into history.

Like us, as people, early hunter-gatherers will have had complicated social relationships within and between families. Their emotions and fears would be familiar to us. Their lifestyle will, however, have been sufficiently different from ours for them to have developed other ways of resolving their conflicts. The ways modern people have imagined Stone-Age societies have often been something of a caricature of our own times and prejudices. Hunter-gatherers have been seen as noble savages (as, for example, in 18th century images of American Indians), as

Modern Hunter-gatherer

When modern hunter-gatherers are used as a source of information it is important to remember that they are modern, not preserved prehistoric relics. All modern hunter-gatherers trade with settled communities and it is not unusual to see apparently odd combinations of traditional crafts and Western goods.
ALAN BARNARD

American Indians in the 17th century

Our impressions of other cultures are always coloured by our own background.
This French artist's representation from the 17th century is clearly a product of the
artist's culture, and reflects then current ideas concerning the 'noble savage'.

hairy cavemen beating each other on the head with clubs, and in the 1960s as peace-loving individuals who resolved all conflicts by debate or by simply agreeing to split up and go their separate ways. All of these models are the result of our looking back at so-called primitives from our point of view as civilised people. Even the idealistic 1960s view depends upon a belief that without ownership of houses, pots and so on and without the investment of labour in fields and stored foods, conflicts could be easily resolved. I hope to be able to make it clear that these people were not so very different from us – they didn't live in a Stone-Age never-never land, but would have had ideas of territory and of resources and objects belonging to people. Having said that, we should not underestimate just how different their view of the world may have been.

As archaeologists, we build up our own images of life in the past. We may claim greater sophistication, but when we want to provide a quick picture, we often fall back on the shorthand of our own stereotypes. Compare the picture below of hunter-gatherers with the picture overleaf of early farmers both found in a recent book. The first picture shows the Mesolithic, and is an image of rather desperate Robinson Crusoe-type characters, all men,

Hunter-gatherer Landscape
A reconstruction of a Mesolithic landscape.
ALAN BRABY, HISTORIC SCOTLAND

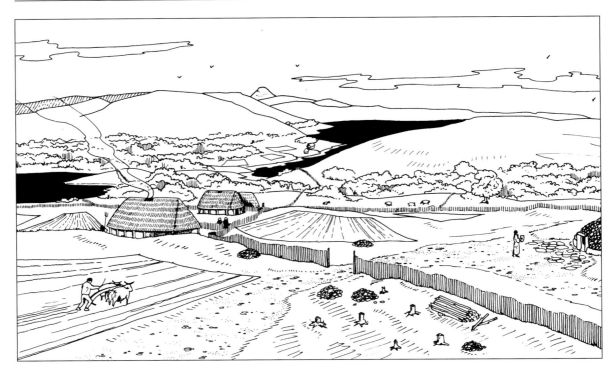

Early Farming Landscape

A reconstruction of a Neolithic
landscape, cleared and domesticated.
ALAN BRABY, HISTORIC SCOTLAND

wearing roughly stitched skins and hunting in a wild wood. The
second picture (above) is of farmers from the Neolithic; the
landscape has become tamed and, as if to emphasise this, we can
see a woman holding a baby. The author of that book does not
consider hunter-gatherers as early farmers in this rather
stereotypical way, and indeed this book reflects the very different
aspects of Mesolithic life, but these pictures do show just how
difficult it is for us to escape such powerful, inherited images.
The shaggy Robinson Crusoe image is of someone who has
been isolated from his culture, and who cannot cope; whereas
the hunter-gatherers of Scotland were in fact living within a
flourishing, functioning society.

Archaeologists call the period after the last Ice Age before
farming began the Mesolithic, which simply means the Middle
Stone Age, but this is just because apart from stone tools used by
the hunter-gatherers, few other objects survive on most sites.
The acid soils of Scotland have destroyed most other tools and
artefacts, but we know from shell midden sites in Scotland, and
from occasional sites scattered across Europe, that Mesolithic
people made bone and antler tools, they made baskets and fish
traps, they lined their floors with bark, and that they built canoes
and decorated elegant paddles.

So, what we need to do is to forget the convenient labels of
Stone Age, or cave men, and to consider the evidence we have
for this period.

Island Hopping

The canoe moved into the bay. The boy sitting at the prow could see that already a large number of other boats were drawn up on the beach, and that camp fires had been lit. He looked back to his sister, who had finally fallen asleep. This would be the first time she had seen so many people in one place. He hoped that this year he would be allowed to go off with the men to fish, while the women collected shells for bait, smoked the fish to store for later in the year and spent the days making the fine leather clothes that his people wore. They would mostly eat shellfish for the next few weeks and he was looking forward to this, even if his brother told him he would be sick of the sight of them before they left the island.

On the island of Oronsay a number of shell middens have been found, piles of shells discarded in great heaps around the old shoreline of the island. These were first examined by antiquarians in the last century, but are best understood through the work of archaeologist Paul Mellars who excavated there in the 1970s. Several very important studies have been made of the material he collected. The collections are particularly well preserved, as the calcium from the shells in the mound produces a less acidic microenvironment than most Scottish soils. Apart from the shells themselves, the type of material recovered includes mammal bones, bone and antler tools, flints and fish and bird bones. Much of the evidence Mellars recovered had not been found in the 19th century as it required careful sieving to pick out the fragments of fish bone. He was soon able to show that although the shells formed the bulk of the mounds, the presence of quantities of fish bones suggests that fish may have been more important to the diet than shellfish. Anyone who has eaten a plate of mussels will know that the size of the mound of shells is far greater than the amount eaten. Another suggestion put forward was that the limpets which form an important part of the mounds were not

Oronsay Middens
Shell middens are not always immediately recognisable as they are now mostly covered by grass.
IAN RALSTON

At Work and Play

The illustration shows people at work and
play on a beach camp site. People are busy cooking,
smoking fish to store for later, preparing shellfish,
making and repairing tools, nets and clothes.
Harpoons are standing outside their shelters. In the
distance you can see the smoke rising from a campsite on another
island. The people are dressed in well-made clothes and wear shells and tooth
beads. We do not know exactly how they were dressed – or how they wore the
beads we find – but we believe that like more recent hunter-gatherers, they will
have cared for their personal appearance.

HARRY BLAND

1 cm

Bone and Antler Tools
These harpoons are typical examples of
the fine workmanship recovered from
shell middens on the west coast.
NATIONAL MUSEUMS OF SCOTLAND

collected for eating, but as bait for fishing. Limpets are a very
rubbery shellfish to eat and would certainly appear to be a
peculiar choice for people who also had fish and oysters to eat.

One of the best pieces of detective work on the material
from the Oronsay middens was conducted on the tiny bones
called otoliths which come from a fish called the saithe. One
student studying these fish bones observed that the sizes of the
saithe otoliths differed from midden to midden. He began a
programme of experimental studies and was able to show that
the different sizes could be linked very closely to the age of the
fish. Looking at the behaviour of modern saithe he was able to
show that the size of fish depended upon the time of year. From
this he was able to show that the different sizes of otoliths found
at the various Mesolithic middens meant that people were
coming to these middens at different times of year, and that in
general the middens were each occupied for particular seasons.
Exactly why they were doing this is more difficult to establish,
but it seems to represent a pattern that continued for a
considerable number of years. Some scholars have suggested that
the same group of hunter-gatherers lived on Oronsay all year,
and moved on periodically around the island in a steady and
constant progression, perhaps because of the weather, or perhaps
as they used up the closest shellfish.

However, I do not believe that this is the most likely course
of events. During the time when the middens were
accumulating, Oronsay was an even smaller island than it is now,
as the sea level was higher than at present, so the population
would have been restricting itself to a very small world at a time
when we know that groups were much more mobile than
people now. Oronsay would have had few, if any, of the other
resources, plant or animal, needed for survival. Indeed, the
mammal bones from the middens suggest that people had
contacts outwith the island – the size of the bones suggests that at
least two different populations of deer were being hunted: one of
rather small deer, probably from a population that had become
isolated on an island for a very long time, and the other of larger
deer, from a bigger population. It seems unlikely that the small
deer would have come from the neighbouring island of
Colonsay, as that island is probably too far from anywhere else
for deer to have become established, which would suggest that
they must be from an island closer to the mainland, perhaps Jura.
The larger deer were probably hunted on the mainland. This
suggests a pattern of wider ranging contacts.

In addition, the particular fragments of bone that have been
recovered are not typical of those you would transport in your
boat if you were interested in meat. The collection has a

Shell Midden Material

This is a collection of the sort of refuse that is
contained in shell middens.

NATIONAL MUSEUMS OF SCOTLAND

1 cm

Antler Mattock

Antler mattocks may have had a range of functions,
perhaps including digging for tubers.

NATIONAL MUSEUMS OF SCOTLAND

Excavation Methods

Mesolithic sites are mostly short term camp sites and the evidence can be
very slight. At the excavations on Rhum fine sieving was conducted to
recover small artefacts, bones, seeds and other small remains.
CAROLINE WICKHAM-JONES

surprisingly large proportion of non-meat bearing bones. This at first appears confusing: why carry parts of animal skeletons all the way to Oronsay if they were no good for eating? The answer to this may explain why people were going back to the same places on Oronsay again and again. There was no need to take meat foods to Oronsay because there were enough fish and shellfish to keep your group fed. What is more, if you knew where the saithe were going to be, and you could predict the shellfish quantities, you would have a very secure and predictable resource. For a few weeks it would be possible for at least part of the group to stay in one place, which would allow them to get on with the various chores that had to be done. One of these was the manufacture of the bone and antler tools that were needed and it is the case that the bone parts taken to Oronsay are the same as those used to make tools, so we can suggest that while part of the group went fishing, another part stayed by the middens making bone tools, such as harpoons.

They also made another tool, a bevel-ended tool shape which has caused some arguments between archaeologists since it was first identified (see p.25). It has been suggested that this tool was used for knocking limpets off rocks, or scooping out the

Saithe
Preserved within the shell middens on Oronsay were the bones of fish. One of the most important was the saithe.
BILL FINLAYSON

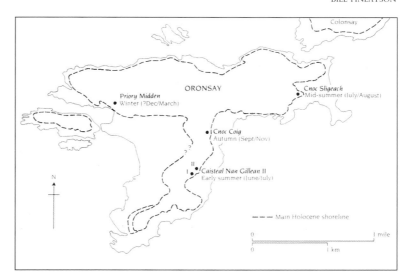

Oronsay Shorelines
Shorelines have changed since the Mesolithic. This plan shows how much smaller Oronsay was when the people who left the middens lived there.
OXFORD UNIVERSITY PRESS

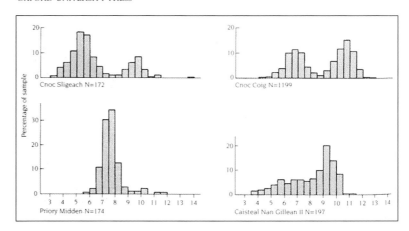

Otolith Size Graphs
Studying the size distribution of saithe otolith sizes and comparing these with modern samples allows us to determine at which seasons the different middens were used.
OXFORD UNIVERSITY PRESS

limpet from within its shell. The presence of these tools in the shell middens has been used to support this argument. This is an example of how modern people tend to assume that life in the Mesolithic was a fairly grim struggle for survival, and that all tools would have been directly related to the business of collecting food. I would argue that these tools are leather working tools and that as well as making tools at the midden sites, people were also using the tools to make leather clothing. This theory may help us to explain why different middens were occupied so regularly at different seasons. Different groups could have had traditional rights to go to exploit the shellfish on Oronsay at different times of year.

Modern Hide Dressing Experiments
Experimenting with prehistoric tasks gives insight into how tools functioned.
CAROLINE WICKHAM-JONES

North American Indians Scraping Hide
Studying traditional crafts helps us understand how the same tasks may have been done in the past.
COURTESY OF CAROLINE WICKHAM-JONES

Bevel-ended Tools

Bevel-ended tools appear as a very simple form of artefact. They are made of bone, antler or stone, and are quite long with a bevelled end. The tools have often been described as limpet hammers (generally when made of stone) and limpet scoops (generally when made of bone or antler). What they were really used for is another matter and serves to illustrate the development of archaeological ideas through debate and also shows how such simple pieces of evidence can begin to play an important role in our understanding of past behaviour.

I have suggested that these tools may have been used for leather working. A colleague at Edinburgh University, Clive Bonsall, argues that the tools are used as limpet hammers, and that their form is the result of their use in collecting the limpets that are common in some middens. Both of us have some experimental data to show that our interpretations are at least possible. Clive has advanced the argument that the association of bone and antler bevel-ended tools with the midden sites supports his case. I have argued that these tools are preserved here by the soil chemistry produced in the middens, and that stone examples are often found away from midden sites, suggesting that the presence of the bone and antler examples is an accident of preservation, rather than a consequence of how they were used. There are

cases, best known in Cornwall, where these bevel-ended tools are not associated with shell middens, but are always found away from the midden sites. Tools with similar bevelled ends are known from other parts of the world, both in north-west America and in Australia, and in all these cases they are used for leather working, both for softening the material and for smoothing seams. Research being conducted while this book was being written has given greater support to Clive's argument, as an analysis of the

microscopic traces on some of the bone and antler tools suggests that they were not used for leather working.

The significance of the disagreement is that Clive's theory sees the tools as firmly placed within the food economy (whether the limpets were being collected to be eaten or used for bait), whereas my suggestion places the tools in the context of understanding social issues, as tools being used to produce well-made clothing.

Bevel-ended Tool Forms
NATIONAL MUSEUMS OF SCOTLAND

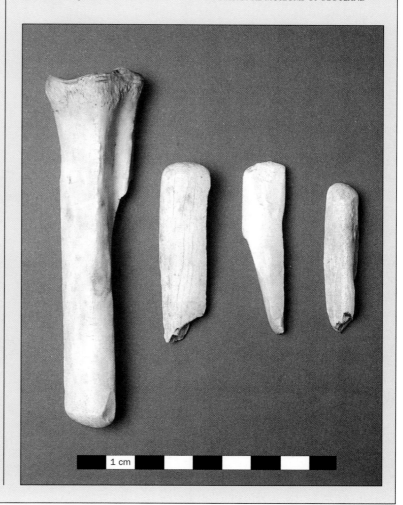

Who made the middens?

One of the apparent problems of the Scottish Mesolithic has been why midden sites are so different from other types of site. Most other sites are dominated by collections of stone tools, including forms called microliths which are not found in the middens. I will describe these in Chapter 4. One of the most interesting recent discoveries has been the site of An Corran on Skye, found by chance during road building, where shell midden artefacts were found mixed with microliths. This confirms information from excavations many years ago on the little island of Risga in Loch Sunart, where a microlith was found apparently associated with the midden. Unfortunately the excavation records made at that time did not make it clear if the midden had just accumulated where someone had previously dropped a microlith hundreds of years before. Finding the microliths and the midden together is very important, as at one time archaeologists thought that the people who left middens were a separate, later culture. They called this the 'Obanian' after a series of middens found around Oban. The Obanian was seen as a late stage of the Mesolithic, separate from the microlith-making stage. Nowadays we see the middens as simply representing one aspect of Mesolithic life, where a different tool kit was required. This new interpretation is to a great extent based on the employment of a new scientific development, where much smaller samples of organic remains can be subject to radiocarbon dating. This not only allows smaller remains to be dated, but means that tools can be dated by taking very small samples without having to destroy an entire artefact.

As with all new discoveries, this revelation required a re-examination of the Obanian. The absence of antler and bone

Hide Working
Many traditional chores have always served as social activities.
HARRY BLAND

Raschoille Cave

One of the small caves in the Oban cliffs. Unfortunately there is often little to see at these sites nowadays. Here access to the cave has had to be restricted as the roof is unsafe.

CAROLINE WICKHAM-JONES

tools away from the midden sites could be explained by the fact that these materials are only preserved because the shell-rich middens provide the right chemical conditions for preservation. It was, however, difficult to explain why no one had ever taken a microlith to a shell midden site and lost it there. An Corran has brought the two types of evidence together. Archaeologist Tony Pollard has now gone back to the site of Risga – or what is left of it – and has discovered that next to the midden is a microlith-rich site. This illustrates two points: firstly, that so far we have only excavated a small number of Mesolithic sites, and our knowledge is so patchy that every new excavation is likely to throw up interesting results; secondly, that in the past archaeologists have excavated middens and because of the good preservation within the midden, have never looked beyond the midden, to find out if there are other discoveries to be made nearby.

Mesolithic Boats

We know from settlements on islands such as Rhum, Colonsay, Skye and Islay and from the fish bones found on their sites, that Mesolithic people in Scotland were successful seafarers. What we are not sure about is how they travelled between islands. There appear to have been two means, one being the coracle, a lightweight frame covered with leather, the other being a canoe made from a log. No examples of either have been found recently to allow them to be dated by modern techniques such as radiocarbon dating. Coracles, because of their lightweight nature, are the more perishable of the two, and none have been discovered. There have been some examples of dugout canoes found, mostly during peat cutting last century, but none survive. Some of these appear to be more recent than the Mesolithic, but other examples may have been Mesolithic. At present, the balance of evidence suggests that Mesolithic waters were travelled by canoe. The examples found, however, have mostly come from freshwater locations, such as former lochs and lakes, and we do not know if these vessels would have been up to crossing stretches of open sea. My guess is that they would have been. They represent a considerable amount of work, and it appears unlikely that this technology would have been adopted if coracles were in regular use at sea.

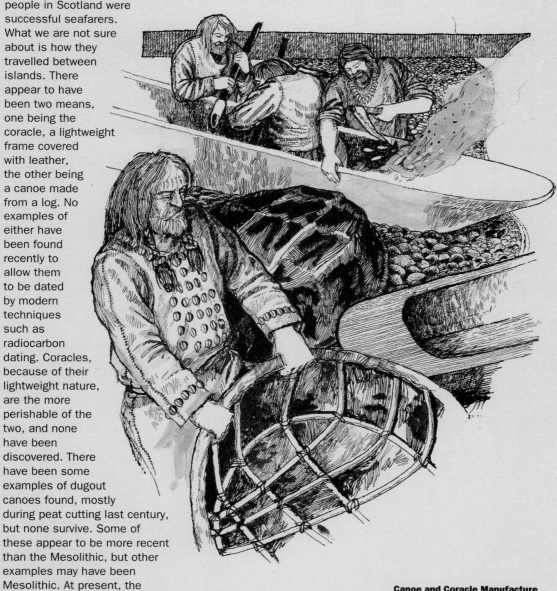

Canoe and Coracle Manufacture
HARRY BLAND

Gathering Hazels

The illustration shows people harvesting hazel shells to take back to their camp. Roasted hazelnuts may have been an important form of stored food for times when fresh resources were scarce. Gathering plant foods will have been important, and will have mostly been done by women.

HARRY BLAND

Life in the Woods

The crowd of children were busy collecting the nuts that were falling from the trees onto the skins laid out underneath. Some of the women were already starting to carry baskets full of nuts back to the camp. From beyond the clearing where the hazels grew, rising above the thick woods that lay between them and the campsite, the smoke could already be seen rising from the fires in the roasting pits where the nuts would be cooked. This was a busy time of year for everyone, as the nuts had to be gathered and processed for storage so that they could be eaten throughout the winter months ahead, when other foods were scarce.

Over the last few years evidence has been steadily accumulating of the deliberate management of the woods that would have covered much of Scotland during the Mesolithic. Most of the direct evidence we have is not from traditional archaeology, but from palynology, the study of pollen (see p.32). We have always known that because hunter-gatherers were so dependent on and involved with their environment that it is very important to establish what that environment was. Palynologists study the evidence for past environments and given the many changes that people have made to the environment in Scotland since they first arrived, the reconstructions that they can make are vital. What is more, we must remember that climate has changed since the Mesolithic. Hunter-gatherers first moved into Scotland not long after the ice sheets of the last glaciation retreated. By the time in which we are interested, when there appears to have been a permanent and significant occupation of Scotland, the climate was somewhat warmer than it is today.

In the past, the work of people interested in the ancient environment was regarded merely as background material by archaeologists trying to

Staosnaig Excavations

Steven Mithen's excavations at Staosnaig on Colonsay have recovered a scatter of stone tools and pits, including a large pit which seems to be full of all sorts plant refuse, including many hazel shells. This is extremely important as such remains are very rarely preserved from the Mesolithic. The polythene greenhouse allows careful excavation work to carry on regardless of the weather.
CAROLINE WICKHAM-JONES

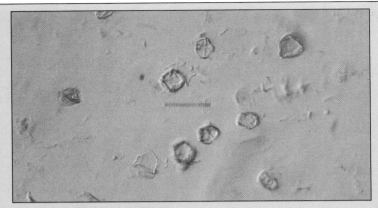

Pollen Grains of Hazel and Alder

Hazel was an important plant food in the Mesolithic.

MIKE CRESSEY

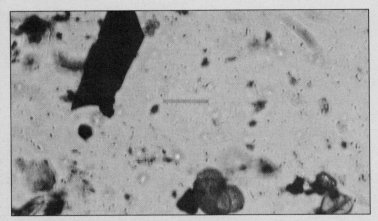

Pollen Grains of Pine with Fragments of Microscopic Charcoal

Such charcoal fragments may be the remains of Mesolithic woodland management.

MIKE CRESSEY

Core Sample

This is a column of peat and soil which has just been collected from a site on Coll.

GERAINT COLES

Pollen Analysis

Pollen analysts (palynologists) identify pollen grains that are preserved in sediments to reconstruct vegetation patterns and changes over time. The best pollen records occur in peat or lake deposits, where the absence of oxygen helps to preserve the pollen grains and the pollen is preserved in a relatively static environment. This means that pollen accumulates pretty much at the same time as the sediments, giving us a column from which samples can be taken in thin slices representing different periods.

In essence this is a straightforward process. A column of peat or lake muds is taken, usually as a core, so that the sequence of growth of the peat or deposition of the muds can be seen. This relies on the same basic principle of stratigraphy upon which much archaeological excavation depends, where more recent material lies on top of older material. By taking slices from these columns and examining the range and frequency of pollen within these slices, pollen analysis can obtain a great deal of information, including information on climate changes (very important when we are interested as a period as far back in time as the Mesolithic) and information on deliberate changes to the vegetation, for example those caused by forest clearance, as well as simply what was growing in the area. There are, of course, all sorts of difficulties, but pollen analysis has become one of the most important ways of understanding this aspect of the early past.

establish the resources available to the first hunter-gatherers. The picture has not remained so simple, however. It now appears clear that from very early on people were modifying their environment; this was, at least to begin with, a rather controversial discovery. Hunter-gatherers were supposed to live a non-intrusive lifestyle, almost as one with the wild, as creatures that were part of the environment. It was generally assumed that it was only when farmers came along and chopped down trees and ploughed fields that people had a significant impact on their surroundings. It now appears clear that hunter-gatherers too were altering their surroundings. This modification would probably nowadays be called management, in the way that a modern park ranger or conservation manager might look after a woodland to encourage certain sorts of rare species to flourish, rather than direct control of an environment, but they were clearly interfering. One of the most obvious traces of this is in the establishment of clearings in woods. We have been able to identify localised clearing of the woods from evidence in cores taken for pollen analysis.

One of the most spectacular discoveries concerning Mesolithic use of woodland resources has been made recently by archaeologist Steve Mithen and his team at the site of Staosnaig on Colonsay. Here, at a site on the old beach a pit has been

Charred Hazel Shells
These are the most common plant remains to survive, but this is probably the result of a preservation bias, as most other plant remains will decay very rapidly.
CAROLINE WICKHAM-JONES

1 cm

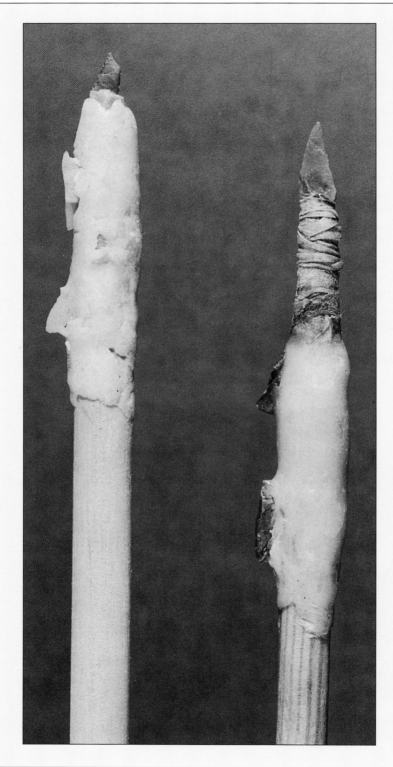

Microliths

Microliths (literally 'small stones') are a very common type of find across much of Europe and the Middle East and date from late in the last Ice Age until the beginning of farming. They are small, generally only a few centimetres long, and sometimes tiny, less than a centimetre long. They are made of long, thin flakes of flint produced by a sophisticated technique designed to produce a large number of fairly standard usable pieces from each flint pebble. They come in a range of shapes, many being geometric forms, such as scalene triangles, crescents, and trapezes. Some of the fine needle-like pointed tools are very well made. A whole range of functions has been ascribed to them, including their use as tattooing needles, drill bits, inserts for sickles, the tips and barbs of arrows, and as elements of graters and other plant processing tools. For a while in western Europe their possible use as the tips and barbs of arrows was the most popular theory, but there is evidence to suggest that other uses were common too. Some archaeologists pointed out that similar tools were, until recently, still used in some parts of the tropics for plant processing, or as fishing equipment. There has been a considerable amount of argument about this, but recent studies of the patterns of microscopic traces of damage

Tool Reconstruction

These arrows were made for experimental use so that the microscopic traces that were then left on the tools could be looked at and then compared with archaeological material.

BILL FINLAYSON

on the tools have shown that they were probably used in all sorts of different ways.

This has formed an important part of the debate about how important hunting was, and how important stone tools were, to Mesolithic people. Based on the use of microliths in arrows, one French archaeologist described the Mesolithic as the period of archery hunting. Other people have tried to identify different communities in the Mesolithic on the basis of different microlith shapes, believing that arrowheads are a very visible tool and that given the importance of hunting, this would be a good way to announce which tribe you belonged to. Unfortunately, most microliths are too small to be very visible, and by the time they had been stuck into a wooden haft (which would have required a socket, and some adhesive materials, such as a mix of resin and beeswax, perhaps also with some binding), not enough would be left sticking out to be useful as a way of letting people know where you were from!

Furthermore, we should not overemphasise how important stone was to the Mesolithic – they may have seen these little bits of flint as very small components of their tools, and have been far more worried about the wooden haft that would have taken much longer to make, but which does not survive for us to study. Most archaeologists looking at the Scottish Mesolithic now suspect that microliths were the world's first plug-in tool replacement part, and that as stone edges wore out, they were thrown away and new ones put in place.

Microliths
A range of fairly typical Scottish microliths.
JOE ROCK, UNIVERSITY OF EDINBURGH

1 cm

found, possibly excavated for a house or shelter. When this structure was abandoned, the pit was filled up with hazel shells. The number of shells is so large that every piece has not been counted, but estimates suggest that hundreds of thousands of hazel shells were dumped into this pit. A microscopic analysis of the pit contents made by a soil scientist has shown that the shells were all dumped at about the same time, in other words during the same harvesting season. This number of shells represents a fantastic harvest and a huge amount of harvesting.

What can have been going on? Steve Mithen has looked at a number of possibilities, and using expert advice from botanists and the evidence from experiments undertaken by his students, has come up with a possible explanation. Around the big pit are a number of smaller pits, and it seems likely that the harvesters were roasting their nuts to help store them. Indeed, once they were roasted they may have gone on to make a paste that would take up far less space that the whole nut kernels. Roasting also improves the flavour of the nuts.

Colonsay may have been a particularly good place to harvest nuts, since, as far as we know, there have never been any squirrels on the island, so eliminating one of the main competitors for the nuts. Even still, the number of nuts harvested is huge, and this may be more evidence that Mesolithic people were not only collecting from wild resources, but were managing them. By burning out clearings in woods they may have

Microlith Manufacture
We don't know whether everyone made stone tools, or whether it was left to experts. In any event, it must have been a craft that was passed on by the elders of the community.
HARRY BLAND

encouraged hazel growth. To increase the harvest still more they may have been pruning the trees, a likely activity given that there is some evidence from Europe that Mesolithic people were actively managing trees by coppicing and pollarding – pruning to encourage the growth of long, straight branches with few knots.

Not only does the harvest suggest woodland management, but it also suggests that a considerable number of people must have been assembled to gather and process all the nuts. The nut harvest and processing may have been an occasion for a number of groups to congregate. The location of this site on Colonsay is interesting, given the nearby middens on Oronsay, but perhaps we should not exaggerate this connection, as it is more likely to be an accident of preservation. Perhaps instead we should think that there may have been many such sites around Scotland.

The most common Mesolithic tool that we find nowadays is the microlith (see p.34). Microliths are typical of most Mesolithic sites away from the shell middens, whether they are up in the hills or down by the coast. They are used as the quickest and surest way of deciding whether a site is Mesolithic or not. People produced vast numbers of microliths, and much of the other chipped stone on Mesolithic sites may be the waste products produced while making these tools. Other stone tools were made, including tools for scraping hides and for shaving wood. These are generally all called scrapers. Unfortunately, people continued to make scrapers after the Mesolithic, and although there are some types that appear to be restricted to particular periods, most could belong to any period of stone tool use.

Excavating most Mesolithic sites involves a considerable amount of time spent collecting the stone needed for tool manufacture. The materials used vary, the most well known being flint, but other materials such as chert and volcanic rocks such as pitchstone from Arran and bloodstone from Rhum have all been used. These stone tools can tell us a great deal about a site and the people who occupied it. We can get an idea of the range of tasks they carried out from the range of tools that are present; for example a tool manufacturing site can be identified from the amount of stone rubbish left. We can see where these people collected their stone by looking for the sources of the stones being used. Looking at sites such as Smittons and Starr in the Galloway Hills and comparing them with the sites down by the coast, both on the west in Ayrshire and to the south along the Solway Firth, we have begun to be able to estimate the movement patterns of these people, who probably travelled from the coast into the hills at different times of the year to exploit different resources. We will explore why hunter-gatherers moved from site to site in the next chapter.

Loch Doon
When the water level was low a series of
Mesolithic sites was found here where the
normal water level had eroded the peat.
Other sites have been found in a similar
manner elsewhere in southern Scotland,
and indicate that the inland hills may have
been extensively occupied, although the
sites are normally hard to find.
CAROLINE WICKHAM-JONES

Making Choices

The group sat together around the fire. The boy's uncle was complaining that he had not caught anything for several days, and although his aunt had teased him that this was because he was getting too fat and everyone had laughed, everyone had agreed and then fallen silent.

After a while the old man let out a long sigh and said perhaps it was time to move on. For a while everyone sat nodding in agreement, looking down at the fire. His wife suggested they should move into the next valley, for the berries would be ripening now and could be picked. The old man, glad to have a chance to get his own back, said that this was a silly idea. His hunting had taken him into the valley and there was no sign that there would be many berries there this year; besides the old man's sister's children had been through that valley just recently and had probably chased off much of the game. A lively discussion followed until gradually they all agreed on the best course of action. They were to split up until the autumn meeting, when the group would join with others to harvest the autumn fruits and salmon to store for the winter.

The boy was cheered up by the thought of the autumn gathering. There were always plenty of people to play with then and strangers to meet. If only they didn't have to split up till then. When he was with just his family, there were fewer chances to play and his father made him work harder.

Hunter-gatherers had a lot of choices to make during the course of their year, but many of these choices were limited by the seasons and the resources available at different times. An important point about humans is that faced by an environment, we can choose how we wish to behave. One of the most interesting things about hunter-gatherer archaeology is trying to work out how people thought about things in the past, and one of the best ways to start to do this is to see if we can understand how they organised themselves.

There are a number of basic ways in which people can organise themselves. The simplest, and the one that we seem to share with our ape relations, is to live in small groups and wander through an area from resource to resource, moving on as each area becomes depleted. Early hominids probably lived like this. It is perhaps easiest in the tropics, where the availability of natural foods may not vary enormously between seasons. It is not so good in a climate like ours, as the seasons may cause big changes in the availability of foods – for example there are few animals to hunt in the hills in the winter, plant foods run out in the autumn, while fish and birds may migrate.

Probably the first major modification to this lifestyle is to design a seasonal round, so that the wanderings through the landscape become more structured. A common and simple

model for Mesolithic Scotland has been that people scattered into small groups in the summer and went to hunt in the hills. In the winter they moved down to the coast and relied on marine resources such as fish and shellfish.

A further adaptation is to have a home camp (often called a base camp), where at least some people live all year. This has the great advantage that you do not have to keep moving around all the time, carrying all your goods, foods and small children with you. Unfortunately, if you are relying on natural resources, you run the risk that you will eat everything within reach and run out of food. Obviously, the more food resources around your

Tanged Points
These flint tools from Scotland look identical to tools called Ahrensburgian Points found in northern Europe and dating to before 10,000 years ago. At present they appear to be the earliest evidence for the human colonisation of Scotland.
JOE ROCK, UNIVERSITY OF EDINBURGH

1 cm

home camp at the start, the longer they will last. This can be helped even more if some of the resources come to you at different times of the year, for example in seasonal migrations, such as with salmon, geese, deer, and so on, or in seasonal availability, such as the ripening of berries and nuts. Unfortunately, there are few places where such year–long abundance is reliable. There are other problems too. If you live in one place all the time, you will start to use up all the available firewood. If people do not get on with each other, but have to carry on living with each other, you may find that arguments

Narrow Blade Microliths
These are the tools that are the most commonly found distinctive evidence for the Scottish Mesolithic.
JOE ROCK, UNIVERSITY OF EDINBURGH

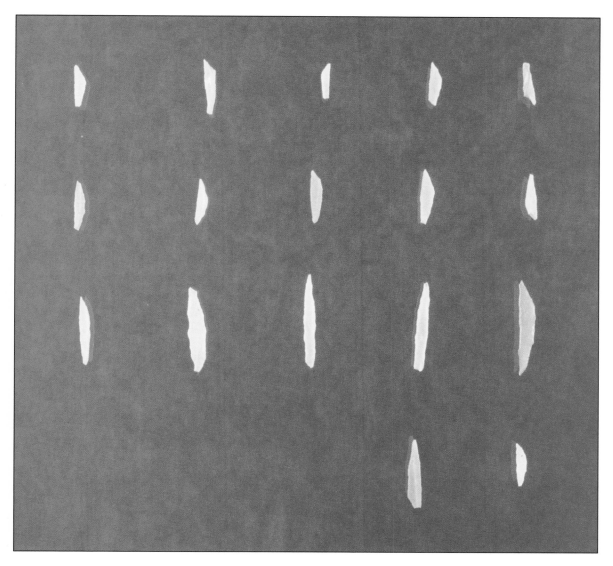

1 cm

become more and more frequent. If something goes wrong with any particular resource that is crucial to feed the community at one time of year, the whole system can collapse.

The base camp idea can be modified too. It is possible to combine some of the benefits of the base camp with those of the seasonal round by using a base camp, but sending out small parties as work groups. These parties can head off to other locations where at certain times of year particular resources are known to be plentiful, and they can then bring back the fruits of their work to the base camp. Work parties could also keep in touch with other groups, keeping the community informed of a larger area and allowing some trading of goods and information.

Where does the Scottish Mesolithic fit into this? Well, it is unlikely that over the period we are interested in any one system would have stayed the same all the time. We can expect some change over time. The evidence is quite interesting.

Early visitors to Scotland

In the earliest part of the Mesolithic in Scotland we see only a few artefacts scattered around. There are no proper sites, just stray tools, of a type called the Ahrensburgian Point, very similar to those found in northern Europe and dating to before 10,000 years ago. They are scattered quite widely over the north and west of Scotland, from Orkney round to Tiree, Islay and Jura. These tools are very distinctive, so we can be fairly sure that the people who made them are part of the same society as that seen in Europe, and therefore of the same period. Archaeologists have argued that if this is the case, we should be finding proper sites, or perhaps that the sites now lie submerged under the sea which has risen since then. I think that this is wrong. We have not found proper sites, despite looking for them. At the same time, it seems unlikely that all of these early people's camps were on the shore. My interpretation is that we see a few scattered tools because of the way people first arrived here. The tools are the remains of small parties of people moving across the landscape who do not establish long-term or large camp sites. Given their distribution around coastal areas, it is possible that what we are seeing are the traces of small hunting parties moving rapidly by boat.

The next phase of the Mesolithic in Scotland is characterised by a particular type of tool, the broad blade microlith. Again there are very few sites, but now the evidence is for proper sites. These people were camping, but perhaps not for long, and there were not many of them. It again appears most likely that we are dealing with people travelling across the landscape with no fixed bases.

The colonisation of Scotland

The next period is quite different. People started to make narrow blade microliths and at the same time seem to have started to settle in Scotland in a much more substantial way. Sites such as Kinloch Farm on Rhum, and Bolsay Farm on Islay, yield hundreds of thousands of bits of flint tools and manufacturing waste. There are pits, holes for stakes, and evidence for hearths. Unfortunately, it is hard to determine whether these sites relate to long periods of occupation, or regular visits every year for short periods over a long time. Either way, we now appear to have people doing something systematically different from what has happened before. It would appear that they had either developed structured seasonal rounds, where they return to the same place on a regular basis, or that they had established base camps.

There does not, as yet, appear to be the sort of evidence to show that these base camps were permanently occupied. If they were, I am sure we would have begun to find evidence for

San Camps
Many hunter–gatherer camps are so slight that we may never find evidence for them.
ALAN BARNARD

better, more solid structures. The islands of the west coast of Scotland are located within a very rich environment, with all sorts of changing resources in the form of fish and migratory birds, so it would have been technically possible to have established a base camp system, but such a system tends to develop a greater degree of social complexity than we see evidence for. Some evidence for this of course may not have been preserved, or has not been found, but if we compare this area with the north-west coast of America, where settled hunter-gatherers did become established, we can see huge differences. This was brought home to me by a Canadian archaeologist, Rick Schulting, who introduced me to the enormously rich material culture of the recent north-west coast American Indians, who carved massive ornate and fantastic totem poles, lived in large substantial houses, and even kept slaves. Our hunter-gatherers were a long way from this. Equally, they were a long way from the highly mobile people of marginal environments, such as the Kalahari Desert.

I think that our people had begun to develop the base camp idea during the Mesolithic period in Scotland. Certainly some of the evidence points to it. As well as these large sites, there are also small flint scatter sites, where the evidence suggests that small numbers of people occupied sites for short periods. One such site lies close to Bolsay Farm at Gleann Mor, and it is tempting to see this as a camp site belonging to a work party from Bolsay Farm. Other sites in other parts of Scotland help to fill in the patterns of movement. There are sites in the Galloway hills, such as Smittons and Starr, which are generally small, and probably represent hunting camps. We should not just think in terms of deer hunting, however: Scottish rivers and lochs provide a considerable resource from fishing and wildfowling, and many of the sites along rivers such as the Tweed are the result of small bands who probably moved up and down the rivers. Water transport is likely to have been an important factor in movement patterns, as otherwise the only way to transport belongings, food and small children would have been to carry them.

Comparable evidence from the final stages of the Mesolithic in northern Europe suggests that the base camp idea was evolving there too. Evidence from Denmark points to large base camps with enormous shell middens, the use of pottery (which, given its heavy and breakable nature, suggests people were not moving around very much), and to small task camps. The latter are very clear, as there are a number of camps where people seem to have gone to intercept migrating resources, such as dolphins or swans, and to have only occupied these sites to exploit these very short-term resources.

Wildwoods

This misty image may be more of a reflection of the landscape our Mesolithic forbears saw than the open expanses of much of modern Scotland. However, this rather romantic view is a modern image. Hunter-gatherers will have known every corner of their environment in great detail to allow them to survive on the wild resources present.
GERAINT COLES

This pattern may have continued to develop through the final stages of the Mesolithic in Scotland too. Nearly all of our surviving shell middens appear to be very late in the Mesolithic. Some, such as Ulva Cave on Ulva off the Isle of Mull, probably continued in use during the early farming period, and perhaps even longer. The presence of groups of middens on Oronsay and around Oban, which mostly appear to have been used during the same period, suggests an intensification of resource use, where groups perhaps may no longer have been quite so free to move due to population pressure. Alternatively, or as part of the same process, people may have been restructuring their economies to rely more and more on predictable marine resources, and less on high-risk hunting.

We may even see a continuity into the early farming period in the west of Scotland. The middens continued in use, but no villages appeared, suggesting that groups of people remained at least partially mobile. What did appear are burial cairns (and later on, burials in middens) and these elaborate funerary structures have often been interpreted as marking land ownership. If people are using particular resources more and more intensively, they do not have to start farming to mark out their own resources. Equally, farming on the west coast and islands may have been adopted only gradually by the local Mesolithic people. The rugged landscape may not have been very suitable for early farming practice, while the rich marine environment and its relatively abundant food resources may have meant that people were unwilling to commence the hard work associated with farming.

At Sea's Edge
The west coast of Scotland provides a wide variety of environments within a small area. These would have provided a range of different resources for hunter-gatherers, reducing the need to travel.
IAN RALSTON

Behaviour and Belief

The young mother had died in the night. Although such things happened all too often, the family were grief-stricken. She had appeared so strong and healthy. Some of the other women in the group now had charge of arranging her body for burial and were gathering together her favourite tools: the carved wooden haft which her grandmother had given her, re-used again and again for new stone knife blades; the leather water bag which she had made for herself in the autumn; and several strings of shells which her man had given her.

It had fallen to the oldest women to wrap up the stillborn baby to keep it warm for the next world.

The men and children stood a short way off, not wanting to interfere, not wanting to get too close. This was not their time and not their place, but in the small group they wanted to show their support for the women, and they felt their grief. The young woman's man squatted down, his face streaked dark with ash from the cold fireplace. Even the dogs sat uneasily, whining quietly.

Burials can tell us a great deal about how people viewed the world around them. Unfortunately, we have no direct evidence of burial from the Scottish Mesolithic. There are Mesolithic burials elsewhere in Europe, notably in southern Scandinavia, the eastern Baltic and Portugal. These show a tremendously rich variety in burial practice – and include some startling examples, such as a baby lying on a swan's wing next to its mother, a man and woman buried together, dog burials, and people buried upright in vertical shafts. People are buried with pierced animal teeth used as beads, resting on antlers, and even some with arrowheads embedded in their bodies, suggesting a violent end.

We do not know where Mesolithic burial sites might be found in Scotland. The combination of mainly acidic soils, patterns of sea level change, and the accidents of preservation may well hide a burial tradition as rich as in mainland Europe. This is a shame, as burials provide so much data on people, not only from the skeletal evidence that lets us see how healthy a population was, but also from the insights they can provide on social structure and ideology. That said, perhaps we can use the knowledge that Mesolithic burials exist to provide us with a general framework of the sort of behaviour that may have been current during the Mesolithic. Burial sites are not the same throughout Europe, and vary over time, so there is no point in examining them in any detail as each local situation would clearly have been different. However, it is clear that societies had developed where the dead were respected, and where the relationships between man and woman and mother and baby

were acknowledged. While we cannot say what exactly the symbolism represented by a baby buried on a swan's wing means, we can infer that these people had a poetic, symbolic side to their lives. Burying dogs and burying people upright also suggests complexities in their lives. It has been suggested that upright burials might have been for priests or shaman, and that dog burials might represent the burials of priests whose spirits had moved into animals after their own deaths. This last interpretation, based on ethnographic analogy, is a good reminder that we must not look at societies just with our own eyes, where we might have been inclined to believe that they buried their favourite dogs out of sentimentality.

Within this world of Mesolithic symbolism, what can we tell about how people in Scotland behaved? We have seen how rich the Scottish Mesolithic is in economic data, but is there anything we can say about society without burial evidence?

Clothing and personal decoration can tell us a lot about society. Clothing is an important issue. Generally, people can survive without much clothing, except in extreme climates such as arctic or sub-arctic zones. There are examples of people, such as the Andaman islanders, who lived in similar temperature ranges to Scotland, who survived with very crude capes. If we can accept that the bevel-ended tools may have been used for leather working, this would allow us to argue that considerable efforts were being put into making leather goods. From the Scottish shell middens we have a large number of pierced cowrie shells. The general assumption is that these would have been strung together as necklaces. There are no examples of strung beads from Scotland, but Scandinavian burials provide some indications of how they may have been put together, and these seem to have been as fairly elaborate head-dresses, or possibly as skirts, and not as simple strings of beads. Once again, because we are looking at the Mesolithic, we tend to suggest that everything would have been very basic but we must remember that these were people with brains just like ours. In north-west America the Indians made very elaborate leather clothing. The cowrie shell beads would suggest that the Scottish Mesolithic people were interested in personal decoration and certainly if the bevel-ended tools were used for leather working, a lot of leather working was going on. In north-west America, the production of fine leather clothes was a way of demonstrating wealth. The Indian men were able to demonstrate that they were rich in that they had enough wives for some of the wives to spend their time on the manufacture of luxury goods, rather than just on subsistence.

There are other, stranger, details in some of the shell middens. Paul Mellars' excavations on Oronsay recovered

Burial

In the illustration are a number of images taken from known burial sites in southern Scandinavia. Corpses were often laid on antlers, mothers were sometimes buried with their babies (presumably if the mother had died giving birth), people were buried with their beads, and sometimes tools were placed in the grave with them. The priest or shaman is wearing a set of antlers – we know from sets found in England that antlers were probably worn.
HARRY BLAND

evidence for numbers of human finger bones buried within the middens. We do not know how they got there. Some people have suggested that they got their by accident, as the inclusion of general material from settlements. It is possible that people in Scotland did not bury their dead, at least not immediately, and that this is why we have found no graves. This may sound a little strange, but exposing bodies to the elements, to allow them to rot, or be scavenged by birds, often as a first stage before burial, is a practice that we know from various places around the world. Some North American Indians did this, placing their dead on raised platforms. Evidence from early farming (Neolithic) communities in Britain has suggested that they may have used the same practice. Similar rites are still followed by the Parsees in India. Such a practice might explain the absence of graves, and might also explain how small bones might accidentally end up scattered in a midden – such bones are small and easily lost once the flesh that holds them together has gone.

Such an explanation would be acceptable, were it not for the fact that some of the finger bones appear to have been deliberately placed on top of seal flippers within the middens. This immediately raises the possibility of the bones providing some intriguing evidence for ideas about burial, death, and indeed life. We can only guess at what significance was attached to such acts, but they not only show a greater concern for human remains, but also perhaps indicate that the shell middens, which we have traditionally interpreted simply as food waste, had other roles in life. Placing human fingers on top of a flipper in a midden suggests that the midden was a special place. The people who used these middens may not have seen a sharp boundary between holy and everyday. Nowadays we recognise a difference between a grave which is symbolic and a midden which is economic. Mesolithic people may not have seen this boundary. People may have buried their dead assuming that after dying life went on in pretty much the same way somewhere else, which is why they buried people with belongings and in their families. Equally, people may have seen their own living world as full of spirits, not just as a mundane and rational place. Australian aborigines see their landscape as rich in special places, a living thing with which they interact, rather than a passive object they use. Indeed, they go further and it is hard for westerners to appreciate fully the way they perceive the landscape and their visions of the dreamtime. Archaeologist Tony Pollard has argued that we need to spend more time thinking

about such spiritual and symbolic aspects of the Mesolithic in Scotland, as without appreciating that such activities would have been essential to the people we are studying, we can never hope to make sense of their lives.

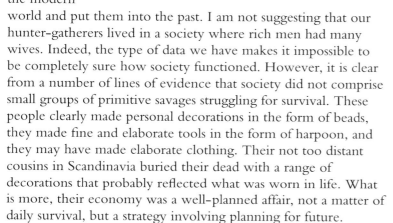

Again, however, it is important, not to simply take known aspects of the modern world and put them into the past. I am not suggesting that our hunter-gatherers lived in a society where rich men had many wives. Indeed, the type of data we have makes it impossible to be completely sure how society functioned. However, it is clear from a number of lines of evidence that society did not comprise small groups of primitive savages struggling for survival. These people clearly made personal decorations in the form of beads, they made fine and elaborate tools in the form of harpoon, and they may have made elaborate clothing. Their not too distant cousins in Scandinavia buried their dead with a range of decorations that probably reflected what was worn in life. What is more, their economy was a well-planned affair, not a matter of daily survival, but a strategy involving planning for future.

Modern clues to the past

One problem we face is the difficulty of imagining the viewpoint of humans several thousand years ago. Nowadays we have a huge amount of information about how other people think, from books, television, and from the ease with which modern people can travel and mix. One of the most striking observations that can be made is just how differently some societies view the world. We need not look at modern hunter-gatherers; the differences between different urban cultures, such as between the modern Japanese and, say, the Italians, are obvious. Importantly, if you think about many of the obvious things we share in common, you can see that these are recent, the products of a general world culture that has been developing since the Second World War. Modern communications, cheap air travel, the telephone, television, cinema, the giant multi-national companies that try to sell the same goods around the world, have all contributed to reducing the differences between cultures. However, even now there are differences, differences often used for example in comedy, where we can laugh at the strange things foreigners do. Now start to think back into the past. It is not that long ago that few people ever travelled far. At the start of this century most people took their holidays in their

Harpoons

Mesolithic harpoons are substantial tools that would have required a considerable effort to manufacture and this investment in time must have been matched by their effectiveness.

NATIONAL MUSEUMS OF SCOTLAND

Mesolithic Landscape
Archaeologists often spend most
of their time looking at individual sites.
It is important, especially during the Mesolithic
when we are studying mobile societies, to look at the
entire landscape. Hunter gatherers will have used every
part of it they could, perhaps hunting in the uplands,
collecting plant foods in the hills and fishing on the coast.
HARRY BLAND

own country. Foreigners really were exotic. Only a few hundred years ago people believed in races of people with only a single eye, or other such stories. Go back several thousands of years and think of the Egyptians, whose religion and burial practices are now the stuff of legend. Yet the Egyptians may well be closer to us in some ways than the hunter-gatherers of Scotland. The Egyptians lived in settled communities, they ate farm produce, they had a government, an army, officials. To get to our hunter-gatherers we have to go back almost twice as far in time.

So, how useful is it to look at modern hunter-gatherers as a way of understanding the past? The trouble with modern hunter-gatherers is that many of them have now been in contact with other cultures for a long time. African hunter-gatherers, for example, were first in contact with farming Africans, and since then have been part of the modern countries that they live in. Modern hunter-gatherers often live in close relationships with settled populations, often trading with them, providing animal herders or a seasonal labour force. They have had 10,000 years to change from the period we are interested in. However, if we can see any general patterns of thought, perhaps these can give us insights into how people may have seen the world.

Kinloch Farm, Rhum
Excavation in process at the site of Kinloch Farm on the island of Rhum. Caroline Wickham-Jones' excavations here sparked off a new wave of Mesolithic research in Scotland.
CAROLINE WICKHAM-JONES

One thing that is clear is that most modern hunter-gatherers do not fully share our way of thinking about where they fit into the world. We tend to divide the world into natural and man-made. We see the world as a series of opposites – town and country, tame and wild. All sorts of ideas are bound up in this. The controlled, man-made situation is generally seen as safe; the untamed wild world is seen as dangerous. Much of this is an illusion, since most of our countryside is of course the result of thousands of years of farming and forestry, and many wild places are far safer than many man-made places, such as roads. It is, however, the way that we view the world. Hunter-gatherers do not see this same divide. In a sense, many of them see themselves as part of the world, part of what we might describe as nature. They do not see themselves in a controlling position.

Hunter-gatherers generally do not have the same ideas about property as most settled societies do. They put less work into developing resources, they do not clear land, cultivate it, sow it, weed it, water it, and so on to harvest a crop. Even where they

Islay
On a calm day it is easy to imagine Mesolithic people travelling between the islands of the southern Hebrides in canoes.
IAN RALSTON

Island Landscape

Many of the landscapes we find hunter-gatherer sites in appear wild. However this wilderness is a modern creation, often caused by a combination of sheep grazing and climate change. In the Mesolithic much more of the landscape would have been covered with trees and scrub, providing shelter, food and the raw materials for making artefacts.

IAN RALSTON

do intervene in the environment to improve harvests, the investment of effort and time is far less than for farmers. Hunter-gatherers have traditional resources, but they are generally less exclusive, and do not revolve around the idea of ownership.

Mesolithic hunter-gatherers probably had quite a lot of spare time, at least for some of the year. Many modern hunter-gatherers spend a fair amount of time resting. Harvesting wild resources may not support the same number of people as farming, but if you know how to do it, it is easier!

They would be familiar with only small groups of people – during their whole lives they might not meet any more than a few hundred individuals – no more than you might see at a school or in a big supermarket.

All modern hunter-gatherers generally seem to share resources. There may be complicated rules as to who gets what and how much, but it is commonplace amongst hunter-gatherers to share food. Many peoples also share other items. In this type of situation theft is rare. There may be a practical reason for

sharing. With wild resources there is a good chance that you will have a bad day hunting or that the grove of trees you visit may not have any fruit on it. Sharing reduces the risks you face, as it is unlikely everyone in the group will have had the same poor luck. When people hunt big animals they often do not manage to catch one every day, but when they do, there is more than enough food for everyone. By sharing with others at the base camp you get food when you do not have any, and supply food when you do. This principle also allows hunter-gatherers to look after anyone who is not well enough to forage, or who has had an accident.

Most hunter-gatherers live in roughly egalitarian societies and have no chiefs. No one is forced to do anything. If one does not like what the group is doing, they can leave. Of course, if you do leave, and if you do not cooperate and share, then you expose yourself to greater risks. Many social conventions may well have been developed to reduce risks, for example it is common for hunter-gatherers to marry outside their band. This helps to ensure that they have friends and relations in other parts of the country, and this may come in handy in times of local hardship when they want to move beyond their normal range. Most hunter-gatherer societies have all sorts of ways they keep in touch with people over long distances, and these can include meeting up during times of plenty for parties, gift-giving and ritual activities. Many of our current social activities probably originate with these.

One common assumption has been that of an ancient division of labour by sex, men hunting and women gathering plant foods. This pattern is largely based on traditional ethnographic analogies with tropical hunter-gatherers where plant foods are possibly the most important food resource. They also relate to our modern conception of hunting as an activity involving big game and being only concerned with the kill. If we look more closely at what goes on in practice, it can soon be seen that women play an important role in hunting and trapping smaller animals and in butchering and processing the kills. They often contribute a substantial part of the meat part of a diet in colder climates where plant foods are not as important as in the tropics. Because of their commitment to feeding and looking after children, many women do not range as far from camps as men, although there are cultures where, both before they have children and after they have stopped having children, women do range as far as the men.

How do these general principles apply to Scotland? We suspect that there would have been variations. If people were beginning to modify their environment through fire or pruning

trees to encourage fruiting or the production of long straight branches, they were beginning to invest in resources and would therefore probably have begun to develop ideas of ownership. Of areas where hunter-gatherers were recorded in the recent past, the Scottish environment is most like the north-west coast of America, and here hunter-gatherers were very different from the general picture. Possibly because of the abundance of salmon in their rivers, some of the North American Indians were able to develop a settled society, with elaborate art, warfare, and many of the traits most commonly associated within farmers and more modern societies. Part of the explanation for this may lie in the nature of their exploitation of salmon. They built permanent installations to trap fish as they went up river. These required a considerable amount of work, as did the processing of the seasonal catch, which then had to be stored over the rest of the year. Although using a wild resource, they exploited it in a manner perhaps more akin to farming.

In another aspect, given our northern latitude, it seems reasonable to expect that women would have played a role in hunting, as well as in fishing and plant gathering. We do not know how important hunting was, but given the sites away from the coast, up in the hills, we can estimate that hunting was an important activity. Some big game hunting did occur; we have the bone and antler tools from the middens to show for it. Some of this may have had a social role like much modern hunting – Steve Mithen has shown from a detailed analysis of Danish bone collections that hunting there, where much of the protein would have been met by sea foods, was probably associated with prestige, with people going out of their way to hunt large animals, rather than following the most economically sensible food collecting strategy. We know that sea foods were important to some Mesolithic communities in Scotland, but we should be cautious about assuming that sea foods were important to all of them. It is likely that communities sailing between the islands of the west coast relied far more on the sea than did their cousins on the mainland. Indeed, in terms of avoiding risks, it might be important that different groups did have different bases for their food economies, as it would be less likely for everything to go wrong all at once.

Discovering the Mesolithic Today

The Mesolithic in Scotland is a difficult period to study. Sites are few and far between, poorly preserved and hard to interpret. To make matters still more difficult, the people who left these few remains would have belonged to a society very different from ours, who may have seen their world through very different eyes. They are likely to have seen a world that was much more alive than ours, where every tree or hill may have had a spirit or been associated with past times or mythical stories, or where the soul of a man might inhabit a dog after his death. They would have known few other people, and had few things they called their own. In some ways it is easy to be envious of them, but then it is worth remembering the Scottish winters spent without houses, the dangers of travelling between islands in primitive open boats, and how comfortable modern life has become.

The Mesolithic was a long time ago, but perhaps we can still learn something about our own view of the world by trying to imagine how these people saw Scotland. The last remnants of their nomadic lifestyle may have finally disappeared as the last tinkers disappeared from the country, but people still sometimes try to hark back to this early way of life.

Do not be fooled by ideas of a people living in a hazy dream time at one with nature. Long before the arrival of the hunting rifle, people were the most dangerous and efficient predators in the forests. Within their own abilities they modified their environment for their own needs. Their way of life was a great success: in one form or another hunting and gathering has been the economic and social way of life for nearly all prehistory, and it has survived until the present day in parts of the world where no other system could work. What it could not do was support the levels of population, or social complexities, on which our own civilisation is built.

Sites to Visit

As little remains of Mesolithic sites other than flint scatters, overgrown shell middens and buried pits, there is little to see at most site locations. What you can see are the positions of the sites in the landscape, but even with these you must bear in mind that sea levels may have changed, and that land use will have altered completely. Some good places to visit are Gleann Mor on Islay, where the location on a knoll above the glen would have allowed good views of game movements, the Oronsay middens, where, although the island is much bigger nowadays, you can imagine the island life, or Kinloch Farm on Rhum, with its location within the bay. On the mainland Loch Doon in Dumfries and Galloway will provide an indication of an upland location favoured by hunter-gatherers. A drive along the north shore of the Solway Firth will let you see an area with many settlements, while a drive around the base of the cliffs at Oban will let you see the general location of the cave midden sites. The Tweed valley provides another general area where hunter-gatherers once lived, richer than most of the other landscapes.

Island Sites

Map showing location of Mesolithic sites around the Scottish west coast and Inner Hebrides.

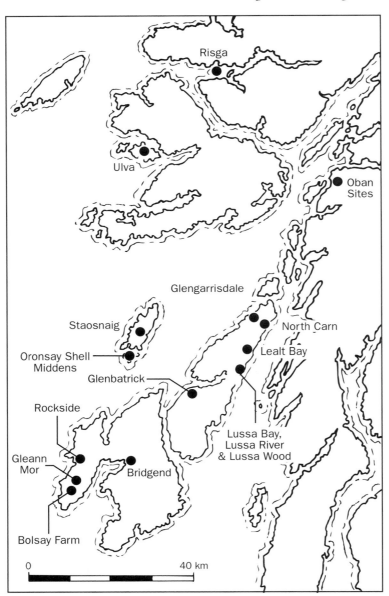

Further Reading

- *The early prehistory of Scotland*, edited by Tony Pollard and Alex Morrison (Edinburgh University Press 1996), contains a set of up-to-date research papers on the Mesolithic.

- *Scotland: Environment and Archaeology, 8000 BC–AD 1000*, edited by Kevin Edwards and Ian Ralston (Wiley 1997), provides sections describing the environment and the Mesolithic.

- *Scotland's First Settlers*, by Caroline Wickham-Jones (Batsford and Historic Scotland 1994) is a general overview of the Mesolithic.

- *Excavations on Oronsay: prehistoric human ecology on a small island,* by Paul Mellars (Edinburgh University Press 1987) provides an account of the principle modern excavation of shell middens.

- *Rhum: Mesolithic and later sites at Kinloch. Excavations 1984-1986* (Society of Antiquaries of Scotland Monograph Series 1990) is Caroline Wickham-Jones's account of her major excavation.

- Peter Woodman published a detailed review in the *Proceedings of the Society of Antiquaries of Scotland for 1989* titled 'Review of the Scottish Mesolithic: a plea for normality'.

- *Farmers, Temples and Tombs,* Gordon Barclay (Canongate 1998), is the next book in The Making Of Scotland series which takes up the story of Scotland's first settlers from around 4000 BC.

Acknowledgements

I would like to thank all those who I worked with on the Mesolithic, and who have provided the inspiration for my thoughts, especially Clive Bonsall, Nyree Finlay, Steve Mithen, Tony Pollard and in particular Caroline Wickham-Jones who commented on an early version of this text and who has helped with the pictures. Alan Barnard, Geraint Coles, Mike Cressey, Ian Ralston and Joe Rock, all of The University of Edinburgh, and Alan Saville of the National Museums of Scotland, all provided assistance with illustrations. The illustrations on p.23 (centre) and p.23 (bottom) are taken from *The Oxford Illustrated Prehistory of Europe*, edited by Barry Cunliffe (Oxford University Press 1994) by permission of Oxford University Press. Harry Bland's questions about how to paint Mesolithic people helped to focus my own ideas. Gordon Barclay not only asked me to write the book but provided encouragement during the process. Thanks are also due to my family, Heather, Amy and Simon, who were forced to read early drafts. The maps were prepared by Sylvia Stevenson and Robert Burns.

HISTORIC SCOTLAND

Historic Scotland safeguards Scotland's built heritage, including its archaeology, and promotes its understanding and enjoyment on behalf of the Secretary of State for Scotland. It undertakes a programme of 'rescue archaeology', from which many of the results are published in this book series.

Scotland has a wealth of ancient monuments and historic buildings, ranging from prehistoric tombs and settlements to remains from the Second World War, and Historic Scotland gives legal protection to the most important, guarding them against damaging changes or destruction. Historic Scotland gives grants and advice to the owners and occupiers of these sites and buildings.

Historic Scotland has a membership scheme which allows access to properties in its care, as well as other benefits. For information, contact: 0131 668 8999.

SETTLEMENT
AND
SACRIFICE

Settlement *and* Sacrifice

The Later Prehistoric People of Scotland

Richard Hingley

Series editor: Gordon Barclay

CANONGATE BOOKS
with
HISTORIC SCOTLAND

THE MAKING
OF SCOTLAND

Series editor:
Gordon Barclay

Other titles available:

WILD HARVESTERS
The First People in Scotland

FARMERS, TEMPLES AND TOMBS
Scotland in the Neolithic
and Early Bronze Age

A GATHERING OF EAGLES
Scenes from Roman Scotland

First published in Great Britain in 1998
by Canongate Books Ltd, 14 High Street
Edinburgh E11 1TB

British Library Cataloguing-in-Publication Data
A catalogue record for this book is available on request
from the British Library

ISBN 0 86241 782 1

Series Design:
James Hutcheson, Canongate Books

Design:
Janet Watson

Printed and bound by
GraphyCems

Previous page
The 2000-year-old broch at Dun Dornadilla, Sutherland.
RCAHMS

Contents

Staircase
Mousa Broch,
Shetland.
HISTORIC SCOTLAND

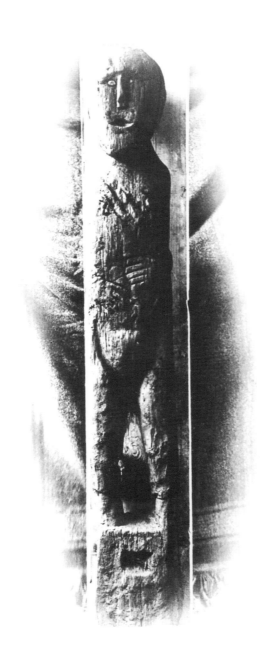

Ballachulish Figurine
A near life-sized wooden figure dating from around 600 BC.
NATIONAL MUSEUMS OF SCOTLAND

The Human Landscape

This book describes the people who lived in Scotland during later prehistory, the 1700 years between around 1500 BC and AD 200. The history of human settlement before this is covered by the titles *Wild Harvesters* and *Farmers, Temples and Tombs*, while *A Gathering of Eagles* gives an account of the Romans who invaded Scotland.

The landscape

The outline of Scotland and its islands would have been very similar to today, but in some places the sea has now moved further out from the shore (for instance, most of the mainland), while elsewhere it has cut into the land and ground has been lost (as in Orkney and Caithness).

However, the appearance of the land would have been very different then. At the beginning of the later prehistoric period parts of Scotland had been occupied for 3000 years or more by farmers who had cleared large areas of trees and made fields in which they planted crops and kept animals.

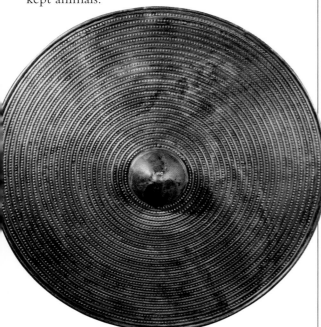

Some areas had not been cleared, and in others people had moved on and the trees had grown again, a process we call 'regeneration'. Other areas were covered in thick peat and the wet climate in later prehistory resulted in this bog spreading to areas that were previously lived in.

Great difficulties were met with in travelling through mountains, bogs and woodlands which were inhabited by wild animals. These included bears and wolves which posed a threat to livestock and people, particularly children. The countryside was not, however, an untamed wilderness. The later prehistoric people had cleared large areas of land by this time, and we shall see that they lived a settled life and for the most part probably felt secure.

Later prehistoric people

It is often suggested that people at this time were warlike and fierce, but this is only part of the story; archaeological work tells us that they were also settled farmers who are likely to have welcomed gifts and tales from visitors from far afield. Until the invasion of the Romans, warfare was probably an occasional and small-scale activity.

The people of Scotland in later prehistory lived in well-built houses, usually circular, and the remains can be found over much of the country. In some places there were villages of roundhouses sometimes enclosed with a boundary. The people grew cereal crops in small fields; they also kept a range of livestock, including cattle, sheep, goats and pigs, and would have lived well on a diet of their own produce – meat, vegetables, bread and cheese supplemented by game, animals and fish.

Bronze Shield
A bronze shield from Yetholm, Roxburghshire which dates to around 800–700 BC. It is very well made but fairly fragile and was probably used for display rather than war.
NATIONAL MUSEUMS OF SCOTLAND

Later prehistoric people wore well-made clothes. They also had ornaments and weapons which displayed their wealth and status. Most of them probably lived their whole lives and died in the same area, but others would have travelled by foot, cart, horse and boat to visit neighbours and kin, or to trade. Life for these farmers was hard and usually fairly short by our standards. Many women and children died in childbirth and most people did not live beyond the age of 40. In these ways their way of life would not have been unfamiliar to recent generations of farmers in Scotland.

Although superficially similar to our recent ancestors in the basic ways of living and farming, some of their customs were very different, even strange, from our point of view. During the later part of our period, for instance, it is possible that when a member of the community died, the body was sometimes exposed on a wooden platform. When the dead body had decayed, the individual bones may have been removed and used in religious acts relating to the memory of the dead person. Occasional evidence suggests that people were even sacrificed to the gods.

They were creative and imaginative, not the primitives who are often portrayed in fiction and on television. Not only did they build complex and substantial houses, but they also made and owned some beautiful objects. Often these objects were deposited as offerings – sacrifices – to the gods. This book explains in more detail what these people were like, how they lived and how you can see and find out more about them.

Prehistoric House

A house dating to about 3500 years ago at Lairg, Sutherland would have looked much like this. Many later prehistoric houses were circular, and were often very impressive and substantial.

CHRISTINA UNWIN: HISTORIC SCOTLAND

During the long period covered by this book there were many changes in the ways that people lived. At the start of later prehistoric times families still buried their dead relatives in substantial stone and earth burial monuments, but later, between 600 BC and AD 200, evidence for the ways in which the dead of the community were disposed of becomes less and less common.

By 1500 BC people were already building large roundhouses, but during the course of later prehistory many of these become more substantial and complex. At the beginning of our period people lived in unenclosed groups of round buildings, but from as early as 1000 BC they started to build various forms of enclosures around their settlements and some of these forts are quite substantial.

The objects that people used also changed through time. Weapons and other objects were common at the beginning and end of our period, but were not so common in between. The appearance of these objects changed according to fashion.

The physical geography meant that families in different parts of Scotland lived in quite different ways. A later prehistoric farm in Caithness would have looked very different from one on Lewis or in the Scottish Borders. Each part of Scotland had its own individual later prehistoric archaeological record.

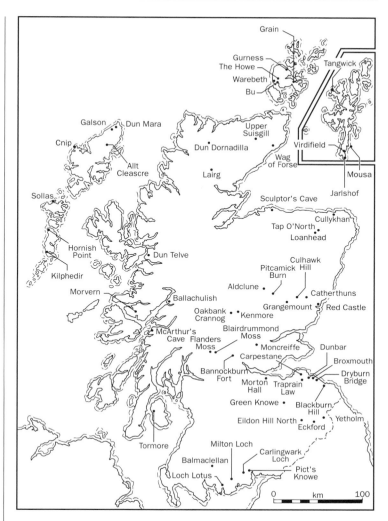

Distribution Map

This map shows the location of archaeological sites and finds which are mentioned in the book.

The People

Who were they?

Scotland as a political entity, where the people thought of themselves as Scots, did not exist until over 1000 years after the end of our period. The people who lived in the area of present-day Scotland during our period would have had a name, or series of names, for themselves and for their communities. We have no knowledge of what these were since nothing was written down and so there are no records which would tell us about the inhabitants. The names for groups of people, or 'tribes', were not recorded until Roman times.

This book will use the term 'later prehistoric' for the people I describe. When archaeologists talk about the period from around 1500 BC to AD 200 they often use the term 'Celtic'. The term

'Pictish' is also sometimes used in Scotland to refer to archaeological remains: for instance, brochs used to be known as 'Pictish towers'. Archaeologists also use the terms 'Iron Age' and 'Bronze Age'. What do these all mean?

The term 'Celtic' seems to me to be too ill-defined to be useful. It is applied to a whole range of people who lived across large areas of central and western Europe in later prehistoric times. In Ireland and western Scotland 'Celtic' is used to refer to a variety of monuments that date to a period of history later than that described in this book. The term is also used today by a range of people in western and north-western Europe, including Scotland, in order to identify themselves for cultural reasons.

Prehistoric People

Later prehistoric people from around AD 100. Two men on horse-back from north-eastern Scotland meet a woman and three men from the south of Scotland. People at this time dressed differently in various areas of Scotland to show their tribal identity. In addition, wealthy and powerful people had access to more impressive ornaments, weapons and clothes. All of the people shown in this drawing are leading figures of the community, apart from a retainer who is looking after the horse. The artefacts shown mostly date from the last two centuries BC and the first two centuries AD. Those shown on the figures to the left have been found in north-eastern Scotland, with the exception of the pony cap, while those on the figures to the right have been found in southern Scotland.

CHRISTINA UNWIN

Later prehistoric people are also not likely to have thought of themselves as 'Pictish'. The Picts were a group of people who live across northern Scotland at a later date. They are first mentioned by a Roman author in the late third century AD, many years after the people discussed in this book were dead. The Picts were probably descendants of the later prehistoric people.

'Bronze Age' refers to the period in which people first used metal (around 2200-700 BC), the first metal in common use was bronze. The 'Iron Age' (around 700 BC-AD 400) was when iron was first used – a harder metal than bronze and considerably more difficult to work. These terms are used by archaeologists to relate to the adoption of certain technological skills, rather than to any real change in the inhabitants of Scotland during these periods. They would certainly have meant nothing to the later prehistoric men and women.

Who were these people? At one time it was thought that many waves of settlers had come to the British Isles, but there is no clear evidence for this, although individuals and groups will have travelled long distances on occasions. Most archaeologists now believe that the men and women who lived in Scotland at this time were descended from many generations who had lived in the same area. Although some new groups of settlers came to live in Scotland after AD 200, including the Scotti and the Vikings, many Scottish people today are likely to be descended from later prehistoric or even earlier inhabitants. If you are Scottish, you are probably descended at least in part from people who lived in Scotland at the time of the Roman invasion.

What did they look like?

We are dependent on the remains that these people left behind for an understanding of what they looked like. In very rare cases, peat bogs can preserve human bodies, including the skin, hair and internal organs. Preserved bodies have been found across Britain and northern Europe, including Scotland. They can tell us a great deal about diet and lifestyle during the later prehistoric period, but to date no Scottish examples have been studied using modern techniques.

Burials of people are more common, although still rare, as the majority of people do not appear to have been buried in a grave. It is usual for only the skeleton to survive as all the flesh has decayed and disappeared long ago. We know from skeletal evidence that later prehistoric people were probably not much smaller than we are. The analysis of 19 Iron Age burials which have been excavated on various sites throughout Scotland provides the following information. The 15 male burials suggest that adults males varied in height from around 1.65 metres

(5ft 5in) to 1.77 metres (5ft 9in). Female skeletons are rarer, but the four excavated examples vary from 1.52 metres (5ft) to 1.66 metres (5ft 5in) in height.

We can also say a little about the clothes and ornaments that these people wore. The Roman author Herodian wrote in the third century AD that people in northern Britain were for the most part naked. He also mentions that they tattooed their bodies with various designs and pictures of animals and that they possessed swords, spears, shields and iron ornaments. Herodian's is one of a number of accounts by Roman authors which dismiss the native people of Britain as uncivilised barbarians. The coldness of the climate suggests that most people dressed suitably for the elements.

Men, women and children wore woollen clothing to protect them from the cold and rain. They are also likely to have had linen, leather and skin garments. Clothing would have been carefully made and dyed in a variety of colours using natural dyes. They may have worn leather shoes, although none have been found so far. Men and women may have had different types of dress but we have very little information on this subject and so cannot be certain. In most situations, the wool and leather that the clothes were made from have disintegrated and leave no sign on an archaeological site. Where organic materials such as wool, leather and wood have fallen or been put into bogs or other wet areas, they are protected to a considerable extent from rotting by the limited supply of oxygen. The few discoveries of ancient clothes give us some idea what sort of clothes the people wore. For example, a hooded woven woollen garment found in Orkney was lost or deposited in a bog slightly

Skeleton

The skeleton of a man of about 35 to 45 years of age from the broch at The Howe, Mainland, Orkney. The dead body appears to have been left in a disused building prior to its collapse. Most of the bones of the body can be distinguished. The skull is to the right and has been crushed, while the remains of the leg bones are to the left.
HISTORIC SCOTLAND

Woollen Garment

A hooded woven woollen garment from Orkney, which was found in a peat bog. Radiocarbon dating suggests that this dates to just after the end of the time covered in this book, but people may have worn clothes of this sort during later prehistory.
NATIONAL MUSEUMS OF SCOTLAND

Burnt Mound

Burnt mound at Tangwick, Eshaness, Shetland. A man is having a bath in the tank in the centre of the burnt mound. Burnt mounds may have been used for bathing or for cooking.

EASE

after the end of the later prehistoric period, but people will have worn clothes of this type earlier too. It is likely that the types of clothes worn at the beginning of later prehistory varied from those worn later. The clothes people are wearing in the illustrations of this book are based on the limited evidence from Britain and Europe.

The later prehistoric people are likely to have been careful of their appearances. Bronze mirrors of later prehistoric date have been found. Sharp bronze and iron tools were probably used during the later prehistoric period to cut hair and shave beards. Many men, however, may have grown beards and moustaches, and combs have been found that were probably used to groom them.

There is evidence that personal hygiene was important. Distinctive horseshoe-shaped piles of stones, called 'burnt mounds', date from 1200 BC to 700 BC. These mounds are formed from stones which have been heated or burnt and often contain evidence of a small tank of stone or wood. Similar arrangements used by North American Indians show that the stones were heated in a fire and placed in a water tank to create steam, forming a communal sauna where people washed and cleaned themselves. The heated water tanks may also have been used for cooking meat and vegetables. Burnt mounds are less common after about 700 BC, although large collections of burnt stones, which may represent bathing facilities, are sometimes found on settlement sites.

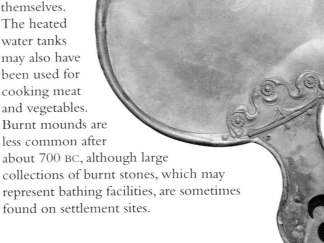

Mirror

A mirror from Balmaclellan, Kircudbrightshire which dates to the first century AD. These mirrors would have been used by important men and women.

NATIONAL MUSEUMS OF SCOTLAND

Personal ornaments were common during later prehistory, including a range of pins and bracelets, which are now over 3000 years old, used to fasten clothes and to keep hair in place. The massive armlets from north-western Scotland, torcs (neck rings), finger rings, pins, armlets, necklaces and brooches were worn 2000 years ago. Some of this metalwork was produced outside Scotland showing that contacts were made with friends, relations and traders in areas of southern Britain, Ireland and on the Continent. A bronze brooch from The Howe, a stone house in Orkney, was probably manufactured in southern Britain and brought into Scotland.

Some of the items of personal adornment were very valuable. The metal would have been expensive and some of the ornate objects must have required experienced specialists to produce them. Jewellery was also made in a range of other materials, such as bangles out of 'jet' and beads of glass. At the end of later prehistory, people wore different types of objects in various areas of Scotland, which suggests that people dressed in a way which showed which community they came from.

Armlet

Armlet in the form of a snake from Pitalpin, Angus. This item of personal adornment is probably about 1900 years old.

NATIONAL MUSEUMS OF SCOTLAND

How did they defend themselves?

From about 1500 BC to 600 BC a range of swords, axes, spears and shields made of bronze was used. An example is the bronze shield from Yetholm discussed earlier. Some of the weapons are (and always were) so fragile that they can only have been used for display, perhaps during ceremonies.

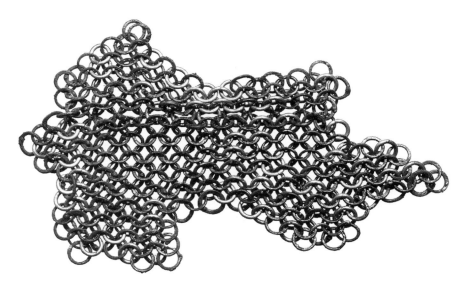

Chain Mail
A piece of chain mail from a collection of metal objects found in a peat bog at Carlingwark Loch.

After this date, until the first century AD, people continued to make and use swords, spears and shields, particularly during the time of the Roman invasions. Some of these weapons would have been more effective in battle than earlier examples, since iron is far harder and longer-wearing than bronze. An example of chain mail was found in a peat bog at Carlingwark Loch, Stewartry, and this demonstrates that some later prehistoric warriors were quite heavily protected. Fittings for horse harnesses were also made by later prehistoric people and illustrate the widespread use of the horse both for riding and draught. Chariots drawn by horses may have been used in warfare.

It is usually assumed that men carried the weapons, but women may also have been armed. Whether people wore weapons whenever they were outside or only during battles and ceremonies is uncertain. Some of the more ornate weapons are likely to have been carried on special occasions by individuals to display their power and status in their local communities.

Scabbard
Sword scabbard from Morton Hall, Midlothian. This highly ornate object is made from bronze and is probably around 1900 years old. It is shown on the back of one of the men in the illustration on p11.

What language did they speak?

These people may have spoken an early form of Gaelic, but whether any of the words used by modern Gaelic-speakers would have been understood by someone from the later prehistoric period is uncertain.

Were they healthy?

The bones from excavated human skeletons can yield a certain amount of information about the diseases and ailments from which these people suffered. The skeletons of a man and a woman found at Galson, Lewis, both showed signs of disease. The poorly developed enamel of the woman's teeth suggested that she had suffered childhood illnesses; slipped discs showed that she also suffered from back trouble. She had given birth to at least one child. The man had probably suffered back pain as he had two spinal conditions (Schmorl's nodes and spondylolysis) and also slight injuries to his spine.

A large stone cist found close to Dunbar in East Lothian contained the remains of at least 21 individuals, all of whom had unhealthy teeth. Tooth loss was not uncommon and chronic abscesses were fairly frequent. Dental decay, however, was not common, possibly due to the fact that people did not use sugar in their diet. Other common ailments included rheumatism, found in six of the East Lothian skeletons.

Not all later prehistoric people would have been unhealthy. Knowledgeable people were probably able to treat some health problems by the use of herbs, medicines and magic.

How long did they live?

Archaeology only provides a limited amount of evidence about how long these people lived. Although it is not possible to tell from their bones exactly how old someone was when they died, an estimate can be made. Analysis of the Dunbar burials provides the following information. The youngest male was 20 to 21 years old when he died, while the oldest was 35 to 40. The youngest woman was in her mid 20s at death and the oldest was about 40 to 50, which must have seemed a great age to these people. These young ages at death reflect the absence of modern standards of health care. Many mothers died in childbirth and death during infancy or early childhood would have been frequent. The remains of the young are rarely found, perhaps because there were particular ways for disposing of their bodies.

Pitcarmick Settlement

A later prehistoric settlement at Pitcarmick Burn, Perthshire. Several hut circles are visible to the bottom right of the photograph and a series of cairns, linear dykes and other features can also be distinguished.
This is a very well preserved later prehistoric settlement which shows up well under a cover of snow.

RCAHMS

Farming and Eating

Most families had a staple diet derived from the meat of domestic animals and the crops that they had grown, supplemented by gathering wild fruits and plants, fishing and occasional hunting.

Patterns of farming

It is likely that almost all families at this time were involved in farming. People worked on the land, and probably had access to a particular area of arable and pasture land. We should not assume that families 'owned' land as we understand it, or that all cultivation plots were marked in a permanent way – in many societies where land is held communally, people are assigned different areas to cultivate every year. In such cases plots need not have been marked very clearly; at Upper Suisgill in Sutherland two plots were found separated only by a line of fist-sized stones.

In upland areas evidence of the fields that surrounded the settlements often survive. In rocky upland areas, people cleared the land of stones to create areas to grow crops. They placed the stones in small piles, which archaeologists call 'clearance cairns'. They also built field and yard walls using these stones. Elsewhere, especially in southern Scotland, people carefully ploughed along the contours of the hills to form level cultivation terraces. Across some parts of Scotland areas are covered in very narrow cultivation ridges which are formed of piled up earth. This is known as 'cord rig' and often appears to be of later prehistoric date. It has been suggested that cord rig was created by the use of spades and hoes, much in the same way that crofting cultivation was carried on into the twentieth century in the west and north of Scotland.

In these fields families planted, tended and harvested crops, which were then processed, stored and consumed. Barley was the main crop and wheat and oats were also grown. People used wooden ards (a simple plough which cut into and turned the soil) to till the fields. When iron became widely available towards the end of the later prehistoric period the ard was sometimes fitted with a metal tip to slice

Ploughing
A man ploughing with a wooden ard.
CHRISTINA UNWIN

into the soil more efficiently. People may have been able to cultivate some of the heavier more fertile soils of Scotland with these improved ards. However, iron plough tips are not frequently found in Scotland and simple wooden ards may have continued in common use; examples have been found in several places, such at Virdifield in Shetland and at Milton Loch in Dumfriesshire. In some places spades were used as cultivation tools, possibly to cut up the turf before the ard was used.

Grain was harvested by hand, possibly on occasion with the aid of bronze sickles. When archaeologists excavate sites they sometimes find grain which has been charred during processing.

Charred Barley
Charred barley found at the broch at The Howe, Mainland, Orkney. This barley would have rotted if it had not been charred.
HISTORIC SCOTLAND

Archaeologists often also find quernstones, grinding stones which were used to turn grain into flour. During the earlier part of our period crude saddle querns were used; while in the later prehistoric period more carefully prepared rotary querns become common. Two circular stones were fitted closely together, so that the upper one could be turned; grain was dropped down a hole in the middle of the upper stone onto the grinding surface on the lower stone and the resulting flour flowed out between the two. Bread, bannocks, gruel and porridge would have been produced from this flour, while barley, other cereals and wild plants may also have been fermented to produce alcoholic drinks.

Saddle Quern
Saddle quern in use. This comprises a simple, flattish, stone on which grain was ground using a smaller stone.
NATIONAL MUSEUMS OF SCOTLAND

Animal husbandry

Each family probably kept several different kinds of animal, although it is likely that the types and proportions kept would have varied between regions. Animal bones that have been found on excavated sites show that cattle, sheep, goats, pigs, dogs and horses were present. All of these animal types may have been eaten, as butchery marks were found on their bones. Horses were ridden and harnessed to carts, and dogs were used for hunting, but even these animals may also have been eaten occasionally. At The Howe in Orkney evidence has been found that cats were kept, possibly to kill mice and for their fur, but they may also have been treated as domestic pets.

Hunting and gathering

In the Western Isles, deer bones are unusually common. Some of the weapons described in the previous chapter could have been used to hunt animals. Nevertheless, the small numbers of wild animal bones from sites suggest that hunting was in fact rare across much of Scotland. On other sites, bones sometimes survive to show that people fished and caught birds. Fishing was particularly important among mainland coastal communities and in the Western and Northern Isles.

During the excavation of Oakbank Crannog on Loch Tay in Perthshire, hazelnuts, cherries, blackberries and raspberries were found. The gathering of wild foods would have supplemented the diet of people throughout Scotland, particularly when the harvest was poor.

Deer
A 2000 year-old drawing of deer scratched on a piece of pottery from the wheelhouse at Kilpheder, South Uist. It is likely that deer were hunted in the Western Isles and formed an important part of the diet. This piece of pottery is reproduced near to its original size.
PREHISTORIC SOCIETY

Storing and cooking food

Later prehistoric people would have had a range of vessels for storing and for cooking food. In the Western and Northern Isles pottery vessels were in common use, as shown by small broken pieces of ceramics found during the excavation of houses. On occasions a whole vessel is found. Fewer pots were in use in mainland Scotland. People also used wooden and bronze vessels to store and process food. Evidence of wooden containers has been found in the remains of crannogs – houses built in lochs and bogs. Wood found deposited in waterlogged conditions can be remarkably well preserved.

In many later prehistoric houses the fire was lit on a single hearth set in the centre of the house, although occasionally a

house had more than one hearth. It is likely that each family cooked and ate food together, probably around the central hearth. Sometimes meat was cooked by placing it into a pit with hot stones or burning turf. Large groups of people met to eat communal meals on special occasions (this is described in more detail in on pages 46–8).

The end product

The evidence for farming, animal husbandry, hunting and gathering demonstrates the kinds of food which families ate. Another source of information for the diet of later prehistoric people is human excrement, or 'coprolites'. These have been found on a few sites, particularly those which have been damp and free from the oxygen which would lead to the decay of organic matter. The coprolites from Warebeth broch, Orkney, came from a number of individuals, probably including a child; one was deposited by an animal, probably a cat or a dog. All of the coprolites contained small quantities of plant remains, but the meals represented consisted mainly of meat; indicated by the presence of animal hairs and small pieces of bone. The animals eaten included red deer, sheep or goat, and birds; seeds within the coprolites included barley and linseed; while traces of peat probably indicated that food came into contact with the fuel of the fire during cooking. The animal dropping contained the eggs of a parasitic worm, but the human coprolites showed no evidence of parasites.

Coprolite Found at Warebeth

A piece of human excrement from Warebeth broch, Mainland, Orkney. Several coprolites were deposited in a well in the broch, presumably after it had ceased to be used, as it is not likely that the occupants would have fouled a source of water that was in use.

HISTORIC SCOTLAND

Making Things

All of the clothes and personal possessions described in the previous chapter, including the ards and quernstones used in the farming and processing of crops, and the pots and wooden vessels used in the storage and cooking of food, were made by later prehistoric people. Everyone within the community may have been involved in making objects. They used a range of locally available materials to make their possessions, but in some cases materials had to be brought into the community for the manufacture of particular items. Pots were produced from local clays and were hand-made and quernstones were usually cut from locally available coarse stone.

Iron and bronze

The production of iron or bronze objects may only have been carried out at certain times by specialists in metalworking. The ore required to produce bronze artefacts includes copper and tin; these are not common within Scotland and must have had to be brought into the communities when metal objects were required. Sufficient heat to melt the ore was created on a small fire. The ore was then melted in a clay container, or crucible, and poured into a mould to cool and produce a cast object. Remains of crucibles, moulds and slag (waste) from melting ores are found during archaeological excavations of later prehistoric settlement sites, demonstrating to the archaeologist that bronze objects were created by people at these locations.

Iron ore commonly occurs as bog iron across much of the country. This probably meant that there was no need to transport materials over such great distances as the constituents of bronze. The production of iron was a more difficult process than bronze-making and may have required specialist workers. The smelting of iron ore requires a very high temperature which could only be obtained by the construction of a clay-built furnace. Smelting involved melting the iron ore, producing a bloom, or cake of raw iron. The bloom was then worked into an artefact through a process called smithing. Both smelting and smithing are complex operations which require a good deal of knowledge. Smelting furnaces are found on occasions and slag, the waste product which results from both smelting and smithing, has been found on a range of later prehistoric sites. The iron artefacts which have been discovered include some very well-made items, indicating a high level of skill.

Pottery
A 3000-year-old pottery vessel from Allt Cleascre, Achmore, Lewis. The grain to the right of the pot was found inside it. The pot and grain were deposited in a peat bog as an offering to the gods or spirits.
NATIONAL MUSEUMS OF SCOTLAND

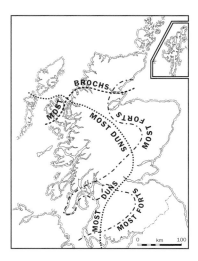

Settlement Map

Map of settlement zones in Scotland. People lived in different types of houses and settlements in different areas of Scotland and this map shows the main areas in which three types occur – brochs, duns and forts.

Houses

There is plentiful evidence from all over Scotland for the settlements and houses of later prehistoric people. If you live in or are visiting Scotland, it is likely that, wherever you are, you are within a kilometre or two of a farm or fort of this period. Different types of house and settlements occur in different areas. Many have been flattened by generations of ploughing and lie in fields, or are buried under modern towns and villages. Hundreds of these sites appear as 'cropmarks' in ploughed fields; the marks are revealed to archaeologists by aerial photography. Elsewhere in the lowlands archaeological evidence is often found during building work or where a quarry is being dug.

One of the remarkable features of Scotland's archaeology, in contrast to that of much of Europe, is that later prehistoric houses and settlements are very well preserved over large areas of the uplands because they were built of stone and have never been damaged or destroyed by later peoples' farms. Scotland has some of the most extensive and best preserved sites and structures of this date in western Europe. When they are excavated they can tell the archaeologist a great deal about our prehistoric ancestors.

Grangemount Cropmarks

Cropmarks of an open prehistoric settlement at Grangemount, Perthshire. The dark marks of ditches surrounding round houses and also souterrains are visible in the centre of the photograph (souterrains are described on p38). RCAHMS

What types of houses did they live in?

The types of houses built and lived in by individual families varied from area to area, although most were circular in plan. This book focuses on the substantial roundhouses which were built across large areas of Scotland; these include roundhouses built of stone, timber (or both), crannogs, brochs, duns and wheelhouses.

Hut circle is the name for a class of monument which occurs across much of Scotland. They are one of the most common prehistoric archaeological remains in Scotland, found over much of upland Scotland at altitudes of up to 400 metres or more. They are common in Shetland, Orkney, the Western Isles, Caithness, Sutherland, much of the northern and western mainland of Scotland and the uplands of Perthshire. There are different types of hut circles in different parts of Scotland, and these were probably built throughout the later prehistoric period. The use of the term 'hut' is rather inaccurate, since many of these houses were large and complex. Although 'hut circle' is well established in the archaeological literature, it would be more accurate to use the term 'house circle'.

Broxmouth Settlement
The excavation of a later prehistoric settlement at Broxmouth (East Lothian). The site has been partly uncovered and traces of several circuits of enclosing ditches and also the slight foundations trenches of timber fences and small timber-built roundhouses are visible under excavation. The site was excavated in advance of quarrying.
RCAHMS

House Circle

A house circle under excavation at Tormore on Arran. The stone footings of a small circular house are visible.
HISTORIC SCOTLAND

(opposite)
Dun Dornadilla Broch

The broch at Dun Dornadilla, Sutherland. The entrance to the broch survives within part of the massive wall. Large parts of the broch wall have collapsed since it was built 2000 years ago but the scale of the surviving masonry is very impressive.
RCAHMS

The house circle was built in an area where stone suitable for building was plentiful and could be used for the walls. The remains of the house circles survive as low walls. On top of these stone foundations would have sat a wall built of turf or earth. The roof would have been constructed of timber covered with a thatch of heather or straw.

Early house circles in Scotland date to around 3800 years ago. Some large examples up to 15 metres across have been excavated, such as at Lairg in Sutherland (described on p.8), which were probably the homes of extended family groups. House circles often have a single central hearth which would have provided a source of heat and cooked food for the family.

Brochs were built mainly in the north and west of Scotland, but a few are known in eastern and southern Scotland. Generally they seem to have been built during the last two centuries BC and the first century AD, although some may be earlier. They are certainly the most impressive of the stone roundhouses which were built by the later prehistoric occupants of Scotland. The tallest surviving broch, Mousa, is over 13 metres high, and stands on a small island just off the mainland of Shetland. Many archaeologists, however, believe that the considerable height of

Mousa was not typical of all brochs. The walls of many other less well-preserved brochs were probably much lower, although they were still very substantial buildings.

(right)
Dun Telve Floor Plan
Dun Telve, Glenelg, Lochalsh, Highland: the ground floor plan of the broch. Opening off the entrance, within the thickness of the wall, was a small chamber, often called the 'guard chamber'. From this small room a watch could be maintained over people entering, or attempting to enter, the building. There would have been a wooden doorway in the passage: traces of the way the door was fitted survive in most brochs.
CHRISTINA UNWIN

(below)
Broch at The Howe
Internal divisions inside the broch at The Howe, Mainland, Orkney. The circular area inside the wall of the broch was divided up by a number of stone partitions which formed private areas for members of the family. Some of the internal stone-built furniture is also visible.
HISTORIC SCOTLAND

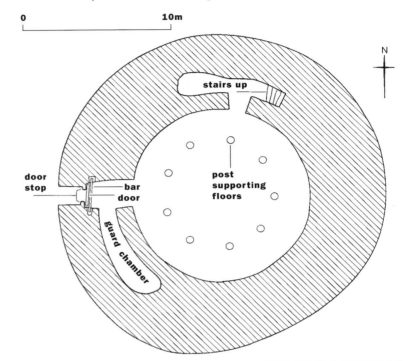

Some brochs were built and lived in for a long period of time. At The Howe in Orkney roundhouses were built one on top of the other over a period of 500 years or more (between the eighth and fourth century BC and the first and second century AD), indicating a remarkable continuity of settlement.

Most brochs had at least two storeys, with a single low entrance on the ground floor through a passageway which passed through the thick wall. It is often necessary to stoop through this entrance to gain access into the interior. On emerging from the passageway and standing up straight a visitor would have entered into a dark space on the ground floor of the tall building.

The floor of the upper levels was built from timber and supported on a stone step

Staircase
Mousa Broch, Shetland. An exceptionally well-preserved 2000-year-old staircase in a broch wall.
HISTORIC SCOTLAND

called a 'scarcement' which is often visible in the surviving masonry of the broch as a continuous projecting ledge. This floor was also usually supported by a circle of internal posts. These wooden posts and the other wooden elements of the broch never survive, having decayed and collapsed soon after the abandonment of the structure. The broch at Dun Telve in Lochalsh, Highland, has two scarcements, suggesting that it had at least three floors including the ground floor. The first and second floors would have been accessible by a flight of stone steps built within the thickness of the broch wall; stone stairs survive in good condition on many broch sites. Brochs are thought to have had conical wooden roofs, probably thatched with straw from the fields, with heather from the moorlands, or with turf.

In Orkney and Caithness stone partitions and furniture often survive on the ground floor, showing that in these cases the main living area may well have been on this level. There would be private areas where people could eat, sleep and undertake other activities. Often a hearth was placed in the centre of the floor.

What Were Brochs For?

In the past it was thought that brochs were built solely to protect the occupants. They were imposing stone structures with no windows and only a single entrance. However, they do not make very much sense in terms of formal warfare, because they could not withstand any form of prolonged siege. Although some brochs have wells, many are without a source of fresh water. Even if fresh water was available within the broch, attackers could have driven off some of the livestock remaining outside, since it is unlikely that all the cattle of a family or community could have

Dun Telve

Dun Telve: a view showing how the broch would have looked after it was built. It was a massive stone building which would have impressed both visitors and occupants.
CHRISTINA UNWIN

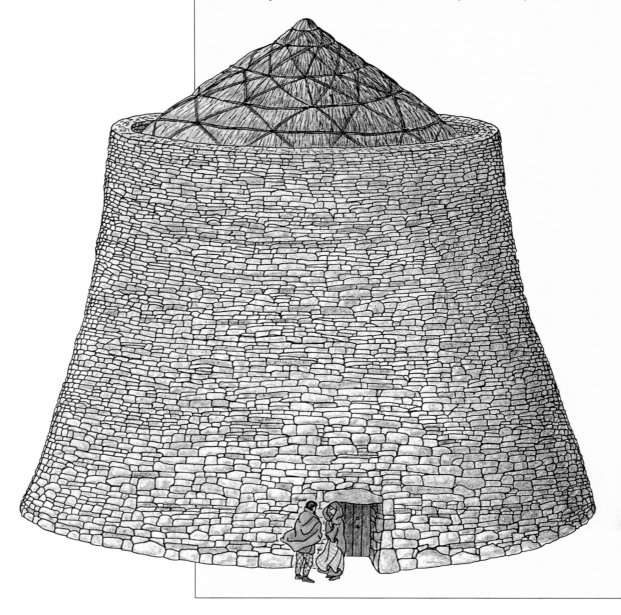

been brought inside the broch for protection. Attackers could have burnt the crop belonging to the broch family, who would then have been likely to die of starvation in the winter. In a similar way to the late medieval Scottish towerhouses, brochs were probably intended to impress others, although they would also have served to protect their occupants from small-scale raids. They are often built on low hills, which would have served to have made them even more impressive.

Dun Telve Cross-section

Dun Telve: a cross-section showing the broch in use. The ground floor space was probably a byre for the cattle of the family and the living space would have been on the first floor level of the broch. This living area probably had a central hearth and wooden partitions dividing up the living and sleeping area. The second floor might have been used for storage.
CHRISTINA UNWIN

Dun houses. In Argyll, Galloway and across parts of Central Scotland, the remains of substantial circular stone-built houses are often called 'duns'. Many of these are large house circles which are not quite as complex as the brochs. They are often placed on the top of hills, helping to make them more imposing. When excavated, as in the case of the two houses at Aldclune, Perthshire, duns turn out to have been substantial and complex roundhouses built of stone and timber, with wooden roofs covered in thatch. They often do not contain the staircases that occur in brochs and many may only have been of one storey.

Wheelhouses. The wheelhouse is another distinctive type of later prehistoric roundhouse. They are called 'wheelhouses' because they look like a spoked wheel in plan. Within the area defined by the stone walls there were stone pillars which supported the roof. These stone pillars resemble the posts in some timber houses (*see below*). Wheelhouses were built during the last few centuries BC and first century AD in the Western Isles and Shetland and perhaps in other areas of Scotland. Some of them are particularly well preserved because they were built by digging into sand-dunes, and often filled with sand after they were abandoned.

Wheelhouse
The wheelhouse at Jarlshof, Shetland. The stone pillars that held up the roof are visible and you can see out through the door of the house. The roof was probably covered with timber and thatch, but this has long since decayed.
HISTORIC SCOTLAND

Timber roundhouses. Elsewhere in southern and eastern Scotland, where stone was less available, later prehistoric roundhouses were often built in a different way. The walls of these houses were of timber, daub and earth and they are inevitably less well preserved, although careful excavation can tell us about the people who built and inhabited them. Unlike the upland house circles, there is usually very little or no trace of the later prehistoric timber roundhouse in the landscape today.

Some of the timber houses may have been built to last, although there is considerable

controversy about how long such houses would have stood – some archaeologists propose no more than 50 years, while others compare them with medieval timber buildings and suggest a far longer period.

Many of the examples which have been excavated do not fall into easily identifiable types. Excavation in many cases uncovers evidence for a ring of post-holes which would have held the bases of upright timbers that supported the walls of the house. Other houses had walls constructed of timbers which were placed in slots cut into the ground in the form of a circle. The long timbers which could be cut from the woodland in these areas meant that houses of great diameter could be built; some are more than 20 metres in diameter, although there are many houses of smaller size. Both types of house often have an internal ring of post-holes which contained timbers supporting the roof and possibly an upper floor.

One particular type of roundhouse which has been defined and studied in some detail is the 'ring-ditch house', examples of which have been excavated in East Lothian and Angus. The interior of the house closest to the wall was dug into the ground and often paved, while the central part of the house comprised a raised area. It has been suggested that the paved floor of the ring-ditch house was a byre for cattle and that the family occupied the first floor level. Ring-ditch houses were commonly built around 500 BC.

Many other timber houses probably had second floors, although the traces of central fireplaces in some of them indicate that the ground floor was not always a byre, and that the family's accommodation may have been divided between two floors. On occasions the roundhouse was located in an prominent position in the landscape, as in the case of the recently excavated ring-ditch house at

Wheelhouse Plan

A wheelhouse at Kilphedir, South Uist. The plan and a cross-section drawing of this well-preserved building shows how it was built and also why buildings of this type are know as 'wheelhouses'.
PREHISTORIC SOCIETY

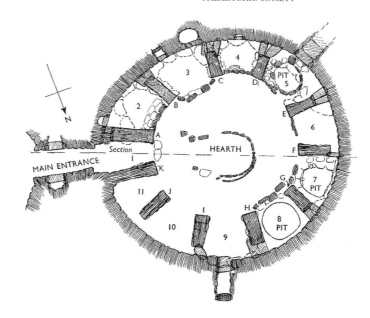

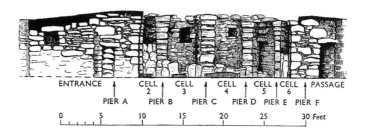

Culhawk Hill in Angus. This large house would have dominated the landscape and the valley below.

Bannockburn House

A later prehistoric house at Bannockburn Fort, Stirling, under excavation. The house was defined by a timber slot which held the wooden outer wall. There were also several circles of vertical posts set in post-holes within the house which held up the roof and possibly a timber first floor. The relative size of the people excavating the house shows how large it would have been.

HISTORIC SCOTLAND

Crannogs. Across Scotland, particularly in the Highlands and south-west, timber roundhouses called 'crannogs' were built on artificial platforms of wood and stone constructed in lochs and bogs. The name 'crannog' is derived from the Gaelic term 'crann', which means 'wood'. Usually a wooden causeway links the crannog to the shore. Crannogs appear to have been built throughout later prehistoric times and were also occupied and built in medieval Scotland.

The reasons that led people to build houses in the middle of lochs are unclear. Living in a crannog in the winter must have been difficult, with cold air blowing off the loch. In the same way that roundhouses and brochs were often located on the tops of hills in order to command the surrounding landscape, the location of the crannog would have created a major impression on visitors, and have made the occupants feel secure.

Owing to the effects of waterlogging the wooden objects used by the occupants and the rubbish accumulated during the occupation of the house are often very well preserved and tell us a great deal about the lives of people at this time. The evidence from Oakbank Crannog, Perthshire, for the diet of its occupants

Crannog

Reconstruction drawing of the crannog at Milton Loch, Dumfries, under construction. This crannog was a large wooden house built upon a stone and timber island in the loch. The canoes are based loosely on the example found at Loch Lotus in Dumfries.

CHRISTINA UNWIN

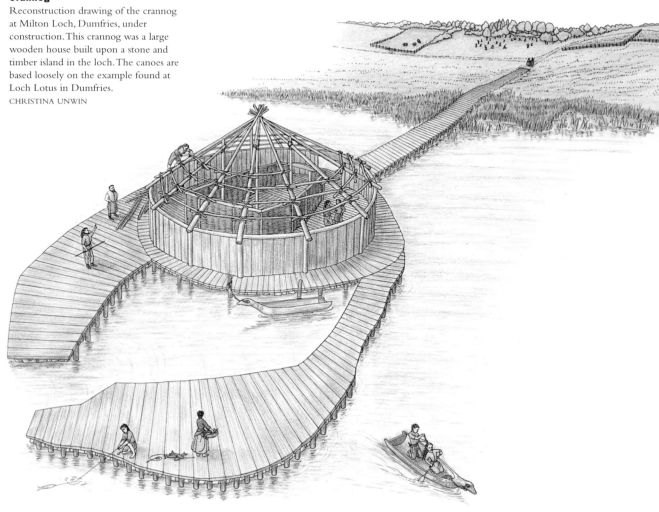

has already been described in on page 21. A crannog has been reconstructed in Loch Tay, close to Kenmore, Perthshire and can be visited by the public.

How many people lived in a house?

The basic structure of most stone and timber roundhouses was very similar, with a wall supporting a roof and often with an internal ring of timber posts or stone columns providing extra support. Some of these houses had upper floors. They varied considerably in size: some are as small as 4 metres in diameter, but many are very substantial, up to 22 metres across.

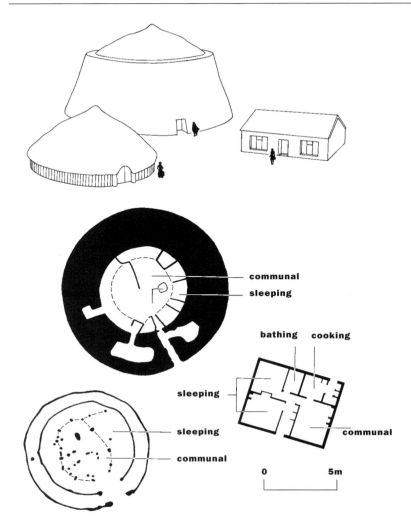

There is enough space in the average broch, or roundhouse, for quite a large number of people to live, especially if the building had an upper floor. The size of the family group in one of the larger timber roundhouses of southern Scotland may have been at least as large as that of the broch-dwelling family, due to the fact that the internal space within a timber house is often greater than the more northerly stone buildings. Some houses might have contained large and complex family groups of perhaps as many as 30 people, or more. As we have seen, in some cases cattle may have shared the family accommodation, a tradition which continued in some areas of Scotland until the beginning of the twentieth century.

House Comparison

A comparison of later prehistoric houses with a modern house shows how substantial these houses were. The large stone house is based on Bu, Orkney, the timber house on a house from Dryburn Bridge, East Lothian and the modern house was built just after the Second World War.

CHRISTINA UNWIN

The family and their home

By studying modern farming societies, we can see that the interiors of these later prehistoric houses would have been organised in very complex ways. Certain areas were set aside for different members of the family, perhaps older members or different sexes. The stone and timber partitions in brochs, wheelhouses and other roundhouses may reflect this. The majority of the stone and timber roundhouses of Scotland have a single doorway, usually facing the direction of the rising sun, to the south or south-east. It has recently been suggested that the occupants did different things at different times thoughout the day in various parts of the house.

The families who lived in these houses were very different from families today. Various Roman literary sources tell us about family groups in northern Europe; they suggest that families were

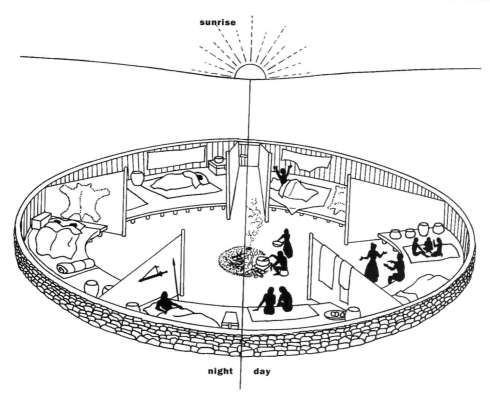

sunrise

night | day

organised according to marriage rules which enabled every man
to have more than one wife (polygamy), but it is also possible that
a woman might have had several husbands (polyandry). The exact
organisation of the family is unclear.

Several generations of a single family probably lived in a
single house. Owing to the fact that life-expectancy was fairly
short, adult responsibilities, marriage and childbearing started
earlier than in our society; grandparents, where they survived,
may often have lived with their children. If a couple had several
offspring, it is fairly likely that their children and their own
families would have lived together in one house, or in a group
of houses. Many of these roundhouses also had a single central
hearth, a communal focus where the family who lived in the
house ate and sat. At Aldclune in Perthshire, one of the two
houses had four hearths, each of which may have been used by
a single family group, or by different parts of a single family.

Whether the property – the house, the fields and the animals
– passed from fathers to sons, from mothers to daughters, or a
mixture of both, or was even held communally is uncertain.
Although it has usually been assumed that property passed from
fathers to sons, this reflects more, perhaps, how our own society
was organised until recently; there is no reliable evidence that
this is what happened in the past.

Roundhouse

A diagram to show the internal
organisation of a roundhouse. Eating
and daytime activities may have occurred
in the south of the house, storage and
sleeping to the north.
CHRISTINA UNWIN

What Are Souterrains and What Were They Used For?

Souterrains are stone-walled underground passageways which occur mainly in Angus, Aberdeenshire, Sutherland and Caithness, and in the Northern and Western Isles. They are usually attached to a stone or timber roundhouse. In the past all sorts of explanations were put forward to explain why souterrains were built; it was even suggested that they were refuges in time of trouble, although this is unlikely because once entered there was often no other way out. Since these underground chambers maintain a constant low temperature, even in very hot weather, it is likely that they were often used for storage, perhaps for meat and cheese. The souterrain at Newmill in Perthshire was connected with a timber house and had two entrances – one from the house, the other from the outside. The excavator suggested that it was used to store grain – at harvest time the grain was put into the souterrain through the outside door and then brought into the house as needed through the connecting door. The idea that some souterrains were used to store grain is supported by the excavated evidence from Red Castle in Angus, where charred grain was found on the souterrain floor. Some of the Angus souterrains are so large that they may have been used as central stores for a community.

It is possible that souterrains have a religious significance, but their exact meaning to later prehistoric people is uncertain. However, the use of a souterrain as a store does not preclude the idea that it might also have been a shrine. The storage of crops though the winter must have been vital for these later prehistoric people and the souterrain therefore would have been associated with magical powers because it was a container and preserver of an essential resource.

Souterrain
The souterrain at Grain, Mainland, Orkney. This is a carefully built stone cellar with pillars that held up the roof. The metal bar has been put into the souterrain in recent years to help to hold the roof up.
HISTORIC SCOTLAND

Settlements

Different types of settlements were built in Scotland during later prehistory. At the start of our period it would appear that most of the population lived in open settlements of clusters of roundhouses, but around 1000 BC people began to build enclosure walls, palisades, or banks and ditches around their settlements.

The open settlement

This was usually made up of a group of houses of similar size, with no obvious indication that any one family was dominant. They varied in size from a single isolated house to loosely associated groups of up to 20 houses and sometimes quite large villages were formed. The individual houses lay within their fields with no prominent enclosure boundary, although in some cases houses were separated from their fields by walls. Some survive as earthworks, while others have been ploughed-out and are only shown by cropmarks. The settlements at Green Knowe in Peebleshire and Lairg in Sutherland are Bronze Age open settlements. During the Iron Age, people in some areas, for instance in Fife and parts of Perthshire, continued to live in these unenclosed settlements.

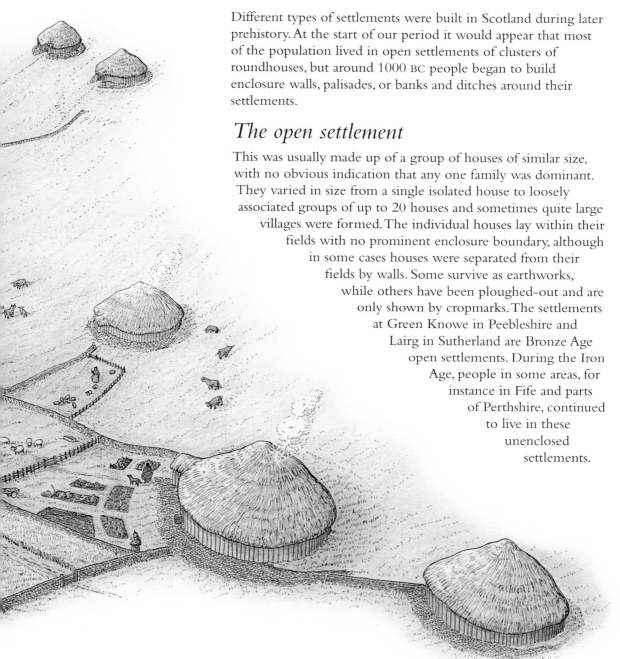

Green Knowe Settlement

The open settlement at Green Knowe, Peebleshire. This was occupied for some time around 3000 years ago. A number of small roundhouses are spread along the hillside, each one built on a small platform. The fields and pasture areas used by each family occur around the houses and are defined by stone dykes.

CHRISTINA UNWIN

The enclosed settlement

Around 1000 BC a new type of settlement – the enclosed settlement – began to appear. They occur across most of Scotland, although only occasionally in the north, and are very common in some areas such as the Borders, East Lothian and Argyll. They vary in scale from small farms to large hillforts. We have seen that some open settlements were divided from their fields by walls, but in the case of enclosed settlements a single bank, ditch, wall or palisade surrounded the whole of the site. This type of enclosure can be compared with a hedge or with a stone or brick wall around a modern house and garden, although some of these enclosures were very substantial and defined the outer edge of the settlement in an imposing way. There was a great variety of enclosed settlements but few have been excavated. The available evidence suggests that enclosed settlements were built from 1000 BC until the first century BC/first century AD, but there was a later revival after the Romans had left Scotland.

Enclosures consisting of a palisade of vertical timbers may have occurred at an early date on many sites. Walls around settlements are common where stone is easy to acquire, particularly in Argyll, the west coast of the Highlands and on the islands. These are often called 'duns'; as we have seen, many duns were large roundhouses while others were enclosed groups of houses. In southern and eastern Scotland people built stone walls where stone was available, but in other areas they built earth banks reinforced with timber. Many of the settlements with earth banks also had ditches outside the bank; the banks were formed by the material thrown up when the ditch was dug. Sometimes only cropmarks indicate the location of these sites.

Most enclosed settlements had a single entrance, in some cases a simple break in the ditch, bank or wall; on the more impressive settlements a stone or timber gate was constructed. Traces of such gates are sometimes found when the sites are excavated, as at Cullykhan in Banffshire where a timber gate was built across the entrance passageway.

Dun Mara

A small enclosed settlement at Dun Mara, Lewis. The dun is visible on the coastal headland and it is enclosed by a stone wall. Traces of post-medieval cultivation are visible inland from the dun.
HISTORIC SCOTLAND

Enclosed settlements were built in different kinds of places. Many were built on the tops of hills, others on hill slopes, and occasionally they occur on low ground. Some enclosed sites are located on coastal promontories and these are often called 'promontory forts' or 'cliff castles'.

Enclosed settlements could contain a single house but many have between two and ten individual houses, each of which may have housed a single related family and which together made up a community. The family of an individual's brother or sister, or aunt or uncle, for example, may have lived in a separate house but within the same enclosure. At Gurness in Orkney the broch dominates a surrounding group of smaller houses within the same enclosure; here the leading family of the community possibly lived in the broch.

The largest of the enclosed settlements were the hillforts, which had strong defences protecting the settlement. The largest and most impressive examples include Eildon Hill North (Ettrick and Lauderdale), Traprain Law (East Lothian) and Tap O'Noth (Aberdeenshire). Eildon Hill North is over 16 hectares in extent and enclosed as many as 296 individual house platforms, each the location of a small roundhouse. Limited archaeological excavation suggests that the hillfort may have been constructed around 1000 BC and that the houses were not all in use at the same time. It may have been abandoned at some stage, after which it appears to have been re-occupied in the period of Roman occupation during the second and third centuries AD. Traprain Law is almost as extensive as Eildon Hill North and appears to have had a similarly early origin. Again there is a lack of clear evidence for occupation between around 600 BC and 50 AD, although we know that activity occurred on the hilltop during the Roman period because finds of this date have been made. The Brown and White Caterthuns in Angus are also impressive hillforts. Recent excavation on the Brown Caterthun indicates that the earliest rampart was built between 700 and 500 BC, although the hill was refortified on a couple of occasions during the time when Eildon Hill North and Traprain Law appear to have been unoccupied.

Cropmarks

Cropmarks of the enclosed settlement at Carperstane, East Lothian. This is a very regular, circular enclosed settlement with at least three circuits of enclosing ditches. The banks have been ploughed out and the ditches infilled. The parallel vertical lines at the top of the photograph are the results of modern drainage while those at the bottom are a result of the way in which the field is currently being cultivated.
RCAHMS

(above)
Gurness
Air photograph of the broch and
settlement at Gurness, Mainland, Orkney.
The large broch is surrounded by a
number of smaller buildings and a
series of enclosing banks and ditches.
RCAHMS

(opposite)
Eildon Hill Hillfort
The hillfort at Eildon Hill North, Ettrick
and Lauderdale. The ramparts of the fort
are visible running around the hill. In
the interior to the left are faint traces of
the platforms left by hundreds of small
houses.
HISTORIC SCOTLAND

Why did some families enclose their settlements?

It is not certain why families in some areas of Scotland built walls and banks around their settlements and others did not. It used to be thought that settlements were enclosed to defend their occupants against the advancing Romans, but we now know that many of the sites date back to at least 1000 years before the Roman invasion, while others are later but were either abandoned or their defences disused by the time of the Romans.

It has also been suggested that worsening environmental conditions around 1000 BC made farming in many upland areas impossible, so that more people needed farmland in lowland areas. Families therefore needed to define and defend their settlements and land from neighbours by building boundaries. Nevertheless, this only occurred in some areas. In some parts of Scotland the contrast is very clear – for instance, to the south of the Firth of Forth, in East Lothian and the Borders, enclosed settlements are very common, while to the north, in Fife, Angus and parts of Perthshire, almost all settlements are open. It is unclear why the population in East Lothian would have required defending while those in Fife were quite happy to live undefended. It is possible that people in later prehistory merely had a tradition of doing things differently in different areas – building enclosures may merely have been a matter of choice.

Perhaps the impressive roundhouses and enclosed settlements were built for the same basic reasons, individual status and group identity. Previously archaeologists have seen both types as solely defensive. It is just as likely, however, that both substantial roundhouses and enclosed settlements helped families to define the identity of the group to which they belonged. Substantial roundhouses and most of the enclosed settlements probably formed the homes for individual families, while some of the more extensive enclosed settlements and open settlements probably formed the homes or the meeting places for extensive communities.

Neighbours and Friends

Having considered some of the houses and settlements in which families lived, we also need to look at how they related to their neighbours. The population of Scotland as a whole was not as substantial as it is now, although large numbers of later prehistoric houses occur in some areas and many areas of the country were more heavily populated than they are now.

Travel

Many of the objects owned by families were transported over great distances – weapons and ornaments found in Scotland show similarities to objects elsewhere in Britain and further afield. This means that some people did travel around and would have carried news and ideas with them as well as objects.

Boggy areas, forests and mountains would have presented considerable obstacles to travellers and visitors in many parts of Scotland. There were no well-made roads and the tracks were unpaved. In some boggy areas wooden trackways were built to help people to cross marshes, such as those found during peat-cutting in Flanders Moss and Blair Drummond Moss, Stirlingshire. Such causeways were not common, however, and most transport would have taken place along dirt tracks which in the autumn and winter must have been very muddy.

Wooden Trackway
A prehistoric wooden trackway known as the Eclipse Track in Somerset, England. The Scottish prehistoric trackways found in Flanders and Blairdrummond Moss might have looked very similar when they were uncovered in the late eighteenth century.
SOMERSET LEVELS PROJECT

Travel would have been easier by water than by land. Families who lived by lochs, rivers or the sea would have had boats for transport and fishing. Different types of boats, including dug-out canoes, have been found preserved in bogs in Scotland and finds from elsewhere in Britain show that more substantial seagoing boats travelled along major rivers, up the coast and across to the islands, Ireland and northern Europe.

Were Large Hillforts Towns?

Some of the largest of the enclosed settlements are so extensive that there is a tendency to view them like modern towns. Eildon Hill North had a large number of roundhouses and the hillfort of Traprain Law had an area equivalent to the medieval centre of the neighbouring market town of Haddington. It has been suggested that some hillforts in the south of Britain served, in effect, as towns for their surrounding populations: that they were places in which people bought and sold goods and were also perhaps local centres of government and the homes of important chieftains.

There are several problems with this explanation. No large hillforts have been excavated on any scale in Scotland but, when similar sites have been excavated in the south, the materials they produce are very similar to those from other typical farms. Large hillforts do not necessarily appear to have been production centres for pots, ironwork or clothes. There is also very little evidence that they were places in which items were bought and sold, or that they were the homes of important individuals. The excavated evidence often suggests that they were just very extensive enclosed settlements and possibly meeting places.

Marriage and kin

The population of later prehistoric Scotland did not live in towns and cities. Some communities lived in groups of houses, others were dispersed in the countryside. Individual families would have had a network of kin and a range of friends in their neighbourhood and further afield, who would have helped to provide security if the harvest was bad and physical protection in times of unrest. Children eventually needed to find partners in order to raise their own offspring. Every society has taboos about who precisely can be married – we do not permit the marriage of brother and sister for example, but in some societies people are forbidden to marry even more distant relations such as first or second cousins, and so the availability of possible marriage partners who are unrelated becomes a matter of great significance.

Fairs and festivals

If they were not towns, what function did these large hillforts have? An alternative opinion is that they were places in which people gathered to celebrate festivals or to deal with disputes or legal matters. Goods might have been exchanged and alliances made between families at these times. The houses within the hillforts may have served as accommodation during the festivities. The large number of houses at Eildon Hill North may indicate that many families were involved, drawn from a wide area. Gatherings may have occurred throughout the year, but were probably more common and popular at times when the demands of agricultural life were not too great.

The houses at these hillforts would therefore have been for temporary occupation only, similar to the 'booths' or the temporary houses set up on the same site every year by the same families at the law gatherings of the Norse settlers over 1000 years later. It is also possible that families retreated to these places in times of war, which may be the reason why they are defended by ramparts.

Gatherings of populations may also have occurred in other places, including the houses and enclosures around settlements. Some of the brochs of the north and west of Scotland are so substantial that they were probably built by a number of families who would have co-operated over the gathering of stone, wood and other materials required to build the structure. The construction of the building was also a major operation and may have involved large groups. Some of the other roundhouses may also have been built by groups of families: for example some pits in the floor of the wheelhouse at Sollas on North Uist contained

Traprain Law Hillfort

The hillfort at Traprain Law, East Lothian. Two ramparts are visible on the right (north) of the hill. Modern quarrying has cut into the hill causing much damage.
RCAHMS

(inset)

Trapain Law Model

A reconstruction of Traprain Law 2000 years ago. Several circular houses have been built in the fort, a gathering of people is occurring close to the top of the hill, while a large fire is burning on the top point of the Law. Traprain Law may have been a place where people met to celebrate festivals. These festivals may have lasted for several days – food and alcoholic drinks would have been consumed.
CHRISTINA UNWIN

the remains of animals which may have been part of a meal partaken by those who gathered to build the house. The burials of a horse under the rampart of the hillfort at Eildon Hill North may represent the remains of a meal eaten by those who built the rampart. The animal remains may also have been in part an offering to the gods, with choice parts of the animal buried or burnt in dedication (see next chapter).

Families may therefore have met for a number of reasons: to celebrate, to build houses or settlements, and probably to exchange produce and stories. Other gatherings probably occurred at particular times, such as the birth and death of members of the community. They may also have occurred at significant spots when groups of people met to make offerings to the gods.

Tribes

We have seen that people lived dispersed throughout the countryside, but loose groupings of families probably felt kinship even in times of peace, an association reinforced by attending meetings. At times of crisis individual families may have gathered together into tribes in order to fight incomers, their leaders having access to impressive swords, shields and ornate personal ornaments, even in times of peace. These metalwork objects displayed the wealth and power of these leaders of the community. The evidence for the dominant broch and surrounding settlement at Gurness may also indicate the existence of a dominant individual and subservient families.

The Roman author Ptolemy wrote down the names of a number of 'tribes' who occupied northern Britain at the time of the Roman occupation. During the Roman invasion in AD 83 native people combined to fight the Roman forces at Mons Graupius under a leader called Calgacus. He led soldiers from a number of different tribes, and it took serious military aggression from the Romans to force the natives to co-operate in this way.

Ptolemy's Map
Map of the 'tribes' of Iron Age Scotland as recorded by the Roman author Ptolemy. These tribes may have been groups of families who felt that they were descended from a common ancestor. They may even have had tribal meetings at the major hillforts or elsewhere.

Sacrifice and Religion

It is difficult to say very much about how later prehistoric people thought and what they believed in. They had no writing and did not record their thoughts and beliefs, but it seems certain that they had a strong oral tradition. They passed on stories, medical knowledge, hunting lore and traditions from one generation to the next, as well as attending to the important matters of naming of places and detailing events which happened at them. Older men and women would have been revered as a source of knowledge and because of their long experience.

The gods

It is probable that they believed in gods, a range of spirits or divine beings who controlled the seasons and the productivity of crops and the animals upon which communities depended. In an age before anyone had a detailed understanding of nature, many aspects of the changing seasons and the growth of crops and animals must have appeared largely beyond the control of the community, and revering the gods would have provided one way of trying to ensure good harvests and a ready supply of food. A wooden figure, found during peat cutting in a bog at Ballachulish near Fort William (Lochaber) in the nineteenth century, may represent a figure of a god.

In earlier periods of Scotland's prehistory, religious activity was centred around burial sites, stone circles, henges and standing stones. In later prehistory these sites fell out of use, although many show signs of later activity, such as metalworking in the stone circle at Loanhead in Aberdeenshire and the henge at Moncreiffe in Perthshire. The Roman authors Caesar and Tacitus mention that druids existed in Britain and on the Continent. The druids appear to have been a group of religious specialists and it is possible that such figures may have existed among the communities of Scotland.

Offerings to the gods

Crops and animals were vital for survival and so it is thought that later prehistoric communities had a range of beliefs relating to the fertility of crops and stock. Significant items are often found in archaeological excavations, such as the remains of a horse buried beneath the rampart at Eildon Hill North, and animal and human bones under the floor of the wheehouse of Sollas on North Uist. Quernstones, used to grind corn, may have also been placed in certain places for religious reasons. At Aldclune in Perthshire numerous quernstones were incorporated into the

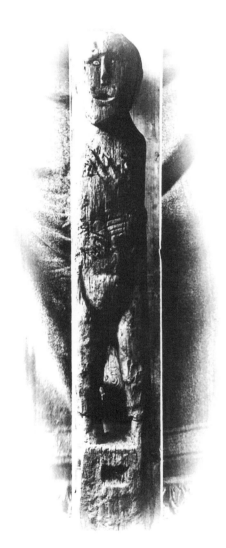

Wooden Figurine
The Ballachulish figurine which was found close to North Ballachulish, Lochaber. It is an almost life-sized wooden figure of a woman dating to around 600 BC who may have been a goddess or spirit.
NATIONAL MUSEUMS OF SCOTLAND

floors of two houses, while at Pict's Knowe in Dumfriesshire quernstones and other objects were found in the ditch of an enclosure which was dug in the first or second century AD and seems to have been built into the remains of a Neolithic henge. These items may have been deposited as offerings to the gods or spirits.

Later Roman writers tell us that the peoples of north-western Europe revered watery places and groves of trees as places of communication with their gods. It is likely that later prehistoric communities in Scotland gathered at places such as the peat bog at Ballachulish Moss to worship. We know this because of the range of items deliberately dropped or thrown into the Scottish wetlands. Some of these are domestic items, such as wooden containers, often packed with a substance called 'bog butter'. Wooden containers full of this substance are a common find in northern and western Scotland and the Western Isles, and several such finds were made during the nineteenth century at Ballachulish Moss, close to the find spot of the wooden female figure. Groups of families may have gathered together to make these offerings and wooden vessels packed with bog butter would have been valuable gifts.

Across the lowland areas of southern, central and eastern Scotland, impressive items of metalwork were deposited in the wetlands, rivers and caves. Some are personal ornaments, but weapons and horse fittings were also placed in bogs. Sometimes collections of

Wooden Vessel
Wooden vessel from Glen Gill near Morvern, Lochaber. This wooden container was full of bog butter and it is dated to the second or third century AD.
NATIONAL MUSEUMS OF SCOTLAND

What Was Bog Butter?

Bog butter has been found in wooden containers during the digging of peat bogs in a number of places across the north and west Highlands of Scotland and in the Northern and Western Isles. It also occurs in other parts of Europe, for instance in Ireland. It is usually a fairly hard yellow mass when discovered and scientific analysis suggests that it was produced from animal fat. It may have been used for cooking, like modern butter, lard or vegetable oil. It may even have been a cosmetic used as face cream or oil for the hair. It has been suggested that it was placed in the bog in wooden containers in order to improve its taste! Bog butter has been found during modern peat cutting so some at least was deposited and never retrieved. It may have been intended as a gift to the gods to pay them back for providing the community with an agricultural surplus. Although to us it may not appear a very appealing gift, it constituted a valuable commodity in later prehistoric times. The pot with grain from Allt Cleascre on Lewis, discussed on page 23, may be another example of a similar gift.

objects were placed in a bronze cauldron which was lowered into a small loch or boggy hollow. Objects dating from the time between 1500 BC and 700 BC are common and widespread. Later deposits are uncommon until the period of Roman occupation in the late first to third century AD.

Some of the deposits contain massive quantities of valuable metal, as in the case of the ironwork hoards from Carlingwark Loch (Stewartry), Blackburn Mill (Berwickshire) and Eckford (Roxburghshire); it has been suggested that these deposits represent gifts made by large groups of families. Whole communities probably gathered to make these offerings,

Ceremony

Deposition of metal objects in a loch during the ninth or eighth century BC. The objects represent an offering to the gods to ensure success in battle. A range of weapons are shown along with a cauldron into which the weapons will be placed. The cauldron will then be lowered into the loch from the end of the jetty. The man on the jetty is throwing some objects into the loch. A group of onlookers have gathered to observe the ceremony.
DAVID HOGG

Bronze Vessel
A bronze vessel which was put into a peat bog during later prehistory as an offering to the gods. This particularly fine example was found during peat digging at Kincardine Moss, Stirlingshire.
NATIONAL MUSEUMS OF SCOTLAND

the hoards may have been placed in the bog y the head of the community. Alternatively, it is possible that the objects were placed in the bog by a religious leader or druid – perhaps the druid and the head of the community were the same person.

What happened to the dead?

Although it is likely that funerals were important times in the cycle of community life, not know a great deal about how the dead were the major burial monuments of the Neolithic and Bronze Age – the chambered cairns and substantial burial mounds – were long disused by the late Bronze Age, although new burials were dug into the surface of old mounds until at least 1000 BC. At the beginning of the later prehistoric period there is evidence that bodies were cremated and the ashes buried in simple cairns surrounded by massive kerbs. During the period from 800 BC to AD 200 the dead were not usually placed in formal graves, but sometimes they were dumped into the disused remains of old houses and settlements as at The Howe, described earlier. Occasionally boxes made of stone slabs, or 'cists', were constructed and contain a single body or multiple burials. Evidence from MacArthur's Cave in Argyll, for instance, indicates that dead bodies were also placed in caves.

As well as the occasional burials in cists, caves and disused buildings, pieces of human bone are found within houses, in pits cut into the floors, behind the walls, or under paved surfaces. At The Howe in Orkney, fragments of two human bodies were found in a drain under the floor of the house, while at Cnip in Lewis a small piece of human bone was found in the entrance passage to one of the houses. When a person died the corpse was probably left in the open until the flesh had decayed. Possibly the body was placed on a wooden platform to prevent animals dragging the remains away. In some cultures the period between the death of an individual and the completion of the rotting of their flesh is seen as a journey between life and death, and the consumption of their body by birds is thought to release their spirit; in others the spirit of the dead person is held to be dangerous, particularly to close relatives, until the flesh has rotted. These sorts of beliefs may have been held by our later prehistoric ancestors; there is certainly evidence for exposure of bodies in the Neolithic period, 2000 years or more earlier. The exposure of the body, therefore, may have been considered to be the final stage in the life cycle of the individual, and the parts of the body that

remained were possibly kept by members of the community as symbols of ancestral power.

The direct connection of these remains with the ancestors of the community meant that, on occasions, they were used in interesting ways which reflected their value. At Hornish Point in South Uist, parts of the body of a dead twelve-year-old boy were found divided among four separate pits dug into the floor of a later prehistoric house. It appeared from a study of the remains that this child's body was first exposed and then separated into four quarters to be placed in the pits, along with remains of cattle and sheep. There is no evidence, however, to indicate that the child was sacrificed and he may well have died from natural causes. Possibly the burial of this child was a foundation ritual and the animal bones represented the remains of a meal that accompanied the ritual. Pieces of people were also turned into objects. At Wag of Forse in Caithness three human bones were found: one had been perforated for use as an artefact and a second bone had been used as a peg.

After-death Ceremony
The exposure of a dead man with a woman weeping. The woman's cloak in the picture is based on one which was found in a peatbog in Orkney and is described on p13.
CHRISTINA UNWIN

Human sacrifice

That human sacrifices occurred on occasions has been demonstrated in the case of 'Pete Marsh/Lindow Man', a body found in a peat bog in Cheshire in the 1980s. Such practices also occurred in Scotland. A cave called the Sculptor's Cave at Covesea in Moray, was excavated earlier this century and produced a wide range of later prehistoric artefacts as well as the remains of humans and animals. The human bones indicated that some of the dead had been beheaded, perhaps as an offering to the gods. Human sacrifice was probably an act carried out only when the community was faced with an exceptional crisis such as a seriously failed harvest which threatened its future. Another example may be the sacrifice of captives after victory in battle.

The exposure of dead bodies and the use of pieces of bone from dead relatives shows that later prehistoric communities had very different ways of living from ours; but our practice of secular cremation might appear barbarous to another society – social values and ethics of behaviour vary significantly over space and through time.

The Impact of the People on their Landscape

Through cultivation and the building of their forts and houses our ancestors changed the landscape, and much of their impact is still visible across Scotland, if you know where to look.

The pattern of the landscape

Most of Scotland was occupied during later prehistory. The country would have been a mosaic of different types of land. Cultivation occurred on the fertile coastal soils of the Western Isles, the west and north coast of the mainland and Shetland; inland areas were covered in bogs and forests. Across other parts of the Highlands, river valleys and straths were heavily settled, as were some areas of modern moorland. Other regions were covered by trees or bog. Orkney, Caithness, and the eastern, southern and south-western parts of Scotland were more heavily settled and, in some places, very few trees remained by AD 50. Across the south and east of Scotland large areas had been cleared of trees, while to the north and west forests may have still been extensive. Woodlands, moorland and the coastline edged the settled areas where communities lived and farmed. This cleared land was farmed by families; some was ploughed and some used as pasture.

Bogs and marshes

The heavy rainfall in many parts of western and northern

Land-use Map
The country formed a mosaic of differing land types. This map shows the rough distribution of forest cover around AD 50. In some areas of central Scotland extensive forest cover survived. The northern and western areas had been largely cleared of trees by climatic factors and human activity. The main areas in which people had cleared almost all the trees were to the south and east of the country.

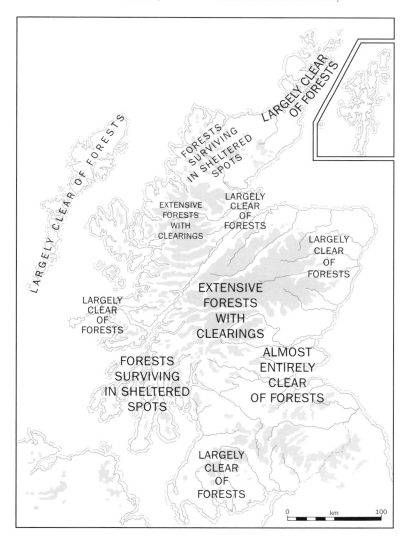

What Other Kinds of Evidence Tell Us About the Past Landscape?

Analysis of pollen found within peat bogs and mires of Scotland has provided us with information about the amount of tree cover and species of trees and plants during the later prehistoric period. Pollen analysis also tells us something of the extent of the peat bogs at this time.

The waterlogged, airless conditions in the bogs preserves vegetable and animal remains due to the fact that the organisms which cause decay cannot live without oxygen. The amount of pollen from different types of plant such as trees and grasses reflects the size of the area covered by woodland or under cultivation. Peat grows in a series of layers which build up through time, the layers of peat below dying and becoming compressed and preserved. These layers can be dated using radiocarbon dating. A peat bog will therefore preserve evidence of the changes in land use around it such as the felling of trees, the regeneration of woodland, the increase in the area of land under agriculture, and even which crops were being grown.

Scotland encouraged the growth of the peat moorland which forms such a distinctive element of the Scottish landscape. Many of these upland peat bogs and some of the lowland bogs, or raised mires, had begun to develop before around 1500 BC. In fact, in some of areas of the west and north we know that bogs started to smother land that had formerly been used for cultivation at this time. These bogs are still fairly common in upland Scotland and were also common in the lowlands before the extensive land drainage campaigns of the eighteenth and nineteenth centuries. For instance, in the central belt of Scotland the area between the modern towns of Aberfoyle and Stirling was covered by a massive bog until it was extensively cleared and drained in the late eighteenth century. During later prehistory the bog would have made travelling across this area very hazardous. Such areas were probably exploited by later prehistoric populations because of their wildlife and because peat could also have been cut for use as fuel.

Forests

It is a modern myth that when the Romans arrived they invaded a largely wooded Scotland occupied by barbaric tribes, but we know from pollen analysis that much of the countryside had already been cleared of trees by that time. The later prehistoric people used the timber to build houses and settlements. Owing to their large-scale clearance across southern Scotland, wood may actually have been hard to obtain; as a result, between 200 BC and AD 200, people had to use more stone to build their houses, settlements and forts. It is likely that people managed the woodland by encouraging the growth of young trees for future structural timbers in certain areas and also by coppicing cut trees, proving that timber formed a valuable resource.

Epilogue – our later prehistoric ancestors

A summary

The evidence for later prehistoric Scotland summarised above demonstrates that people at this time lived in small communities but had widespread contacts with other communities across northern Britain and northern Europe. This is how styles and ideas spread across Scotland.

The main theme in the evidence is the settled agricultural nature of life at this time. The impressive roundhouses and forts of later prehistoric Scotland may suggest that people needed to defend their families, cattle and crops from raiders, but it is also likely that these structures were intended to make an impression – to indicate the power of the individual family who built the house and of the community who worked together to construct the fort. The major hillforts of Scotland may have been places in which large groups of people from a wide area met to exchange goods, tell stories and settle disputes. We have plentiful evidence of houses, settlement, forts and fields, but only limited evidence of how communities disposed of their dead during the Iron Age. We do, however, have some information about their religious beliefs.

The later prehistoric evidence does not suggest that prehistoric Scotland remained the same over the 1700 years covered by this book. In fact, it indicates that families changed their ways through time. At the beginning of our period, the main metal in use was bronze and a range of weapons, tools and ornaments was manufactured from it. By around 700 BC iron had come into use and the creation of iron plough-shares may have enabled families to cultivate heavier, wetter soils. This may have had a dramatic effect on the landscape, as larger areas were cleared for cultivation, demonstrated by the evidence from pollen analysis. In addition, iron weapons were made. These were more effective in killing and maiming humans and animals than bronze weapons and the fact that they may have been used for more aggressive behaviour possibly provides one reason for the building of enclosures around settlements and the construction of large imposing roundhouses.

People also lived in different ways in the different areas of Scotland. For instance, we have seen that a contrast exists between open settlements in Fife and Perthshire and the enclosed settlements of East Lothian and Borders. From 200 BC to AD 200 there was a contrast between the deposition of

Brown Caterthun Hillfort
The hillfort at the Brown Caterthun, Angus. The multiple ramparts of this hillfort are very obvious from the air. This is one of a large number of very well preserved later prehistoric settlements in Scotland which you can visit.
RCAHMS

religious offerings across Scotland – metalwork items were used in the south and east of Scotland and wooden and organic items in the north and west. Numerous differences also occurred in the types of houses and settlements that people built in different parts of Scotland.

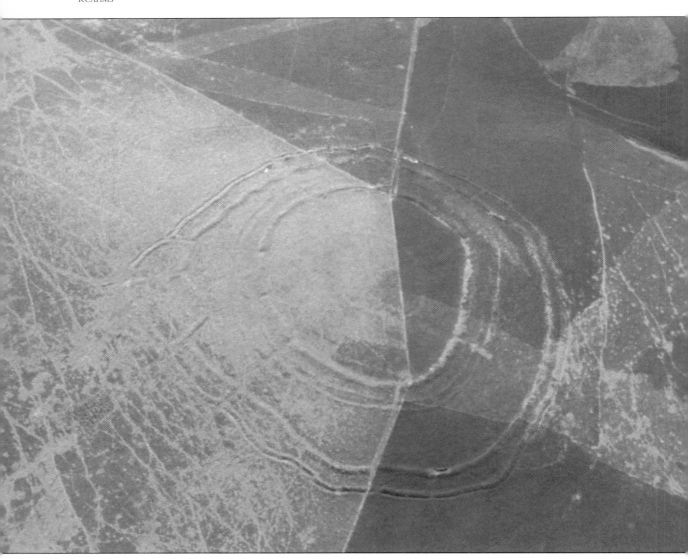

How important is the Scottish evidence?

The evidence for Scotland's later prehistory is particularly important, although there are large gaps in our knowledge about how people lived at this time.

The later prehistoric settlements are particularly significant from a British and European perspective because they are very well preserved. In Highland Scotland, the islands and upland areas of the east, south and south-west there are substantial remains of later prehistoric houses and settlements. When well-preserved buildings are excavated they produce particularly important evidence for the domestic life of the people who built and lived in them.

Across much of southern and eastern Britain the majority of sites of later prehistoric date have been flattened by the plough or built over. Modern cultivation methods can destroy much important information, and many sites in southern and eastern Scotland have already been ploughed flat. Ploughing nevertheless does not destroy all of the evidence and the surviving remains of these buildings and sites often demonstrate different ways of life from that of the inhabitants of the north and west of Scotland. We therefore have to preserve and understand later prehistoric sites from the whole of Scotland if we are to maintain a balanced record of our past in the future. The protection of these sites is important because understanding the past illuminates the present and enriches the future.

Lochan Druim an Duin

Lochan Druim an Duin, Sutherland. A substantial roundhouse, possibly a broch, on the north coast of Scotland.
Many later prehistoric settlements are still impressive features of the modern landscape.

DAVID SMITH

How Do I Find Out More?

Sites To Visit

The remains of the later prehistoric people are scattered all over Scotland. Some areas have a range of sites that are excavated and interpreted but most areas have something worth seeing. The list is ordered by area, alphabetically. I have tried to give a broad geographic coverage, concentrating on monuments that are open to the public by Historic Scotland or by other bodies. The initials (HS) means that the site is open to the public by Historic Scotland; (P) means that the monument is opened to the public by another agency. Where there are no initials the site is on private land and the permission of the owner may be required. Ordnance Survey grid references are provided.

Aberdeenshire

Archaeolink – (P) archaeological interpretation centre. This includes the remains of a hillfort, house circle and a modern reconstruction of a roundhouse. Plans exist to build reconstructions of other archaeological monuments in the future.
NJ 667 252.

Angus

Souterrains (all HS) –
Ardestie NO 503 344,
Carlungie NO 511 357
and Tealing NO 412 381.

The Brown and White Caterthuns hillforts – (HS) a pair of fine hillforts. Recent excavation has produced later prehistoric dates for the construction of the ramparts.
NO 555 669 and NO 548 661.

Argyll

Kildonan – a small dun or fort which was probably built in later prehistoric times and reoccupied during the Early Historic period.
NR 780 277.

Arran

Torr a'Chaisteal dun – (HS) the remains of a small prehistoric house or fort.
NR 921 232

Berwickshire

Edin's Hall – (HS) – a hillfort, broch and group of hut circles. This is an unusually complex later prehistoric settlement.
NT 773 601

East Lothian

The Chesters – (HS) a heavily fortified hillfort containing traces of later prehistoric houses.
NT 507 782

Traprian Law – (P) a hillfort on the top of a steep-sided hill. Traces of the ramparts of the fort are visible on the north and west faces of the hill and there are faint traces of internal buildings. Excavations produced evidence for Late Bronze Age and Roman-period occupation and the finds are in the National Museum of Scotland.
NT 580 747

North Berwick Law – (P) a hillfort located on a steep-sided hill.
NT 556 842

White Castle – a small hillfort.
NT 613 686

Ettrick and Lauderdale

Eildon Hill North – a very extensive hillfort, with traces of ramparts and many internal houses. Evidence for later Bronze Age and Roman-period occupation has been found.
NT 554 328

Inverness

Craig Phadrig – (P) a hillfort which was built and occupied in the later prehistoric period and also under the 'Picts'.
NH 640 453

Kincardineshire

Culsh – (HS) a souterrain.
NJ 504 054

Lewis
Dun Carloway – (HS) a very well preserved broch.
NB 189 412

Lochalsh
Dun Telve broch and Dun Troddan broch – (HS) two very well preserved brochs located close together in Glenelg.
NG 829 172 and NG 833 172.

North Lanarkshire
Castlehill, Barhill – (HS) a small fort close to the line of the Antonine Wall. The ramparts of the fort are difficult to distinguish.
NS 525 726.

Orkney
Gurness – (HS) a very well preserved broch with a surrounding settlement all placed within a encircling rampart.
HY 381 268.

Midhowe – (HS) a very well preserved broch.
HY 371 306.

Souterrains (both HS) Grain (HY 441 116) and Rennibister (HY 397 125).

Perth and Kinross
Kenmore – (P) a reconstructed crannog based on evidence recovered from excavated examples in Loch Tay and elsewhere.
NJ 667 252.

Queen's View – (P) a small homestead which was probably a later prehistoric roundhouse.
NN 863 601.

Ross and Cromarty
Culbokie – (P) a small hillfort.
NH 602 584.

Shetland
Clickhimin – (HS) a broch and settlement on a small island in a loch.
HU 464 408.

Jarlshof – (HS) a broch and settlement. The settlement includes wheelhouses and later Norse and medieval buildings.
HU 398 095.

Mousa – (HS) the best preserved broch, located on a small island.
HU 457 236.

Ness of Burgi – (HS) a small fort of a distinctive type called a 'blockhouse'.
HU 387 083.

Skye
Dun Beag – (HS) the remains of a broch.
NG 339 386.

Sutherland
Carn Liath – (HS) the remains of a broch. Recent excavation has demonstrated that the site was used for hundreds of years before the broch was built.
NC 870 013.

Dun Dornadilla (HS) a broch with an impressive triangular lintel over the entrance.
NC 451 450.

Skelbo Wood – (P) a broch which has not been excavated and survives as an earthwork.
NH 782 944.

West Lothian
Cairnpapple Hill – (HS) this is a Neolithic henge but burials were made into the site during the later prehistoric period.
NS 987 717.

Castlelaw – (HS) an impressive hillfort with a souterrain which was later inserted into the ditch of the fort.
NT 229 638.

Western Isles
Dun Vulan – a broch which has been recently excavated. The excavations indicated areas of settlement outside the wall of the broch.
NF 714 298.

Wigtonshire
Barsalloch – (HS) a small fort or dun.
NX 347 412

Rispain Camp – (HS) a small rectangular fort. Excavation has suggested that it was the home for a later prehistoric community.
NX 429 399.

Further Reading

- The Exploring Scotland's Heritage series published by The Stationary Office explains how to visit various later prehistoric sites in Scotland. Different volumes deal with different areas.

- *Wild Harvesters*, B Finlayson (Canongate 1998), examines the hunter-gatherers of prehistoric Scotland.

- *Farmers, Temples and Tombs*, G Barclay (Canongate 1998), considers the Neolithic and early Bronze Age ancestors of the late prehistoric period.

- *The Ancient Celts*, B Cunliffe (Oxford University Press 1997), is a large, colourful book about Iron Age Europe, which helps to place the Scottish evidence in context.

- *Iron Age Britain*, B Cunliffe (Batsford 1995), is a helpful introductory book with some information about Scotland.

- *Celtic Scotland*, I Armit (Batsford 1997), provides both a fuller study of the evidence than has been possible in this book and a very different approach to the Celts.

- *A Gathering of Eagles*, G Maxwell (Canongate 1998), discusses the Roman invaders.

- *Roman Scotland*, DJ Breeze (Batsford 1996), gives an alternative view about the Roman invaders who came to Scotland.

Acknowledgements

I am very grateful to Fraser Hunter for help with the illustrations and advice on the text; to Ian Armit, Steve Dickinson, Jackie Henrie, Christina Unwin, David Breeze, Niall Sharples and Gordon Barclay for advice on the text and to John Coles, Graeme Wilson and Andrew Fitzpatrick for permission to use various illustrations. Thanks also to Historic Scotland, The Royal Commission on the Ancient Monuments of Scotland and the National Museums of Scotland for permission to use their illustrations. The work of a wide range of authors is quoted in this book, but there has not been space to acknowledge individuals. Much of the evidence quoted is taken from the pages of the *Proceedings of the Society of Antiquaries of Scotland*. Many of the references to the original places of publication can be found in my review article in Volume 122. The maps were prepared by Sylvia Stevenson and Robert Burns.

A GATHERING
OF EAGLES

A Gathering of Eagles

Scenes from
Roman Scotland

Gordon Maxwell

Series editor: Gordon Barclay

CANONGATE BOOKS
with
HISTORIC SCOTLAND

THE MAKING
OF SCOTLAND

Series editor:
Gordon Barclay

Other titles available:

WILD HARVESTERS:
The First People in Scotland

FARMERS, TEMPLES AND TOMBS:
Scotland in the Neolithic
and Early Bronze Age

SETTLEMENT AND SACRIFICE:
The Later Prehistoric People
of Scotland

First published in Great Britain in 1998
by Canongate Books Ltd, 14 High Street
Edinburgh E11 1TE

British Library Cataloguing-in-Publication Data
A catalogue record for this book is available on request
from the British Library

ISBN 0 86241 781 3

Series Design:
James Hutcheson, Canongate Books

Design by:
Janet Watson

Printed and bound by
GraphyCems

Previous page
A Monument for Posterity
The Antonine Wall at Watling Lodge, near Falkirk.
HISTORIC SCOTLAND

Contents

Trajan's Column
The Roman army at the start of the second century.
ANGUS LAMB

'Eight eagles were then seen, which flew off into the woods,
a splendid omen...."After them", shouted Germanicus,"they are the
Legions' guardian spirits."'
Tacitus, *Annals*, II, 17.

'The chief standard of the entire legion is the eagle,
carried by the eagle-bearer.'
Flavius Vegetius Renatus, *Epitome of Military Science,* II, 13.

'If, however, it is put into italics, in a conversational form, separate
from the actual scholarship, then the hypothesis remains only a
hypothesis and doesn't undermine the seriousness of the work.'
Umberto Eco, *Foucault's Pendulum.*

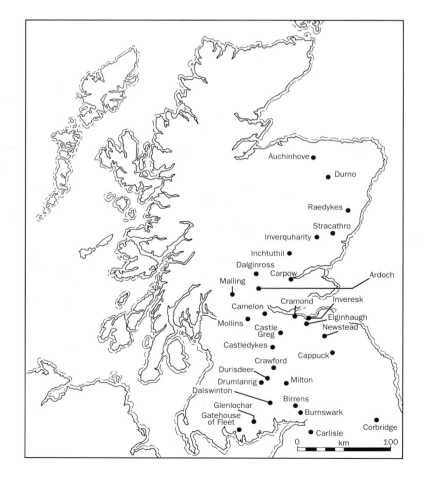

Roman Scotland
A map showing the
location of the main
Roman sites
mentioned in
the text.

Prologue

The year is AD 383, and the Spaniard Magnus Maximus, newly appointed to a senior command in the five-province Diocese of Britannia, has been persuaded to make a bid for control of the Western Empire, challenging the two sons of the emperor Valentinian I, Gratian and Valentinian the younger, and hoping to become the colleague of his former comrade-in-arms and distant kinsman, the Eastern Emperor Theodosius the Great. From York, the capital of the northernmost province of the Diocese, he writes a letter to an old friend. . .

MAGNUS MAXIMUS, DUX BRITANNIARUM, JUSTINIANO FRATRI SUO AC CONTUBERNALI ANTIQUO PLURIMAM SALUTEM.

scr. Eboraco xii Kal. Apr., Gratiano Augusto et Merobaude conss.

Ridiculosior sane tibi viderer, frater, si me ad scrinia mea nunc deprehenderes. . .

To Justinianus, his old messmate, Magnus Maximus, Duke of the Five Provinces of Britain, sends his warmest greetings!

Governor's Lodge

York

21st March

You really would smile to see me now, sitting at a desk piled high with obsolete military intelligence: dusty maps, dog-eared plans of forts, reports of long-dead Governors of the Five Provinces of Britannia; rosters of regiments that no longer exist. Rarefied reading for this time of night! Yet for several days now I have been engrossed by my task, a night-owl picking over the bones of the Eagles; and you would not smile to learn the reason for my labours.

Britannia is in excellent shape, but across the Channel, as you will have heard, things are in a poor state. Germany is overflowing with her pernicious brood: Frankish invasions today, Vandals, Alans, and Suevi tomorrow. Not that we in this island have lacked troubles of our own, but a firm hand can work wonders. It was much worse sixteen years ago, when we also had to deal with internal treachery. Picts and Scots are never slow to sniff out any weakness, and could not fail to notice the destabilising effect of all the civil unrest under Constantius, but when our own men, our eyes and ears beyond the frontier Wall, were bribed to act as double agents, the situation became hopeless. What a stroke of luck that Valentinian eventually decided to send out the elder Theodosius with his field-army!

The point of all this reminiscing is twofold: first, to confirm that the secret of ensuring peace and prosperity in Britannia is to maintain an effective northern military command, both by having well-trained, well-equipped troops in the right places, and by keeping our ears close to the ground on both sides of the Frontier Wall; and secondly, and more

Magnus Maximus
'You really would smile to see me now. Sitting at a desk piled high with obsolete military intelligence…'
CHRIS BROWN

importantly, to realise that, although Theodosius is a thoroughly reliable Emperor, his sphere of action lies beyond the Adriatic, while the entire Western Empire must risk ruin under the feckless sons of Valentinian.

You'll have guessed where all this is leading, the more so because it is something you have always encouraged me to do. Well, yesterday, I finally acceded to the requests of the Legions; within a day or two I shall be acclaimed as emperor by the Diocesan Council in Augusta [London]. I not only invite you to join with me now in this venture, I also want you to help me determine how the next phase must be managed: namely, how Britannia is to be kept safe while you and I, and a sizeable part of the British garrison, risk our lives on the far side of the Channel. From intelligence reports, it seems unlikely that the Prefecture of the Gauls will present much opposition to our move, although the barbarian levies might make a token stand. I will not, therefore, need to strip the frontier of its guards. Nevertheless, something must be done to bind the people of the north more firmly to us, and somehow we shall have to make sure that the garrisons we leave behind understand our tactical and strategic objectives in that quarter.

That is why I have ransacked the provincial archives here in York, and why I am asking you to come directly here while I play politics in London. What you must do is to go through these documents, omitting nothing, and get an overview of the entire course of frontier history. Examine the successes and failures of our dealings with the north, and assess the effectiveness of our modern, and past, garrisons and installations. Incidentally, a fellow-Spaniard, Vegetius Renatus, showed me the material he was collecting for a publication on just this subject. It's a pity his work isn't yet complete; you would have found it useful.

In the meantime, have fun with the files. I'm off to gather in the Eagles.

Farewell!

A Legionary Eagle
Britannia places a tiny wreath in the beak of the eagle-image crowning the Twentieth Legion standard. From a second-century carved stone found near Bearsden.
HUNTERIAN MUSEUM, UNIVERSITY OF GLASGOW

Within a fortnight, Maximus receives the following reply:

To His Imperial Highness Magnus Maximus, Justinianus, Commander of Frontier Forces, Britannia, sends greeting!

Governor's Lodge
York
2nd April

Well, I've done all that you asked, to the best of my ability. Taking you at your word, I've concentrated on the north, but omitted nothing, even though the files go back to the expeditions of the late Republic. (Knowing your weak grasp of history, I've added the consular dates, where necessary, and provided notes about the strength and organisation of the province's early garrison.)

Julius Caesar was the first Roman actually to land an army on these shores [in 55 and 54 BC], and several of the early emperors had plans for Britain: Augustus thought about invading it on several occasions [between 34 BC and AD 7], and Caligula aborted an invasion at the last moment [AD 40], but the island did not become part of the Empire until Claudius personally oversaw its conquest [in AD 43]. These plans were all preoccupied with the south-east corner of the island, and with the usual confused mass of pretexts and objectives – the political glory conferred by a victory won beyond the narrow strip of Ocean, the military need to destroy a possible refuge for our enemies, and, of course, the diplomatic claims that numerous British refugees have had on our protection.

Once begun in earnest, the conquest proceeded in a series of waves. In the reigns of Claudius and Nero [i.e. until AD 68], we secured our grip on the south-eastern lowlands and began to address the problems of controlling the western and northern uplands. After Nero's removal [in AD 68], the successive emperors of the Flavian dynasty presided over the most extensive annexation of British territory since the original invasion. Under Vespasian all the land west of the River Severn and northwards as far as the fringes of Caledonia was either overrun or occupied, first of all when Petillius Cerealis was governor, then by his successor, Julius Frontinus (who wrote several of the memoranda I've been reading), and latterly by Julius Agricola. When Vespasian died [AD 79], his elder son, Titus, re-appointed Agricola with orders to consolidate everything south of the isthmus between Forth and Clyde. However, Titus' brother, Domitian [succeeded AD 81], soon had him advancing through Caledonia again, and within two years Agricola had fought the northern tribes to a standstill at the battle of *Mons Graupius*. If it hadn't been for the troubles on the Danube, which resulted in the need to cut back on manpower (some things never change!), Agricola's successor might have led the legions to the very furthest tip of the island. As it was, the files of this period record nothing but retrenchment – first of all withdrawal from territory north of the Forth [by AD 87], and then, about twelve years later, humiliating retreat to a line between Tyne and Solway, at which time Trajan was on the throne. Not surprisingly, there's a lot of information available for the Flavian period, due in part to the fact that Agricola's son-in-law (and biographer) was the historian Cornelius Tacitus. Considering this relationship, I'm not sure we should trust everything he says!

The following years are much more sparsely covered: innumerable folders of administrative papers – unit-strength returns and the like, but few detailed situation reports. It's almost as if there had been a complete reversal of strategy: from the open, fluid frontier-zones of the Flavians, to the fixed, continuous barrier which is still with us today. At first this barrier was the wall of Hadrian, constructed between Tyne and Solway at the lowest ebb of Flavian retreat [begun AD 122]; then 20 years later, a replacement wall, this time

ROMAN ARMY ORGANISATION – FROM THE FLAVIAN TO SEVERAN PERIOD				
Unit/CO	Status/Average number in Britain	Sub-units/ officers	Total manpower per unit	Ranker's pay (in *denarii*)
Legion/ Praetorian Legate	Roman citizen (elite)/ 4 until AD 86/7, 3 thereafter	Nine 6-century (500 man) cohorts + one double cohort of infantry, under centurions + c. 120 cavalry	c. 5500 per legion	300 (infantry) 400 (cavalry)
Auxiliaries	Mostly non-Roman (second line troops)			
Quingenary infantry cohort/Prefect	c. 18	Six 80-man centuries, each of ten (8-man) *contubernia*, under centurions	c. 500	100
Milliary infantry cohort / Tribune	2	Ten 80-man centuries each of ten (8-man) *contubernia* under centurions	c. 800	100
Quingenary cavalry *ala* / Prefect	c. 15	Sixteen 30-man troops, under decurions	c. 500	333
Milliary cavalry *ala* / Tribune	1	Twenty-four 30-man troops, under decurions	c. 750	333
Quingenary equitate cohort / Prefect	c. 30	Four 30-man troops of cavalry, under decurions + six 60-man centuries of infantry, under centurions	c. 500	100 (infantry) 200 (cavalry)
Milliary equitate cohort / Prefect	c. 5	Eight 30-man troops, under decurions + ten c. 70-man centuries, under centurions	c. 1000	100 (infantry) 200 (cavalry)

A member of the Roman re-enactment group The Antonine Guard.
THE ANTONINE GUARD

Note: The numbers of auxiliary garrisons varied over time and are approximate.

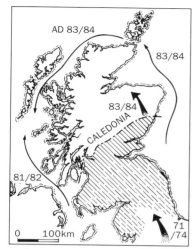

AD 83/84

83/84

83/84

CALEDONIA

81/82

71/74

0 100km

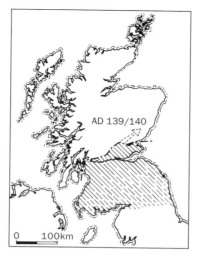

AD 139/140

0 100km

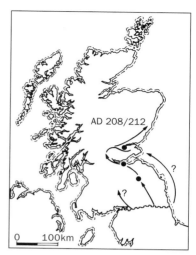

AD 208/212

?

?

0 100km

Third Century

CALEDONII

MAEATAE

Britannia Inferior

York

Britannia Superior

London

0 200km

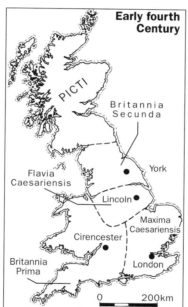

Early fourth Century

PICTI

Britannia Secunda

Flavia Caesariensis

York

Lincoln

Maxima Caesariensis

Cirencester

London

Britannia Prima

0 200km

Late fourth Century

Britannia Secunda

? Valentia

Carlisle

Flavia Caesariensis

York

Lincoln

Maxima Caesariensis

Cirencester

London

Britannia Prima

0 200km

Conquest, Occupation and Administration

Military activity in Roman Scotland in the Flavian, Antonine and Severan periods, together with later provincial sub-divisions of the Diocese of Britannia, as well as later capitals.

Bronze Visor Mask

A visor mask from the fort at Newstead, near Melrose, which would have been worn by a member of a well-paid cavalry unit.

NATIONAL MUSEUMS OF SCOTLAND

of turf, was built between Forth and Clyde, on the orders of the emperor Antoninus Pius – a project which necessitated re-occupation of much of what had been conquered in Flavian times. Although in some ways less ambitious, this Antonine frontier lasted much longer than its predecessors, and cost less to build and maintain, despite some hefty repair bills in its middle years, than the wall of Hadrian. Nevertheless, about two years into the reign of Marcus Aurelius [say around AD 163], after only two decades of productive life, the Antonine Wall was abandoned, leaving only a handful of outpost forts to maintain a Roman presence north of the recommissioned Hadrianic wall.

The files of the next 40 years are either hopelessly jumbled or tantalisingly nibbled by mice. Yet it is clear that the unsupervised northern tribes had become a menace, constantly threatening to break through the frontier defences. They succeeded at least twice in this period, first under Commodus [around AD 184], and again in the early years of the emperor Septimius Severus [between AD 197 and 200].

These Severan campaigns [AD 208-211] were the last real attempt to take a full Roman army into the heart of barbarian territory; most of what came later was an extended field-exercise, when all we risked was having our pockets picked by the locals. However, it was more than pilfering that Severus was up against when he came to Britain. To begin with, there was the awkwardness of a previous governor, Clodius Albinus, who had decided [AD 193] to attempt to win the imperial throne, and had taken a sizeable detachment across to Gaul to fight for him. When he was killed, our 'friends in the north', with whom he seems to have had an 'agreement', decided that his death had cancelled all debts, and they began to overwhelm elements of the reduced frontier force. Virius Lupus, Albinus' successor, for want of men, was forced to buy off the nearer threat, the Maeatae, who live just beyond the Forth, and so stop them from joining forces with the nations of the Caledonian heartlands beyond. However, within a few summers the same troublemakers were at it again, and this time only an imperial expedition could sort it out.

In those days, such an expedition was truly imperial. Indeed, I cannot find any reference to a greater land-force than that which assembled to invade Caledonia, or Pictland, as they now call it. In addition to the bulk of Britannia's mobile reserve, the emperor took with him his personal Guard, legionary detachments, and auxiliary regiments from several other provinces. It would appear that they penetrated, although with serious losses, almost as far as any Roman army has ever gone; in the early phases they followed the existing road-system, but beyond the Tay the metalled roads give out, and they had to rely on their scouts and the field-notes of previous commanders. Twice they made the long haul from friendly districts, through the Maeatian lands, into the depths of Caledonia; at first they met with success, the two halves of their army operating independently, but later, in the teeth of renewed opposition, they combined into one crushingly massive force. The rigours of the march did for Severus; when death claimed him here in York he was preparing for one last push, confident that outright victory was in his grasp. Unfortunately his unworthy son Caracalla abandoned all his conquests, including the innovative scheme of isolated coastal bases south of the Tay and the Forth, supplied by sea and more than 100 miles from the frontier wall.

Were it not for his son, who knows how long Severus' plans for frontier control might have lasted? Nothing that came before it quite matched it for originality; nothing that followed has attracted more than a line or two in the pages of history. At any rate, despite such swift abandonment, the Severan campaigns ushered in a period of tranquillity, unbroken even when Britain became part of the breakaway Gallic Empire [AD 260-273]. It ended only when a bid for independence

[AD 287–96] under the ex-admiral Carausius, and later his finance minister Allectus, brought down another imperial expedition, led by Constantius Chlorus, on our heads. Chlorus and his son, the future emperor Constantine, returned a decade later [AD 306] to deal with trouble in the north; unfortunately, Chlorus too died in York.

Around this time official reports begin to refer to the northern hostiles as *Picti* (although you and I know that they went under various names). At any rate, up to the time of Count Theodosius' campaigns, they figure in three or four brief situation-reports, mostly in association with the *Scotti*, and once [AD 360], they are laughably described as 'breaking the agreements on the frontier' – as if a Pict would ever admit to an agreement on any topic! But,

joking apart, it is clear there have always had to be 'arrangements' on the frontier, beyond the purely military requirements. Our spies beyond the frontier, whose treachery [in AD 367] precipitated the disaster that we ourselves had to address under the elder Theodosius, were part of a surveillance system that was put in place long before our days: we've always had to depend on cloak-and-dagger men operating behind the Wall, but we shall need more than spies to secure the hearts and minds of the frontier people in the months immediately ahead. How tragic that we cut back on cross-border contact after the last debacle!

So much for history. What, you may ask, about the maps and plans? Well, there's nothing, at any scale, later than the revised map of the Diocese made by governor Alypius

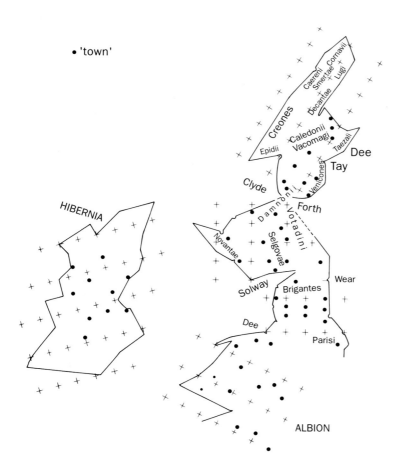

First-century Britain
Coastal and tribal information gathered during the Flavian advance and later compiled by Ptolemy of Alexandria, as it might have appeared in separate sheets, correctly aligned and with ten 'towns' per sheet.

[AD 357–360], and the only available road-book goes back 60 years before that to Diocletian! Looking at those old maps (neither of which shows much north of the Frontier Wall), it was strange to see a Britain that consisted of just three provinces, instead of the present five. Of course, for a hundred years before that, there were only two provinces, Inferior and Superior, and, amazingly, for the first 150 years of its existence, Britannia was under a unitary provincial control. Funnily enough, it was a map from that early period, which showed most clearly the home territories of those northern tribes with whom we are most concerned at present. The map comes in two versions: one that was published by the geographer Ptolemy in book format at Alexandria; and a second, presented in rather sketchy outline, illustrating the whole island (and Hivernia) on seven separate sheets, each indicating the ten most notable 'towns' (forts, I suppose) in the relevant district. Ptolemy's version has clearly been compiled from the other, but unfortunately some of the sheets have been joined to each other at the wrong angle, which gives an occasionally bizarre effect, especially as the scale also varies disconcertingly.

It is from the three northernmost sheets of this map that we learn the original names of our closest neighbours, the Novantae, Selgovae, and Votadini (who extend from west to east across the outer zone beyond our present frontier), as well as their neighbours, the Damnonii and Venicones, and the peoples of the Caledonian confederacy beyond. But, in my opinion, the most startling feature of these sheets is that they indicate as dense a deployment of Roman forts to the north of the Tyne-Solway isthmus as they do to the south. Since the latter area on the map

seriously under-represents the number of forts that were actually built, we must presume that a comparably dense pattern once extended right into Caledonia! I'm therefore convinced that there is a direct correlation between this intense northern activity and the bulging portfolios here in York, which contain blueprints for elaborate military installations of a size and type we never see these days. So it must be the camp-sites and stations of those early campaigners (and their immediate successors) whose eroded earthworks we can still trace beside the upland roads of the north country. These installations should now inspire us as we prepare for the coming redeployment. They were designed and built by armies in rigorous pursuit of well-defined objectives, and their classic form doubtless reflects this. And that, in turn, reflects the enormous respect the commanders of that time entertained for their northern adversaries. Since we too must shortly consider how best to handle matters with their descendants, may I recommend that you read carefully the accompanying memoranda on the works of the Eagles of old?

Farewell till we meet!

Forced Entry: Invasion and Conquest

'No one now for a long time has built a camp with a ditched perimeter and a stockade fixed above it'.
Flavius Vegetius Renatus, *Epitome of Military Science*, I, 21.

'The erection of the outer defence and the buildings inside it is accomplished faster than thought, thanks to the numbers and skill of the workers'.
Flavius Josephus, *The Jewish War*, Excursus III.

The evidence of the marching-camps

It is ironic that the invasions of Scotland by the Romans, whose immediate objective was to conquer and lay waste, should have left behind such a rich legacy. No other country can boast so wide a range or so many examples of structures built by the legions during their campaigns, when professional armies, often tens of thousands strong, advanced across the northern landscape. They went wherever duty or glory called; they stopped only when the day's march, or military quest, was ended. At the end of each day, they pitched their carefully-aligned rows of leather tents, each row in its set space and location within the defences

Roman Legions on the March
It is Spring, and the the army is on the move. As the rear of the column approaches the end of its day's march, legionaries of Agicola's army are hard at work completing the overlapping *claviculae* that protect the gate of the Stracathro-type marching-camp which will be their temporary base.
CHRIS BROWN

The View from Above

Aerial photographs of a Roman temporary camp (top) and a permanent fort (bottom), both in Dumfries and Galloway, are revealed by cropmarks. Over the buried ditches of the camp at Ward Law, the greener growth of corn defines the single-ditch perimeter; within the more complex defences of Glenlochar fort lighter tones indicate the internal street grid.

RCAHMS

of the camp: on occasion, a low bank of sods would have sufficed to defend it, but more often the camp was surrounded by a V-sectioned ditch, its size proportionate to the scale of danger faced, and within there stood a rampart crowned by the wooden stakes each soldier carried. It is little short of a miracle that any traces now survive of these temporary structures, so swiftly erected by the teams of diggers and spoil-shifters, that onlookers almost doubted what they saw. The rare quality and quantity of the Scottish material, in great part the result of decades of aerial survey, especially through the recording of cropmark evidence, allow archaeologists today not only to reconstruct the successive invasion routes, but also to figure out the intentions of those in command, and tentatively reconstruct the Order of Battle of the army.

But how can these sites yield such complicated information? At the lowest level, although most Roman camps share certain characteristics, resembling a playing-card on plan, with straight sides and rounded corners, there are various structural details – for example, the camp's proportions, the design or spacing of its gates, and possibly its relationship to other structures – which may indicate its date. When camps of the same size and appearance are found at regular intervals along a line of movement, we can assume they are marching-camps built by legionaries of the same battle-group as it advanced through enemy territory. Occasionally, however, we can deduce more, for in every instance the camp's appearance is determined by unseen operational requirements. Most obviously, its size is directly

related to the number and status of the troops it needed to accommodate: according to the military manual, each *contubernium*, or messing-unit, of eight legionaries, occupied a tent measuring 10 by 10 Roman feet (a Roman foot is about 296mm, compared with a British Imperial foot of 305mm). The six rows of 10 tents apiece required for a complete legionary cohort were assigned a tentage area measuring 120 by 180 Roman feet. Unfortunately, it is not clear how much space within any camp might have been allocated to such additional elements as equipment, draught animals, or indeed accompanying auxiliary troops (whose numbers usually matched those of the legionaries); nor is it known how much space was so 'awkward' as to be unusable.

Nevertheless, much can be gleaned from close scrutiny of the remains. The distance between each camp in a chain and the scale of the defences at each site should indicate the degree of danger faced by the invasion force; the identification of rows of rubbish-pits (flanking the lines of tents) will suggest a longer than overnight occupation and may furnish invaluable information about the camp's internal layout. Being the weak spots in the perimeter, since they lacked proper gates, the entrances frequently display structural features designed to lessen their vulnerability; the various flanking or covering devices employed for that purpose constitute further evidence of the perceived level of threat, but more importantly they gave scope to the individual legionary construction-teams scope to 'sign' their handiwork. Thus the wide range of marching-camps discovered in Scotland do more than just identify the strategic targets of ancient invasion forces or the areas of greatest resistance; their structure also reveals the nature of the forces that brought them into being, and the late first-century, or Flavian, examples are the most informative.

The Flavian campaigns (c. AD 77–83)

We are extremely lucky that the Roman campaigns in Scotland took place during the heyday of military field-engineering in Britain, long before the decline which Vegetius decried in the later fourth century (quoted at the beginning of the chapter); and we are luckier still that, when the governor Julius Agricola

Campaigning Before Agricola
The 8.1ha camp at Rey Cross, County Durham, on the line of march from York to Carlisle, belongs to a many-gated class of marching-camp possibly dating to the advance of Petillius Cerealis in AD 71–74. RCHME

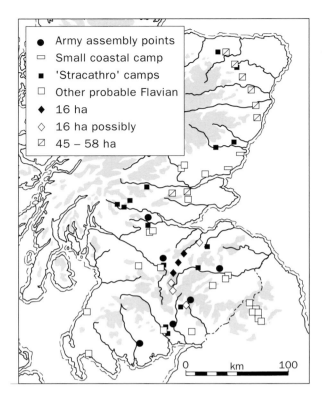

Legend:
- ● Army assembly points
- ⬚ Small coastal camp
- ■ 'Stracathro' camps
- ☐ Other probable Flavian
- ◆ 16 ha
- ◇ 16 ha possibly
- ▨ 45 – 58 ha

0 km 100

Where the Flavian Armies Marched

Map showing the distribution of marching-camps that probably housed the battle-groups engaged in North Britain under the emperors Vespasian, Titus and Domitian.

turned his attention c. AD 78/79 to the annexation of the lands beyond Tyne and Solway, he commanded an army which had, over the previous decade or so, begun to accustom itself to the discipline of regular marching-camp construction. It is possible that, in the first stages of their advance beyond the Solway, Agricola's troops passed or even re-used the camps built during the earlier conquest of the lands of the Brigantes by the governor Petillius Cerealis.

Several criteria can be used to identify those marching-camps most probably the work of Agricolan forces; they include a tendency to squareness of plan, and a method of gateway defence incorporating the *clavicula* (an extended arc of ditch and rampart that compelled an attacker to expose his unprotected side to the camp's defenders). Using these and other criteria we can show that in southern Scotland Agricolan, or at least Flavian, armies operated in strength in most of the main river valleys, apparently moving north from bases at Carlisle and near Corbridge on the Tyne; the coastal districts of Lothian and Berwickshire seem to have received scant attention, probably because the local people, the Votadini, had adopted a pro-Roman policy, whereas the reverse is true of the shores of Clyde and Solway. The largest camps in eastern Scotland were some 16-20 hectares (ha) in area, while those on the west occasionally attained 25ha. (A hectare – roughly 2½ acres – equals 10,000 square metres, or about two football pitches.) The actual distribution of camps is uneven. Some clearly represent major lines of advance, for example, the two claws of the pincer movement from mid-Clydesdale and Northumberland towards the Forth. Others appear in clusters, often beside river crossings, as at Newstead, Castledykes, Beattock, and Dalswinton, identifying them as the assembly points for armies engaged in the two years of consolidation which followed.

One such cluster, on the south bank of the River Carron near Camelon, marks the springboard for Agricola's ultimate conquest of Caledonia, which Tacitus tells us was the objective of his last two campaigns, in AD 82-83. The earliest penetration of Caledonia, however, had been effected three years earlier in Agricola's third campaign, when, we are told, the legions advanced as far north as the Tay estuary. The cropmark traces of

two or three exceptionally large camps recorded in the lower valley of the Earn indicate the probable course of that push. Elsewhere north of the Forth, there is only one other instance of temporary camps revealing an Agricolan line of march – the series of seven camps that extends north and north-west in a great arc from near Stonehaven to the Pass of Grange, just east of the Spey, which I will discuss later. The dozen or so others are of widely differing size, doubtless representing a range of temporary duties which individual detachments might be called on to perform: fort-building (several adjoin *castella* of Agricolan date) and overseeing coastal installations, to name but two. Several are of a size and character, however, that point to a more significant role, especially given their location astride important natural corridors.

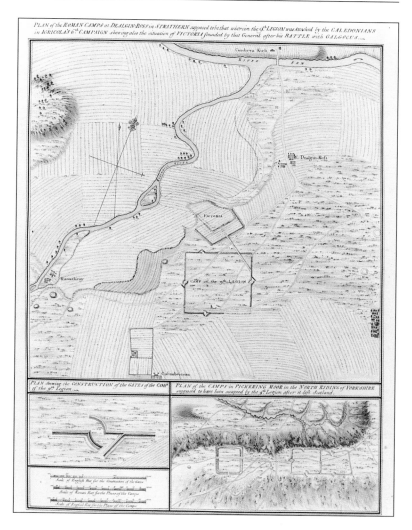

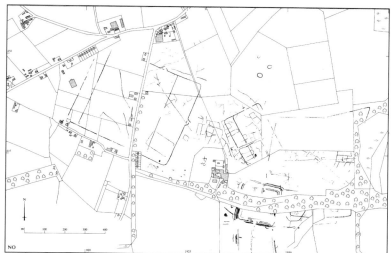

(above)
Early Plan of a Roman Site
Manuscript copy of the survey of the Agricolan fort and Stracathro-gated camp at Dalginross, near Comrie, made by William Roy in 1755. The inset (bottom left) shows the combination of *claviculae* and traverse.
SOCIETY OF ANTIQUARIES, LONDON

(left)
Gathering-ground for Eagles
Transcribed aerial photograph of the multiperiod Roman fort at Castledykes, near Carstairs in mid Clydesdale, with marching-camps of the various field-armies which halted here.
RCAHMS

All of the latter are further distinguished by a singular type of gateway defence, called the 'Stracathro gate' after the site south of Edzell in Angus where it was first recognised in cropmark form; its original appearance is nevertheless best illustrated by the examples at the camp of Dalginross, near Comrie in Perthshire, which was surveyed by General Roy in 1755, before the earthworks were levelled by cultivation.

The Stracathro entrance, featuring opposed *claviculae* and an oblique traverse, is found only in Scotland. Furthermore, its distribution in Scotland, though widespread, is localised in distinct areas – south-west Scotland, Strathclyde, central Scotland, Strathmore, and Aberdeenshire – corresponding to five of Agricola's six 'Scottish' campaign-areas, which suggests that it was the product of one particular legion engaged in those campaigns. There are good reasons to believe that the legion responsible was the Second Adiutrix, then based at Chester. It seems likely that both it and the Twentieth *Valeria Victrix*, from Wroxeter, were present at almost full strength throughout the Agricolan conquest of the north, together with a weakened Ninth *Hispana* (from York).

It was with these forces that Agricola approached the climax of his six-year governorship. We read in Tacitus that, after a campaign in which the cunning of the Caledonian warlords had almost engineered the slaughter of the unlucky Ninth Legion, both sides had determined that matters must be brought to a head. The North Britons had united under the leadership of an outstanding warrior named Calgacus, 'Swordsman', and taken up a position, allegedly more than 30,000 strong, on a hill which the Romans were to remember as *Mons Graupius*. Precisely where that field of battle lies cannot yet be determined. Nevertheless, if the chain of large marching-camps that curves through Aberdeenshire towards the Spey can be dated to the Flavian period, as their appearance suggests, it would be difficult to find a more appropriate context for them than the *Mons Graupius* campaign. Indeed, it has been proposed that the largest of the series (c. 57ha), situated at Logie Durno, facing the peak of Bennachie, directly adjoins the field of battle.

Regardless of the accuracy of that identification – and there are reasons for suggesting that the battle was fought even further to the north-west – the importance of Logie Durno lies in the information it may reveal on marching-camp capacity: basically, how many troops to the hectare. The Durno camp is significant because it is 13 to 14ha larger than the other camps in the series – a figure which appears quite frequently in temporary camp statistics. In this case it is the average area of the two camps with Stracathro gates (at Ythan Wells and Auchinhove) which housed a

The March to *Mons Graupius*?

The chain of marching-camps probably built by the two units of Agricola's army on their way north to the battle of *Mons Graupius* in AD 83. When united, as at Durno, opposite Bennachie, the army was possibly 40,000 strong.

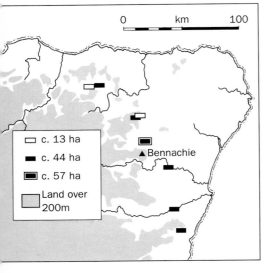

| | 0 | km | 100 |

c. 13 ha
c. 44 ha
c. 57 ha
Land over 200m

▲ Bennachie

unit apparently accompanying the main force on this campaign, but, except at Durno, operating independently of it. At the site of Ythan Wells, one day's march to the north, the smaller 13–14ha camp was built over by the larger, indicating that there the minor detachment, representing about a quarter of the whole army, had led the advance. It is not unreasonable to presume that the smaller force was one that could easily have been split from the rest, in other words, a standard detachment based on a single legion (which the Stracathro gateways reveal as the Second *Adiutrix*). At neither Ythan Wells nor Auchinhove can an estimate readily be made of the total troop strength involved, but comparison with another possible Second Legion product, the 9.4ha camp at Dalginross, is instructive. A combination of aerial photographic data with Roy's 1755 survey makes it possible not only to obtain a precise measurement of the camp's defences and internal structures, but also to deduce it was built to accom-modate the equivalent of a legion with little or no auxiliary support; the probability that Dalginross was not a marching-camp but a temporary base for local reconnaissance and intelligence duties makes such an assessment even more reasonable.

On this analysis, Ythan Wells and Auchinhove, with half as much capacity again as Dalginross, probably accommodated not only the full legion but also 2–3000 auxiliaries, or some 8000 men in total. In consequence, Durno would have held a combined force well in excess of 32,000, suggesting in fact that Agricola used all his resources to ensure victory over the Caledonians. The 13–14ha camps may therefore represent a not uncommon Agricolan troop-deployment, recorded by his son-in-law Tacitus as 'a legion and a modest force of auxiliaries'.

Similar links between tactical capacity and size or shape should doubtless be sought in other Agricolan camps. Thus, Stracathro itself, at 15.7ha, could have accommodated an auxiliary supplement equal in size to the legion it accompanied, or up to 11,000 in total, while Dalswinton or Castledykes, at 25ha, could

Legionary Labour-camp
Cropmarks reveal a uniquely detailed picture of the internal arrangements of the camp housing the builders of Inchtuthil fortress, to the south-west of Blairgowrie, Perthshire; the rows of dark dots indicate the rubbish-pits adjoining the legionary tent-lines.
RCAHMS

Dalginross from the Air
About 240 years of cultivation have
removed the earthwork defences
recorded by Roy (see page 19), but
internal details of both fort and camp
can now be revealed by cropmarks.
R.CAHMS

have accommodated more
than 20,000 men, or two full
legions each with a
moderately large support
force. Since it seems likely that
the Ninth Legion would have
contributed to the Agricolan
advance by moving north
from York, the two legions
operating together to operate
in the west of Scotland must
have been the Second *Adiutrix*
and the Twentieth (which
contemporary records suggest
may have left detachments at
Carlisle). Until the final
campaign, the respective legionary objectives are less easy to
distinguish, although it is reasonably certain that the Second
remained in the thick of things. It was not, however, the unit
detailed to remain in Scotland as the garrison of the new fortress
at Inchtuthil, on the banks of the Tay in Perthshire.

The two-phase construction-camp that housed the builders,
and eventual occupants, of the new legionary fortress at
Inchtuthil is probably the latest temporary enclosure of the
Flavian period north of the Forth, dating perhaps to AD 84. In its
earliest form, carefully positioned to avoid obstructing the direct
route from the front gate of the fortress, the camp covered almost
20ha, an area sufficient, given the more relaxed peacetime
conditions, for not only most of the legion that would eventually
occupy the fortress, but also a generous support team. It is usually
assumed that the future garrison was the Twentieth Legion, based
until then at Wroxeter, a position which had become too remote
from the action. Whatever the identity of the builders, aerial
photography has recorded within the camp the cropmark traces
of numerous rows of tent-line rubbish pits, confirming the
lengthy period the building party spent under 'canvas', while
they constructed the permanent defences and internal structures
of the legionary base. Ironically, the 'permanent' fortress they
laboured to build may have enjoyed an even shorter period of
use than their temporary quarters; within a couple of years or so,
due to events on the Danube frontier, one of Britain's four
legions had to be sent abroad, and soon the fabric of the
Agricolan victory began to unravel. Inchtuthil and all the
northern conquests were abandoned, while Newstead on the
Tweed, along with other forts in the south of Scotland, was
refurbished to serve as forward positions on a new frontier.

The Antonine campaigns (c. AD 140–142)

'As far as possible, a camp's length should be half as much again as its width, to ensure that the lines have sufficient ventilation.' Hyginus, *On Building Camps*, 21.

The evidence relating to the campaigns that preceded the building of the Antonine Wall is totally different – not least in the apparent absence of serious activity north of the Forth. Gone is the variety of structures; in their place, we find only workmanlike regularity and uniformity, effective but unexciting. The Antonine camps are mainly distinguished by the more elongated plan of Hyginus, especially one in which the long side is half as long again as the short, and an avoidance of the *clavicula*; gateways were protected by a device also used in Agricolan camps, the *tutulus*, a detached bar of ditch and rampart set forward from the entrance to prevent direct assault.

The builders of the Antonine marching-camps evidently followed the pre-existing road in their operations, and frequently appear to have used the road embankment as the baseline from which to set out the camp fortifications. As a result their commanders were able to capitalise on experience gained during the Flavian advance. Knowing what to expect in the way of route-mileage and possible resistance, they could operate at the minimum necessary strength and calculate supply requirements to a nicety. The apparent inactivity of the tribes north of the Forth–Clyde isthmus meant that they did not need to maintain a large strategic reserve – their main objective was to secure what would become the hinterland of the new frontier, showing the Eagle in all the main centres of population, with field-forces usually well below their maximum disposable strength. The forces used were nevertheless large enough to indicate that a question-mark still hung over the loyalties of the peoples in southern Scotland and northern England. If camp area was still allocated in accordance with Flavian standards, the invasion force of AD 139-140 included units resembling Agricola's single legion with moderate auxiliary support (in c. 13ha camps), but more often it employed the individual legion with full support (in c. 16ha camps). On occasion, and particularly evident in the series of c. 20ha camps that adjoin Dere Street from between the modern Border and the Forth, larger groupings, possibly of more than one legion, were deemed necessary.

Three legions were available for duties in these operations: the Second *Augusta*, the Twentieth (now based at Chester), and the Sixth at York (replacing the departed Ninth). However, the characteristic regularity and uniformity of plan of the Antonine

Antonine Marching-camp
Typical of the camps of the second century, with its regular, elongated plan and six, tutulus-guarded gateways, Pennymuir, in the south-eastern Borders, aligns itself with the Roman road Dere Street, now a modern track visible to the left of the camp, along which its builders had advanced over the Cheviots.
RCAHMS

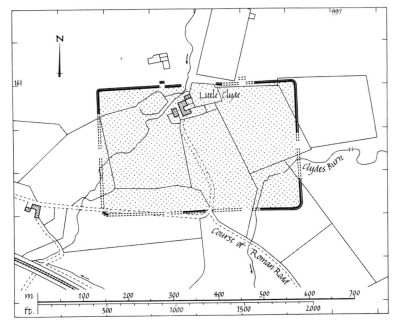

Severan Marching-camps.
Ardoch (53ha) and Kirkbuddo (25ha)
represent the two classes of early third-
century camp found north of the Forth.
Contemporary structures south of the
Forth were 13ha bigger than Ardoch (top);
the average permanent fort was about the
size of the Kirkbuddo annexe (bottom).
GORDON MAXWELL, MERCAT PRESS

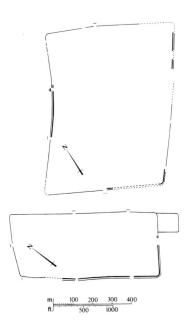

camps also make it difficult to distinguish between the products
of different legionary drawing offices. The camp at Little Clyde,
possibly one of the Second Legion's halts on the watershed
between Clyde and Annan, splendidly illustrates the general
appearance of the majority. It is a regular rectangle measuring
precisely 1500 by 1000 Roman feet, its 13.2ha area being appropriate to a 'legion with moderate support'. Two features stand
out: the greater number of gates, both long sides being provided
with two; and the marked regularity of the plan, maintained
despite the extremely broken nature of the ground occupied. The
six entrances, a number found mostly only in the very largest
Flavian camps, may reflect either the greater self-confidence of
the Antonine legions or simply a desire to facilitate entry and exit.

The Severan campaigns (c. AD 208–212)

'The Britons having broken their agreements and taken up arms,
Severus ordered his soldiers to invade their territory and put to
the sword all that they met, adding the Homeric quotation that
"they should let nobody escape, not even the children hidden in
their mothers' wombs"'.
Cassius Dio, LXXVI, 16.

There is one significant difference between Antonine (second-
century) and Severan (third-century) camps – their size. Whereas
the Antonine examples rarely exceeded 20ha, we know of no
Severan camps below 25ha; on the contrary, the two largest
series average respectively 53ha and 65ha.

The Severan sites, in contrast to the Flavian, are all marching-camps associated with one of three campaigning phases. The four camps of the 65ha series indicate three successive days' march along Dere Street from the Tweed to the Lothian Tyne; each day, a journey of eight Roman miles was accomplished, a creditable distance for an army whose strength, based on camp-capacity already estimated, probably exceeded 40,000. Such vast numbers, comprising not only most of the British legions' strength together with auxiliaries, but also detachments of the Praetorian Guard and contributions from overseas legions, show that Severus' campaign was a truly majestic undertaking. Assuming some 25-30,000 of the army were on foot, and most of the cavalry were deployed off the road, Dere Street would have been packed with columns six files wide for up to three miles. The several hundred carts, carrying baggage and provisions for men and beasts, would have lengthened the column by another two miles. The advance party would have surveyed the next night's resting-place when the rear had barely caught its first wind on the march!

At some point beyond the northernmost c. 65ha camp at Pathhead in Midlothian, probably near the coastal base of Cramond, the Grand Army seems to have left a detachment to attend to matters on the Forth-Clyde line, and then regrouped for separate duties, for there are two separate categories of Severan camps in the country north of the Forth – c. 53ha and 25 ha. Significantly, the party left behind near Cramond accounted for a 13ha diminution of the available force – a reappearance of the 'legion with moderate support'. Of the two northern series, the 25ha camps are the earlier: however, their combined distribution pattern seems likely to represent two equal parts of the reduced army, operating separately.

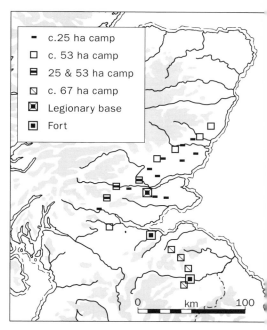

Imperial Campaigns AD **208–211**
Temporary camp-sites indicate the route of Severus' army from the Tweed to the Forth and, in two equal units, throughout Caledonia. Over much of the area they are set a day's march apart.

Legend:
- — c.25 ha camp
- ☐ c. 53 ha camp
- ◒ 25 & 53 ha camp
- ◪ c. 67 ha camp
- ◼ Legionary base
- ◼ Fort

Trajan's Column
Trajan's column provides the most authoritative picture of the Roman army at the start of the second century – here it contrasts the second-line auxiliaries (left) and the elite soldiers of the legions (right).
ANGUS LAMB

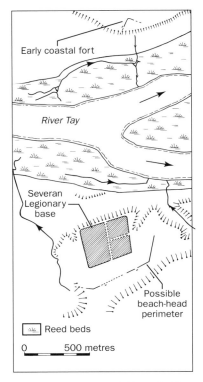

Third-century Coastal Stronghold

At Carpow on the south shore of the
Tay estuary aerial survey by the
University of Cambridge revealed not
only a Severan legionary base, but also
a polygonal ditched enclosure which
might possibly have defended the
beach-head of a Roman assault.
After St Joseph

Gold Coin

Aureus (gold coin) from the Severan
base at Carpow showing the head of
the Emperor Antoninus Pius, under
whom the Antonine Wall was built.
NATIONAL MUSEUMS OF SCOTLAND

The northernmost 25ha camps may thus belong to a
detachment pressing constantly north-eastward from the Teith
through Strathmore to the North Esk, and probably returning by
a coastal route.

The presumably simultaneous operations of the other half of
the army are less easy to interpret. It is possible to imagine a divergence from the first group somewhere south of Ardoch, and then
an eastward march along the south side of the Earn to Carpow,
with subsequent forays into the heartland of Fife. However,
although an eastward advance is supported by the positions of the
camps at Auchtermuchty and Edenwood in Fife, Forteviot in
Perthshire, on the west bank of the Water of May, would appear
more likely to have been used by a force moving westward, that is,
returning to the Forth. The odd multi-sided enclosure at Carpow
has an important role to play here. Originally seen as a 25ha camp
somewhat deformed to cover the end of the bridge of boats used
to cross the Tay, but also explained as an outwork to the later
legionary fortress, its widely spaced gateways combine with the
available ground to suggest a capacity well in excess of 25ha.
Now, as there is roughly contemporary evidence pointing to the
involvement of elements from the fleets of three other provinces
in the British campaign, we may ask if Carpow should be
interpreted not as a bridgehead, but rather as a beachhead.

Since a legionary presence was eventually established here,
and almost certainly supplied by sea, why should the northern
campaigns not have included a seaborne assault? Intended to
divert attention from the land advance through Strathearn, and
directed at the rear of the Maeatae, the landings would have tied
up the potentially troublesome tribes of Fife, while the other part
of the army tackled the Caledonians. An operation on this scale,
involving the ferrying of almost 20,000 armed men, probably from
a temporary base on the Forth, would constitute one of the major
feats of the Roman army in Britain.

The operation was not repeated, for during the next campaign
the separate groups had to recombine in a renewed onslaught on
the now-rebelling Maeatae and Caledonians. The march of
this army, advancing relentlessly at an average of ten
miles a day along the inland route pioneered by
Agricola, has left, in the series of 53ha camps, one
of the most eloquent statements of Imperial power
to be seen anywhere in Britain. It is the track of
an army that methodically trampled everything
underfoot, even, as at Ardoch, the installations of
its predecessors, but certainly all foolhardy enough
to stand against the authority of Rome.

The Sinews of Power

'The effect of these operations was that many previously independent nations, who had laid down their arms and handed over hostages, were now guarded and watched over on all sides, with such judicious care, that they became part of the province of Britannia free from any external interference, something that had never happened before'.
Cornelius Tacitus, *The Life of Agricola*, 20, 3.

The aftermath of invasion

After each campaigning episode, especially during the Agricolan conquest, there was a period of consolidation during which assessments had to be made – of the population-density and the main natural resources of the conquered land, of the attitude of the different tribes to their conquerors, and of the vulnerability of the area to its unconquered neighbours. How best could the available Roman manpower be deployed to guarantee the security of the newly annexed territory, without prejudicing the prosperity and safety of the more settled areas?

What the situation called for, on the one hand, was a survey, to enable the effective 'farming' of the local economies, and thus defray the costs of maintaining an army of occupation; on the other, a thorough strategic review, to shake out the auxiliary garrisons, transferring them from relatively peaceful southern parts of the province. We must remember that this was a rolling process, with various stages. In AD 80–83, even while the advance moved north, fortified posts were being built for fixed garrisons, in some cases, not far behind the active war-zone. The size and nature of these *castella* and *praesidia*, as Tacitus calls them, have not yet been precisely determined.

Between Campaigns and Colonisation

Before regiments could be assigned to permanent bases, the garrison needs of newly overrun territory had to be assessed. The Flavian solution in southern Scotland apparently involved a provisional network of forts and intermediate fortlets.

The provisional network

Nevertheless, Agricola and his successor probably addressed this problem in a similar way, by sub-dividing units and spreading them out, to begin with perhaps more thinly than either might have wished. Newly conquered territory would have been overlaid by

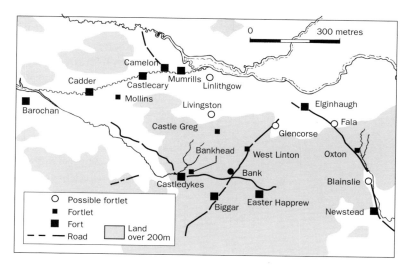

An Early Flavian Fortlet
On remote moorland, miles from any Roman road, forestry ploughing advances upon the earthworks of Castle Greg, Lothian, where the parrot's-beak ditch-terminals at its single entrance indicate an Agricolan origin.
R.CAHMS

Off the Beaten Track
Faint cropmarks reveal the position of the square Flavian fortlet at Kirkland, a node in the provisional network, guarding a side-valley off Nithsdale, not far from Moniaive, Dumfries and Galloway.
R.CAHMS

a provisional network of fortified posts in which smaller and larger garrisons alternated, so carving up the tribal lands into a pattern of fields, whose edges, as yet unprovided with regular roads, were patrolled by the locally stationed troops. Eventually, as the tide of war rolled further north, or as the perceived threat diminished, individual posts, or even lines of posts, might be abandoned, after perhaps only a matter of months. In such cases, we would expect the physical remains to be extremely slight, so making the site difficult to identify in modern times unless by aerial photography. The well-preserved early Agricolan fortlet of Castle Greg, which lies in isolated moorland on the north side of the Pentland Hills, miles from the Roman road network, represents a remarkable exception.

Further instances of abandoned early semi-permanent posts have been identified actually on the line of the later road-system: the sites at West Linton and Glencorse, Peeblesshire, on the route leading north-eastward from Biggar along the south side of the Pentland Hills, are particularly significant, being positioned at respectively one day's march and half a day's march from the Agricolan fort of Elginhaugh, Midlothian. Similar subdivision of standard fort-intervals can be identified on Dere Street between Elginhaugh and Newstead. The main characteristics shared by these posts appear to be the absence of elaborate defences or prolonged occupation, an area of less than 0.4ha, and a tendency to be spaced half a day's march (c. 10km) apart.

Communications by land

'Of course, the farther North you go the emptier are the roads. . . and the wind sings through your helmet-plume.'
Rudyard Kipling, *Puck of Pook's Hill*, 'On the Great Wall' 1906.

The next stage of occupation – the establishment of more permanent garrisons – meant that the communications requirements had to be addressed. The machinery of military government simply could not have functioned without adequate supplies of materials and information. These needs were met by a relatively sophisticated system of roads and watch- or signal-towers.

The roads and towers took longer to complete than the forts they linked, and in some areas (such as Strathmore in the Flavian period) the construction programme lagged two or three years behind that of the forts. However, the road network should be considered first, as probably the biggest capital expenditure project associated with the occupation. Until this strategic road system was built, the land routes used would have been tactical, following where possible in the tracks of the campaigning

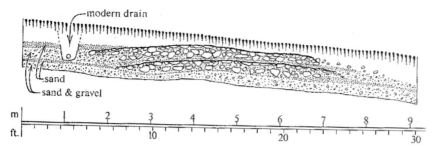

columns and little altered from their natural state; pack–animals would have been used to transport materials, and only for important tasks would a specially engineered sector of road have been provided in advance of the main programme. During the construction of the legionary fortress at Inchtuthil, for example, a handsome wagon-road was laid to bring the stone from the distant quarries to the building-site. This road included a one–way loop, more than three Roman miles in extent, which ensured easier gradients for heavily laden wagons descending from the quarry, and restricted the more direct but steeper route to empty vehicles. If it took 6000 man–days to complete 10km of road of basic tactical standard (involving little more than clearing vegetation, filling in holes, and essential rock cutting), the scale of surveying, designing, and constructing more than 400 Roman miles (590km) required for the Agricolan conquest is almost unimaginable.

Given that much of the road-making took place in the frequently harsh environment of the Scottish uplands, the resulting product was remarkably uniform. Two-thirds of the system was apparently built to a standard carriageway-width of 20 Roman feet (5.9m), but what one might term the central spine of the road system, Dere Street, exhibits a more generous standard, perhaps as wide as 25-30 feet; the quarry-roads at Inchtuthil were of a similar standard.

A wide variety of construction techniques was used, reflecting the changing character of the terrain through which the roads ran. In areas with well-drained and firm subsoil little effort would be made to provide boulder bottoming – only enough to ensure the correct cambered profile. On softer ground, the road builders either excavated down to the bedrock, as on Craik Moor, or 'floated' the road mound on a raft of sand or gravel, as occasionally on the Biggar-Elginhaugh sector.

The Well-beaten Track

A cross-section of the Roman road to the east of Castledykes in Clydesdale, showing the two periods of smooth, cambered running-surface, with boulder bottoming, and underlayer of gravel bedding.

Straight as a Rule

A typical stretch of Roman road, with cambered running-surface flanked by rows of quarry-pits, is seen to advantage in this aerial view, as it crosses uncultivated upland on the south-east slopes of the Pentland Hills.
RCAHMS

(below)

The Road Network

The securely identified sectors of the
Roman road-system of all periods,
together with coastal installations
possibly associated with Flavian
military operations.

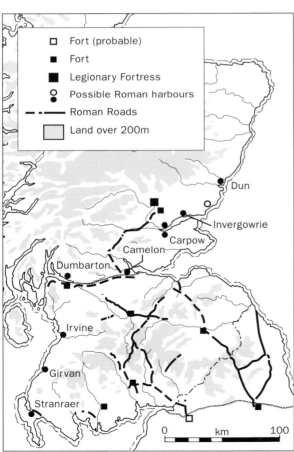

□	Fort (probable)
■	Fort
■	Legionary Fortress
○ ●	Possible Roman harbours
▬ ▬	Roman Roads
▨	Land over 200m

Dun

Invergowrie

Carpow

Camelon

Dumbarton

Irvine

Girvan

Stranraer

0   km   100

Most of the material for bottoming and
metalling came from roughly circular or
oblong quarry-pits flanking the road and lying
5–15m from it. Typically 3–8m across and
originally about 1.3 mdeep, the pits, in places,
are so numerous that they overlap, suggesting
that some may have been dug by later road-
repair gangs. Where the roads have been heavily
denuded by later activity, such pits may be the
only evidence of the road's existence and its
Roman origin: mere straightness of alignment
is not evidence that a road is Roman – many
eighteenth-century and later roads share this
characteristic.

The road system fulfilled its function
superbly: it ensured the safe, economical, and
reasonably swift movement of men and
material between the military establishments.
The design of the road was governed by the
needs of its most important traffic – wheeled
vehicles. The worst gradients encountered on
Roman roads in Scotland were about 1 in 4,
but only infrequently and for short distances,
while slopes of 1 in 6 seem the maximum
generally allowed for longer climbs. Traffic
negotiating such slopes would have been
considerably aided by the generous road-width;

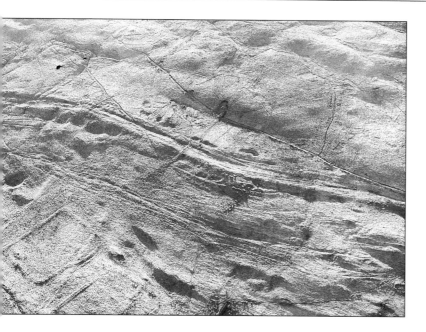

Take the High Road
In the valley of the Daer Water, upper Clydesdale, the dying rays of the midsummer sun pick out the quarry-pits, artificial shelf and cambered mound of the Roman road as it climbs towards the watershed, avoiding the deeply scooped house-platforms of an earlier age.
RCAHMS

as shown by the wheel-ruts in roads at Inchtuthil and other Roman sites, wagons were probably built to a standard gauge of 4ft 8 inches [British Imperial] (1.42m) and on the normal 20ft-wide Roman carriageway, it would have been quite possible to pass on-coming or slower-moving vehicles.

The road system would also have greatly eased the passage of information – the reports, returns, and requisitions upon which the Roman army, like the modern, depended for its very existence. As is shown by the correspondence recovered at Vindolanda on Hadrian's Wall, paperwork and the military mind are connected by an indissoluble link, and the official couriers responsible for its dispersal back and forth along the roads were further burdened by personal letters. For more immediate transmission of urgent or sensitive information, a totally different channel was required, an extensive system of intervisible towers. The means of transmission ranged from beacon-fires and trumpet-call to elaborate semaphore, and its speed of operation would have been invaluable in an emergency.

Heavy Goods Vehicles
The Roman road system was designed to accommodate wheeled traffic, including such ox-drawn wagons as appear on Trajan's column.
ANGUS LAMB

Telecommunication in Roman times

'And some hang wooden arms on the towers of forts and
cities, to indicate what is going on by alternately raising and
lowering them.'
Flavius Vegetius Renatus, *Epitome of Military Science*, III, 5.

All of the known examples of towers in Scotland were massively
built timber structures, two or three storeys high, and most were
roughly square in plan, with sides 10–12 Roman feet long; they
were enclosed within one or two penannular ditches, and
sometimes also protected by a rampart. Their close resemblance
to the towers that flanked or surmounted the gateways of
permanent forts may indicate, in some cases, that they were built
by the same work party. Although a few are found in high
positions, for example, on the summit of the North Eildon Hill,
most adjoin a sector of the Roman road system. The towers
had a twofold role: to see and be seen, that is, to serve both as
watch-towers (particularly evident when they appear in a
close-set series) and signal-towers. The best example of the
former role, dating to the Flavian period, is known as the Gask
frontier, after the ridge south-west of Perth along which it runs.
Here, towers were integrated with forts and fortlets to maintain a
close watch over an extended front which may originally have
been drawn from the Forth to the banks of the Tay. News of
hostile movements across or along this line (which may partly
have coincided with a tribal boundary) would have been passed
down the chain of posts with requests for immediate action.

The four examples in the sector of the Gask
'frontier' to the north and south of the fort at
Ardoch merit particularly close attention.
As a group, they are remarkable in
their uniformity, being of similar
size and spacing – 40 Roman

To See and Be Seen
Reconstruction drawing of a
typical Flavian watch-tower.
HISTORIC SCOTLAND;
MICHAEL J MOORE

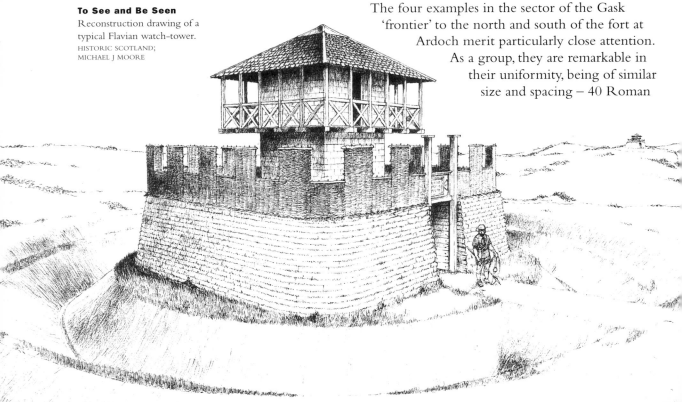

feet (over the rampart) and enclosed by double ditches; at the centre of each, occupying a quarter of the 20ft square interior, stood a 10ft square tower. It would be hard to imagine a more obviously modular product of a Roman military drawing office. Each tower was not only built by the builders of Flavian Ardoch, but also manned by the unit serving at Ardoch. The tower-detachment strength cannot be proved, but all the likely duties of the watch could have been adequately performed by a single *contubernium*, or messing-unit, of eight men; the tower's ground-space of 100 sq. ft, with at least one room above, would approximate to the barrack space allocated to this unit in the fort.

We know much less about the Antonine equivalents of such towers. Only two free-standing towers of that date have so far been identified – Beattock Summit and White Type. Built on a smaller scale than the Flavian towers, they lie, five Roman miles apart, on either side of the 2nd-century fortlet of Redshaw Burn, watching over the road that straddles the watershed between Clyde and Annan.

For more instructive parallels we must look to the Antonine Wall; yet even here only little understood fragments of the signalling system can be identified. The best-known groups comprise pairs of platforms abutting the south side of the Wall itself: one pair lies on each side of the fort at Rough Castle, and one to the west of the fort and fortlet on Croy Hill. The pairs are reckoned to have operated in combination, transmitting and receiving messages by beacon-fire to and from the Wall's eastern

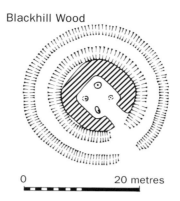
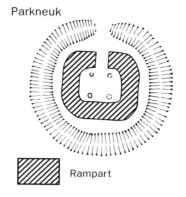

Peas in a Pod
Comparative ground-plans of two types of watch-tower on the Flavian frontier, as they might have been filed in the engineers' drawing-office of each respective legion.

Similar Function, Similar Form?
The communications needs of the second-century Walls were similar to those of earlier frontiers, the role of the watch-towers being discharged by turrets on Hadrian's Wall (right), and, on the Antonine Wall, by 'expansions' (middle) and possibly minor enclosures (left), all of comparable 'internal' area.

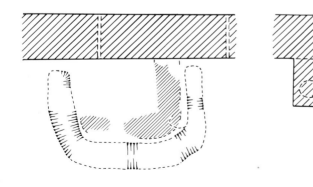
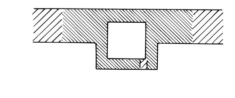

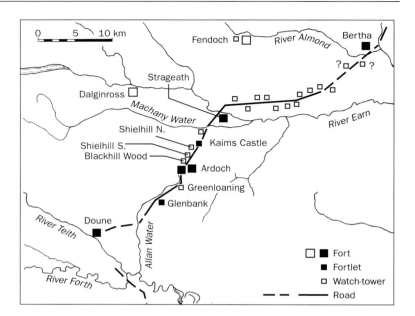

Integrated Watch and Ward
The southern sector of the Forth-Tay frontier demonstrates how, in the Flavian period, surveillance and communication were maintained by complementary series of towers, fortlets, and various sizes of fort.

outposts and western hinterland. The nature of their super-structure, which was of turf, cannot be determined, but they were raised on stone-edged bases 18 Roman feet (5.2m) square. Resembling these in some respects, is the group of three minor enclosures discovered during aerial survey beside the Wall-fortlet of Wilderness Plantation; they too abut the south face of the Wall, but are defined by a single rampart and ditch, enclosing a space about 20 Roman feet square. From the excavation of one example little was learned, save that, like the Flavian towers of the Gask Ridge, or the stone turrets on Hadrian's Wall, a square module of 20 Roman feet appears significant in their construction; we may deduce that they had a related purpose.

Naval communications

'So one legion was detailed to each of the fleets at Misenum and Ravenna... with the capacity to go by sea, without delay or detour, anywhere in the world... for in wartime speed is usually more useful than courage.'
Flavius Vegetius Renatus, *Epitome of Military Science*, IV, 31 (Precepts of Naval Warfare).

Communication by water is often mentioned in accounts of Roman Scotland, but seldom substantiated by hard evidence. Yet the major role played by the *Classis Britannica* (the fleet of Britain) in Agricola's campaigns, whether in reconnaissance or tactical support, suggests that the advantages of water-borne transport would not have been ignored. We have little evidence other than an anchor allegedly found near Camelon, Falkirk, and

a possible steering-paddle discovered at Newstead. It is also true that, apart from the still-unconfirmed forts at Stranraer and Irvine (Rerigonium and Vindogara), few Agricolan installations are situated within walking distance of the seacoast, far less exploit natural harbours there. Indeed, reviewing the known Lothian sites, where Dere Street approaches the Forth, it is significant that a specifically inland route appears to have been chosen in the Flavian period; coastal positions like Inveresk and Cramond lay undeveloped until the second century.

On the other hand, with such major navigable rivers as the Forth or Tay penetrating deeply into the interior and offering the possibility of transhipment of cargoes to shallower-draught vessels, the army may not have got round to harbour construction before the withdrawal of AD 86/87. However, the reference in Ptolemy to a base called *Horrea Classis* implies that, somewhere on the coast of Fife, Perthshire, or Angus, a supply base was maintained for the Roman fleet in British waters, at least temporarily. Such a base would presumably have required a larger defensive perimeter than is found in such small camps as Dun on the Montrose Basin.

The only camp of reasonable size to occupy ground near enough the coast to justify a connection with naval operations is at Invergowrie, on the western outskirts of Dundee; however, the camp overlooks a coastline that has been much altered in recent centuries, and its capacity to provide safe harbourage in the past is largely unknown. The possibility that a Flavian naval base underlies the third-century works at Carpow a little way

Waterborne Suppliers
Whenever practicable, Roman commanders would have used the fleet to supply forward positions as shown here on Trajan's column.
DAVID BREEZE

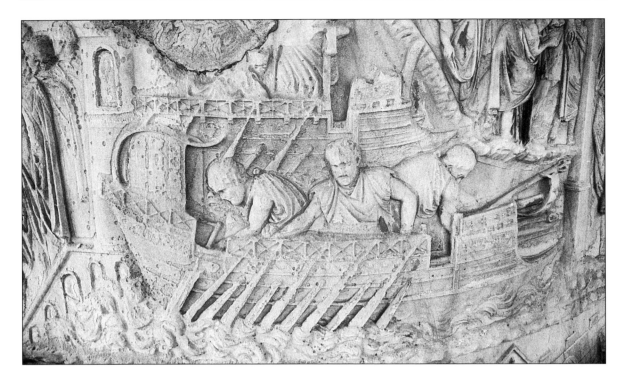

Roman Sea-power

In both communications and offensive operations, the Roman fleet in British waters *(Classis Britannica)* had as important a role to play as Danubian units in Trajan's war against the Dacians.
ANGUS LAMB

upstream on the opposite shore of the Tay, has often been considered, but since no early artefacts have come to light during excavations there, only a temporary landing-site seems feasible for the Agricolan campaigns. Perhaps it is just such an ephemeral installation that appears on Ptolemy's map; the very presence here in the Severan period of an isolated fortress, supplied by sea, demonstrates that such a location was a practical proposition.

No harbours have as yet been identified in the Flavian west, nor have any which may have accompanied the building of the Antonine Wall. There are, however, traces of a chain of second-century fortlets which follows the heights above the southern shore of the Clyde estuary and, reaching the sea near Largs, could have linked up with whatever military dispositions Agricola had earlier made from Irvine south to Stranraer. The discovery of such coastal installations might cast light upon one of Tacitus' more enigmatic observations – that Agricola was 'obsessed' with the possibility of an invasion of Ireland. The political pretext for this adventure – the arrival of a refugee Irish princeling – was no less fanciful than that which Claudius had exploited for the invasion of Britain in AD 43. There is thus a good chance that these unconfirmed western harbours were selected as the invasion bases for some never-realised naval assault.

Occupation

If communications-chains represented the sinews of the Roman occupation, the muscles were provided by the individual garrisons. And like the muscles of the human body, the garrisons of Roman Scotland differed in size and character depending on their function. As with the temporary camps, the Flavian permanent sites offer a key to understanding comparable installations of succeeding occupations. We have already looked at the physical remains of the Flavian watch-tower system that adjoins long stretches of the Forth-Tay road. Closer examination of the same sector will furnish us with illustrations of similar relationships, but on a larger scale.

Flavian fortlets

We noted earlier that a *contubernium* of eight men was probably adequate to operate each of the watch-towers in the vicinity of the fort at Ardoch. Fortlets were also an integral part of the system. The Ardoch-sector examples, Kaims Castle and Glenbank, both measure about 120 by 100 Roman feet (35m by 30m); the long axis of one lies at right angles to the road, that of the other parallel to it. On the analogy of the similarly sized, but later, fortlet at Barburgh Mill in Nithsdale, they would have accommodated a century of infantry, ten times the presumed strength of the tower garrisons. A clue to the relative capacities is provided by the spacing between neighbouring structures, which in this sector (unlike elsewhere on the Gask frontier) is a regular 3000 Roman feet, regardless of the type of structures at which the stage terminates. Since Kaims and Glenbank are very nearly six Roman miles (30,000ft) apart, it would seem that the ten intervals thus defined match the ten *contubernia* that make a century, and thus the theoretical density of deployment over each six-mile stretch was two centuries or 160 men: one in the fortlet, the other divided between the towers.

It was once thought that subdividing of garrisons and closer positioning of fortified sites was what distinguished a formal frontier from a standard communications route. However, recent study of fortlet types suggests strongly that these differences have a more complex origin, stemming sometimes from shortage of resources or purely temporary need. Mollins, to the south-west of Cumbernauld, at 60 metres square (0.4ha) is typical of the larger Flavian fortlets; probably one of Agricola's Forth-Clyde frontier chain of AD 80-81, it belongs to a group that seems equally at home in rural backwaters and on the front line.

Flavian Forth-Clyde Frontier
Air photograph of the large fortlet at
Mollins, one of a chain of posts drawn
by governor Julius Agricola across the
Forth-Clyde isthmus during his
fourth campaign.
RCAHMS

Flavian forts

Subdivision of standard military units need not be expected
solely among the smaller classes of installations. Excavation at
Strageath, the next fort north of Ardoch, revealed that, during all
periods of occupation, the garrison comprised one complete
regiment of auxiliaries and part of at least one other. The early
investigation of Ardoch itself indicated that the mixed garrison
there might include a legionary detachment. The presence in
Flavian times of fractions of whole units at both sites would be
totally understandable if they represented the residue left after
detailing men to serve in the adjacent towers and fortlets. We
have long known from actual unit reports such as those found
at Vindolanda on Hadrian's Wall, that regiments were quite
frequently well below their supposed strength. Since excavation
at Strageath not only confirmed this but even suggested that the
internal buildings of forts might have been designed from the
beginning to accommodate only such reduced units, it might
appear nearly impossible to use fort size alone to assess garrison
strength, especially as different kinds of garrison − infantry,
cavalry, and composite regiments − had different accommodation
needs. However, the adoption of a rule-of-thumb approach by
construction parties in the field seems to have had the perhaps
unexpected effect of standardising fort size. The small Agricolan
fort at Crawford (0.8ha), for example, which may have held half
a cohort of mounted infantry, is the physical equivalent of two
fortlets of the Mollins type set side by side. Although incapable
of holding a complete regiment, excavation revealed that
Crawford possessed a standard headquarters-building; it is
therefore convenient to class it as a fort rather than a fortlet,
despite its restricted capacity.

Bases for Sub-units
Computer-generated ground-plans from
air photographs of Flavian installations
near Ardoch − two types of watch-tower
(1 and 2), and the small fortlets at
Glenbank (3) and Kaims Castle (4),
compared with the large fortlet at
Inverquharity (5), by Kirriemuir, Angus.

0   50 metres

Elginhaugh, guarding the point where Dere Street crosses the North Esk west of Dalkeith, demonstrates the advantages and disadvantages of using fort-size to estimate garrison-size. Measuring about 445 by 405 Roman feet (132m by 120m) over the rampart (1.6ha), it represents, both in physical appearance and capacity, the equivalent of two forts of the type found at Crawford built side by side; and yet excavation has shown that the interior, packed with timber buildings, accommodated many more troops than size, or comparison with Crawford, would have led us to believe. However, there are hints in the layout of the buildings that a less densely packed interior was originally planned.

Roman forts, like temporary camps, can also be classed according to their stylistic features. Inturned gateways, intended to make attacks on the entrance more difficult, are relatively common in early Roman fort architecture. This depth of defence could be achieved by recessing the flanking gate-towers some way back from the line of the rampart, often creating a long corridor of approach, or else by incurving the rampart itself. An alternative method was to provide a double or triple ditch system outside the rampart. By uniting and incurving the ditches on either side of the entrance, a funnelled approach was created in the form of an opposed pair of what are called 'parrot's beaks'.

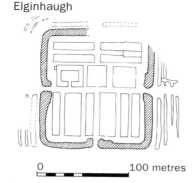

Elginhaugh

0   100 metres

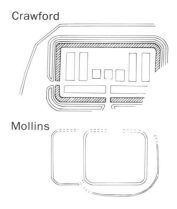

Crawford

Mollins

Graded Garrison-posts

Evidence of a modular approach to fort construction in Flavian times provided by the large fortlet of Mollins, the small fort of Crawford, and the fort at Elginhaugh, each increase doubling the area available for use.

Discovery and Excavation

The initial aerial view (left) of the fort at Elginhaugh, where Dere Street crosses the North Esk, near Dalkeith, reveals only the parchmarks of the external and internal roads. When completely excavated (right), post-trenches for timber buildings appear everywhere within the interior.

RCAHMS

The 'parrot's beak' type of gate has advantages for the archaeologist: it can be recognised easily in cropmark form and it can be reasonably accurately dated, for at no site is it associated with structures later than the Flavian period. Its geographical distribution within Britain, on the other hand, is relatively wide, aerial survey having greatly increased the number of sites recognised. There are quite distinct groupings in Scotland, with particular frequency in the south-west, central Scotland, and in Strathmore; they are totally absent from the south-east. Since this distribution pattern agrees broadly with that of the Stracathro-gated type of camp, the 'beak' may also indicate the handiwork of the Second *Adiutrix* Legion. This suggests that legionary command responsibilities endured from the campaigning stages through to at least the initial phase of the occupation. To confirm this association we must look to the seven or eight known or suspected sites in England and Wales; their restricted distribution in north Lincolnshire/south Yorkshire, as well as in north Wales/Lancashire points unequivocally to the activities of the Second Legion, transferred from the lower Rhine to Lincoln around AD 71 and moved across to Chester some time before Agricola's governorship.

The 'parrot's beak' gates in several of the forts in Strathmore – at Cardean, Cargill, and possibly at Stracathro, shows that the Second Legion was active in the north up to and perhaps beyond the end of Agricola's Caledonian campaigns. As to its status when the

Timber Gateway of Flavian 'Parrot's-beak' Fort

At many of the earthwork-and-timber forts which housed the auxiliary regiments of the Agricolan garrison in Scotland the gateways are accompanied by 'parrot's beak' ditch-terminals, possibly an indication that they were built by the legion also responsible for the construction of 'Stracathro' camps.

CHRIS BROWN

withdrawal from the northernmost conquests was ordered in AD 86/87, the evidence is ambiguous. The defences of the last period at Dalswinton, Bankhead, in Nithsdale, did not use the 'beak'; at Milton, Annandale, on the other hand, both the early and the later defence-systems employed the device. On balance, it seems likelier that, by this stage, the Second Legion was on its way to the Danube; shortly afterward, facing the inevitable, Rome had decided to abandon all the Agricolan conquest.

Antonine frontier policy

'Through the actions of his lieutenants, Antoninus waged a great many wars: on his behalf Lollius Urbicus, the provincial governor, conquered the Britons, having driven off the barbarians and built another wall, of turf.'
The Augustan History, Antoninus Pius, V.

When the legions marched north again almost 40 years later, new officers and new ideas had appeared in the field of military engineering, and the effect was noticeable. Authority decided that if a line now had to be drawn between Caesar's land and *barbaricum*, the new line had to be a physical barrier which could fittingly express the superiority of Rome, rather than a chain of discrete garrisons. The Antonine Wall was certainly 'physical': for over 40 Roman miles its turf-faced rampart snaked, 10ft high and 14ft thick, along the escarpments and crags marking the southern side of the Central Scottish Rift Valley, with a massive ditch in front and a Military Way behind. Abutting its southern side were at least 17 forts, about 40 fortlets, and an unknown number of lesser installations, while at intervals, embedded in each face, stood handsomely carved stone tablets, Distance Slabs that recorded the completion of successive sectors of Wall-building by individual legions.

Legionary Trademarks
At Malling, on the Lake of Menteith, the auxiliary fort with its conspicuous parrot's-beak gateway and (to the left) the Stracathro-gated marching-camp display the equivalent of architectural signatures, possibly those of the Second Adiutrix Legion.
RCAHMS

The Turf Curtain
On the Antonine Wall, running from Bo'ness in the east to Old Kilpatrick on the west, there were at first six forts and about forty fortlets. This plan shows it in its final, much strengthened form.

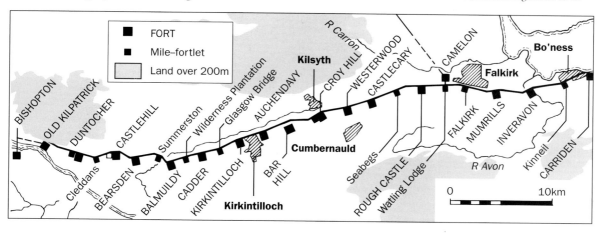

(above)

Arthur's O'on

At the end of another season in the field, early in the Antonine occupation, the senior staff officers of the Second Augustan Legion attend a *suovetaurilia* (sacrifice of pig, sheep, and bull) to celebrate the successful completion of the Wall-building task. The scene, depicted on the Bridgeness Distance Slab, has been transferred to the temple of Victory on the opposite side of the Forth at Stenhouse, whose imposing remains later generations called Arthur's O'on (Oven).
CHRIS BROWN

Vanished Glory

The Roman temple known as Arthur's O'on (Oven) on the banks of the Carron, which was barbarously demolished to provide material for the dam of an early ironworks, is here seen in a sketch made by the eighteenth-century antiquary and surveyor William Roy.
SOCIETY OF ANTIQUARIES, LONDON

The most magnificent of these slabs was set up by the Second *Augusta* Legion at Bridgeness, in Bo'ness, probably at the eastern end of the frontier. It bears two carved panels, one depicting a victorious cavalryman, the other a religious ceremony, which conveyed to a conquered population the same propaganda message as the Wall itself: that the combination of military might and divine favour made Rome irresistible. Although divine favour may lack relevance in modern times, to a Roman the sacrifice to Victory depicted on the Bridgeness slab would have demonstrated the renewal of a living contract between Rome and her gods at the end of a successful campaign. The same ceremony may well have been performed by officers of the Second Legion at Arthur's O'on, a possible victory monument or temple of Antonine date, which long survived at Stenhouse on the other side of the Forth, some nine miles to the west, only to be deliberately destroyed in 1743.

The Flavian armies would never have dreamt that a continuous curtain of walling would one day replace the open frontiers, yet there were elements of the new Antonine frontier which they would certainly have recognised. The most significant of these would have been the forts and intervening fortlets supplemented by occasional watch-towers. In its original form the frontier had six forts, set half a day's march apart, linked not only by the curtain wall with its sentry-walk, but also, at roughly one-mile intervals, by fortlets. At an early stage this system had

Imperial Propaganda

The easternmost Distance Slab on the Antonine Wall, at Bridgeness, is also the largest and most impressive. The dedication to the Emperor Antoninus Pius, recording the building of 4652 paces of the Wall by the Second Augustan Legion, is flanked by scenes of victory and ritual sacrifice.
NATIONAL MUSEUMS OF SCOTLAND

View of the Antonine Wall at Croy Hill

Winter is drawing on. In the lee of the Antonine Wall on Croy Hill and looking north-west we can see that the original fortlet has now been replaced by a fort; in the foreground, soldiers of the Sixth Legion, engaged in either repair work or support duties, gather in the garrison cemetery to attend the funeral of a comrade.
CHRIS BROWN

been strengthened by the addition of about a dozen forts, each about two miles apart. The density of garrisons might have appalled, and the wide range of plans and sizes bemused, a visitor from the past; he might also have looked in vain for evidence of a comprehensive series of watch-posts. But the fortlets he would have known and understood. Although smaller than most first-century examples and manned by garrisons not more than half a century strong, with their towered gateways the fortlets would not only have fulfilled the 'see and be seen' role that was the mainstay of the earliest defence-lines; they would also have served as architectural 'signatures' of the separate legionary parties at work on the Wall, since each Legion's fortlets were built on a slightly different plan. The Twentieth Legion apparently built fortlets whose short axis lay at right angles to the Wall-curtain, whereas in the fortlets of the Second Legion it was the long axis that was so aligned.

Of course, the association between legionary troops and the Wall did not end with the building phase; some played a role in its eventual manning, but not necessarily in the sectors they had built. Thus, at the long-axis fort at Croy Hill, possibly built by the Second Legion, a Sixth Legion presence is also attested by building dedications and, more grimly, a tombstone. Does this mean that a legionary engaged in building the fort which replaced the fortlet died during the construction-work? Or was it a centurion who had stayed behind to command the fort's auxiliary garrison?

Turning to the area to the south of the Wall, we shall find further parallels to the Flavian experience, which confirm that comparable stimuli tend to produce comparable responses. Antonine Crawford in upper Clydesdale, for example, differed

Roman Gravestone

A gravestone found at Croy Hill depicting three legionaries.

NATIONAL MUSEUMS OF SCOTLAND

Frontier Modifications

Plan of the Antonine Wall near the summit of Croy Hill, showing the primary fortlet on the west, and the slightly larger fort which soon replaced it, overlying the site of an enclosure that may have belonged to an even earlier phase of Antonine occupation.

GLASGOW ARCHAEOLOGICAL SOCIETY

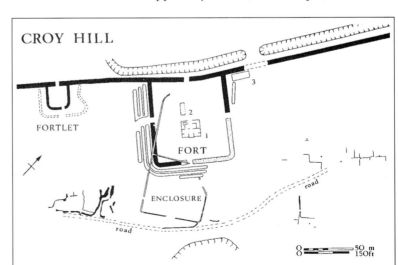

minimally in size and shape from its Agricolan predecessor, and, although its interior layout was completely redesigned, it still contained a standard headquarters building and half-size barracks sufficient for half a 500-man auxiliary regiment. In this period it did not stand alone; dispersed around it in the upper valleys of the Clyde, Annan, and Nith, were earth-and-timber fortlets which would not have looked out of place on the turf section of Hadrian's Wall. In close association with one of these, the fortlet at Redshaw Burn, we have already seen that a pair of timber watch-towers maintained surveillance along the road; so slight are their remains, that many others, now destroyed, may once have lined the roads that linked the fortlet chain. How many of these recognised Crawford as their mother-fort we cannot tell. Doubtless some were manned by detachments from larger forts, like recently discovered Ladyward to the west of Lockerbie or Drumlanrig in upper Nithsdale. The existence of this integrated system unambiguously identifies this part of south-west Scotland as a potential threat to frontier security – not least because of its proximity to the once-troubled kingdom of Brigantia; the scale of that threat may possibly be better indicated by the remarkable site at Burnswark in eastern Dumfriesshire.

(above)
High Passes and Lonely Outposts
An aerial view of the well-preserved Antonine fortlet near Durisdeer, Dumfries and Galloway, protecting traffic on a remote sector of the road from Clydesdale to upper Nithsdale.
RCAHMS

(left)
A Monument for Posterity
In some stretches, as here at Watling Lodge, near Falkirk, where the ditch has survived centuries of erosion, we can understand why early post-Roman peoples thought the Antonine Wall was the work of a superhuman race.
HISTORIC SCOTLAND

Burnswark, a firing range for Roman field-artillery

'The artillery-pieces of all the legions were superbly constructed. . . their stone missiles weighing thirty kilos travelled 400m or more, and no one who got in their way remained standing. The enemy look-outs, posted on towers, gave warning whenever an artillery shot came hurtling towards them, with a shout of "Baby on the way!"'
Flavius Josephus, *The Jewish War*, V, 6.

Burnswark in lower Annandale constitutes a treasury of archaeological evidence, which illustrates aspects of Roman military activity seldom represented by upstanding field-monuments. Situated on the steeply sloping south face of Burnswark Hill, the complex commands a wide view southwards to the Solway and Cumbria. It comprises a Roman long-axis fortlet, a temporary camp, and various types of minor settlement of the local population, as well as a number of possible post-Roman burials; a smaller Roman camp, of irregular plan, is sited at the foot of the Hill's northern slope. The distinctively shaped summit of the Hill is occupied by an equally wide range of structures, dating from the early prehistoric to the mediaeval and later periods. Of these, the most relevant to this account is the hillfort whose timber-revetted ramparts once enclosed the entire summit area (at roughly 7ha the largest fort in south-west Scotland); within the interior a number of wooden round-houses provided accommodation for a local community several hundred years before the Romans arrived. By the time the Romans came the defences had fallen into disuse, and it is probable that afterwards the summit was only occupied at intervals.

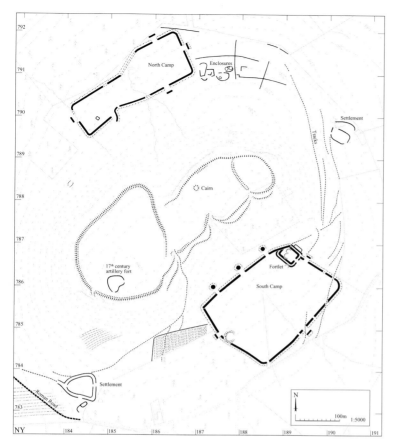

Roman and Native in Conflict

On either side of the large native hillfort of Burnswark lies a Roman temporary camp, the southern example differentiated by the three massive mounds that block its north-west gateways and the long-axis fortlet nestling in its northern angle. The long-abandoned theory that it once marked the scene of a bitter assault may need to be reviewed.

RCAHMS

North Rampart of Burnswark camp

In the languid days of summer legionary units are out on the artillery range at Burnswark Hill, where, in the Antonine period, ballista-firing exercises took place. The heavier weapons occupied massive emplacements at the gateways of a possibly re-used temporary camp, their targets, like those of the cart-mounted catapults, being the dilapidated defences of the abandoned native fortification on the summit.

CHRIS BROWN

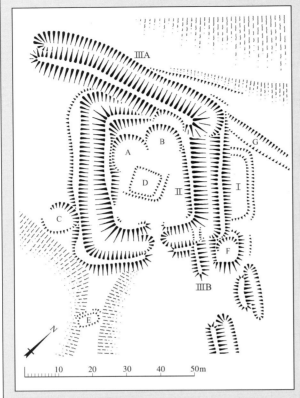

Evidence of Structural Change
This recent detailed survey of the long-axis Antonine fortlet
not only shows how it has been overlain by the north–west
side of the temporary camp, but also hints at the existence
of an even earlier camp.
RCAHMS

The fortlet, defended by a rampart, ditch and
counterscarp bank, was probably built early in the
Antonine period, around AD 140, and may have held
most or all of a century of auxiliary infantry, presumably
one detached from the 1000-strong First Cohort of
Germans at Birrens, 4.5km to the south-east. Why it
differs from all other members of the fortlet group in
lying at such a distance (500m) from the Roman road is
not immediately obvious, as its position has no obvious
tactical advantage. Nevertheless, some time after its
construction, it was incorporated in the northern angle
of a temporary camp of about 5.5ha, one of a pair of
camps, whose partner, about 2.5ha, occupies a similar
position on the opposite side of the hill. The southern
camp might have accommodated a little more than half
a legion – allowing for any specialist equipment required
for its duties here, probably about 3000 men. Under
normal conditions, even if only half the force had

been assigned to camp-building, while the rest stood
guard, each two-man team of diggers and basket-
carriers would have been allocated only 4 feet of the
defence perimeter and the entire circuit could have
been completed in little more than an hour.

The nature of the camp's main purpose is shown
by the three massive mounds built at its entrances on
the side that faces uphill towards the summit and
hillfort. These mounds served as *ballistaria*,
emplacements for the huge artillery pieces of a
Roman legion. From here were fired the stone missiles
that have been found during excavation, scattered in
profusion around the three gateways of the hilltop fort.
Made of local sandstone, and weighing 0.7–1.1kg,
such ballista-balls would have had a deadly effect, but
they formed only part of the lethal barrage, which also
included smaller stone shot (probably fired from lighter,
cart-borne weapons, *carroballistae*), leaden slingshot
and arrows tipped with iron. Since the killing-range of
bow and sling are 140m and 200m respectively, both
could safely have directed fire at the hillfort's gate
from within the camp. Yet the missiles in question
were all targeted at defences that had already
collapsed; in short, they were merely the spent shot
of a field-firing exercise. For a week or two each year,
legionaries would have stayed here under canvas,
improving their skills with torsion-gun, trebuchet, sling
and bow, probably under the supervision of engineers
(*architecti*) seconded for that purpose to nearby
Birrens. The location of the targets they bombarded,
in the dilapidated entrances of the hillfort, would have
had symbolic significance.

So far, the picture is of the pragmatic and
methodical Roman army, practising till it was perfect,
training its troops until the battlefield held fewer
terrors than the parade ground. Yet the story
Burnswark has to tell may be a little less prosaic,
for closer study of its splendidly preserved Roman
remains suggests a more complicated and much more

Ballistic Missiles
Excavation of the hillfort and
training camp at Burnswark
produced many examples of
the stone ballista projectiles
and leaden acorn-shaped
sling-shot which saturated
the target areas at the
hillfort gates.
NATIONAL MUSEUMS
OF SCOTLAND

dramatic history. Detailed examination of the evidence on the ground may indicate that the camp was used on two separate periods, and only in the second was it used for artillery firing practice. The oddly sited fortlet would thus have been built in the north-east angle of an earlier camp, the advantage of re-using the earlier defences outweighing the disadvantage of the site's greater distance from the road. The presumed early Antonine date of the fortlet, together with the camp's 'un-Antonine' lack of regularity, makes it very likely that the latter dates to a much earlier campaign. Moreover, if all three *ballistaria* occupy original gateways, then the first phase camp can be most closely compared with a series of multiple-gated, irregularly-shaped camps in northern England. Being also equivalent in average area to the *combined* areas of the north and south

camps at Burnswark, the English sites, attributed to the campaigns of Petillius Cerealis in AD 71-74, provide a perfect match. IIf that analysis is correct, Burnswark may be the first site in Scotland at which we can identify a scene of military activity preceding that of Agricola, a temporary base of the army of Petillius Cerialis campaigning against some northern part of the Brigantes.

Casting a Long Shadow

The deep shadows of a late summer evening pick out the structural complexities of the artillery training camp at Burnswark, notably the reconstructed north-west side with its three massive ballista-platforms and the inset fortlet.
RCAHMS

Epilogue

It is now AD 411. Magnus Maximus is dead. Although initially successful, having disposed of Gratian, won control of Gaul, Germany, and Spain, and driven Valentinian II out of Italy, in AD 388 he had been drawn into battle with the forces of Theodosius the Great near Aquileia, at the head of the Adriatic. Maximus was defeated, captured, and executed. Seven years later when Theodosius died, the Empire was divided between his two sons, Arcadius and Honorius, under the tutelage of the Vandal generalissimo Count Stilicho; almost immediately the peace was shattered by a rising of Gothic mercenaries led by Alaric, who went on to sack Rome in AD 410. Britain, meanwhile, though rescued from Pictish harassment by Stilicho, had become dissatisfied with the level of support from central government and seen no fewer than three usurpers claim independence from Rome – the latest of these was Constantine III. Constantine, accompanied by the aged Justinianus, now a senior general, had taken an expeditionary force across the Channel to the continent in AD 407, partly to head off a Germanic invasion, and partly to establish an independent western empire of his own. However, in Gaul his luck is running out – one of his lieutenants, Gerontius (Geraint) has taken over a large part of the army and left Constantine under siege in the provincial capital of Arles. His former supporters in Britain have disowned him, seeking – unsuccessfully – to re-align themselves with Honorius. Loyally awaiting the end with his master, the aged Justinianus begins to write a letter to the daughter of his old friend, Magnus Maximus. . .

Execution of Maximus
'A dawn appointment with the headsman, three miles outside Aquileia.'
CHRIS BROWN

JUSTINIANUS COMES, SEVERAE MARCELLINAE SUAE, MAGNI MAXIMI AUGUSTI FILIAE, SALUTEM

scr. Coloniae Juliae Paternae
Sextanorum, Id. Mart., Constantino A. I. et Ignoto conss.

Rogabis forsitan qua re nunc demum scribam. . .

To Severa Marcellina, daughter of the Emperor Magnus
Maximus, Count Justinianus sends his greetings!

The City of Arles,
Gallia Viennensis,
15th March AD 411

You are probably asking, 'Why does he write now? It's more than twenty years since Aquileia.' Well, having thrown in my lot with our new British Constantine, I find myself once more on the losing side, penned up in Arles together with my imperial master and about a third of our field army.

Since the end cannot be far off, there are things I must tell you about your father and the unwritten legacy he bequeathed to Britannia. In the days when all the West was his, from the banks of the Rhine to the Pillars of Hercules, he had me join him on the continent to discuss the worsening situation. He had clearly foreseen the dangers that would threaten not only our provinces in Britannia but also the whole Empire. What use did it serve to have our armies securely lodged in their fortresses if they were surrounded by an ever more alien land? How long can we endure if the armies that defend the state are increasingly composed of the barbarian warriors who most recently battered at our gates?

Buried Treasure and the Church
The hoard of late-Roman hack-silver found in Trapain Law hillfort, East Lothian, included a flagon (right) depicting the infant Christ and Magi as well as a spoon (left) with the Chi-Rho symbol.
NATIONAL MUSEUMS OF SCOTLAND

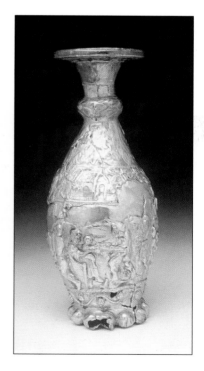

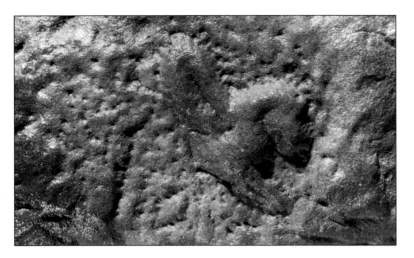

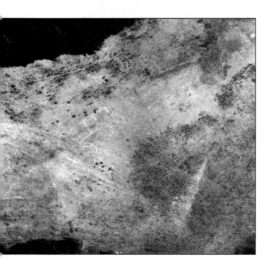

Your father saw that it didn't have to be like that. 'The commanders on the frontier have a duty of care,' he used to say, 'and those in their charge should expect that care to be exercised prudently'. In Britannia, he sought to reduce the military burden by cultivating harmonious links between the people and the administration, on both sides of the frontier. 'The Picts are not the real trouble,' he would say; 'like a wasps' nest, quite harmless till meddled with'. The problem, as he saw it, was to stop the *other* northern tribes becoming too meddlesome; if the Picts were half as bad as folk painted them (and the pun was his), their southern marches would lie closer to York than they do!

In consequence, before he took the troops across to Gaul, he made it his business to develop a real community of interest on the periphery of the outer provinces, not just Britons with Romans, but Britons with Britons. And the people he worked hardest to persuade were the rural magnates of the west and north: he was very successful with the rulers of the tribes beyond the Wall, especially the Damnonii and Novantae, who were already Romanised to the extent of adopting Roman names (partly a result of their conversion to the Christian faith). These were the sorts of people your father would single out for close attention. Of course, it helped enormously that, being a convert to Christianity, he could also claim the kinship of faith – kinship being so important to them.

However, as we knew, what could not be secured by prayer had to be procured by politics. And so we also bound the frontier peoples by solemn oaths and treaties, not just to Rome, but to each other. In theory, this means that if one sector suffers external attack, another will come to its aid, but, in practice, since most neighbouring groups are perennially at each others' throats, it will be a more distant sector (one probably not affected by the same threat) that brings assistance. Thus, if the Ordovices were attacked by the Scotti, it wouldn't be the Brigantes who responded but one of the more northerly tribes, and vice versa.

I'm glad that the arrangements made by Magnus in Britannia have so far proved successful, as I saw at first hand on my last tour of inspection north of the Wall. Apart from opportunistic raids,

the Picts have been discouraged from southward expansion, and the Scotti no longer find the Demetae on the coast of Wales such an attractive target. It's the seaborne threat from the Saxon east which has proved most dangerous, all the more so in the absence of the Expeditionary Force on the Continent. Heaven knows where that leaves us: a disinherited usurper with his army in Gaul, and Britannia defenceless in the face of Saxon assaults.

In short, I have the gravest misgivings. I know what weakness and divided loyalties can do to a country. You haven't seen, as I have, the grass growing rankly on the silent upland stretches of the Eagles' road that once linked the garrisons of the Wall with the shores of Tay and Forth. Only the wind moves now through the ruins of watch-posts and fortlets, way-stations and strongholds. Here and there local people have moved in to loot or squat, or quarry. At Trimontium [Newstead] it was a settlement of northerners, complete with underground storehouses, but even these are now dilapidated and abandoned; a little further on, their kinsfolk have dismantled a wayside monument built by the Second Legion in the time of the Antonines. A day's march beyond that, where a fort guarded the fords across the North Esk, the unit bath-house is being removed stone by stone, whenever

Heirs to the Roman Legacy
Among the traces of the rectilinear
field-system that once supported the
garrison and followers at Inveresk,
cropmarks reveal the presence of
oblong sunken-floored houses built by
Dark Age settlers exploiting the same
natural resources.
RCAHMS

there's a need for well-cut masonry. On the other hand, some of
the forts for example at Inveresk and Cramond have been given a
new, and not inappropriate, lease of life as the focus for local
native communities, reoccupying the lands that were theirs before
the Romans came. At Inveresk, the fort stood guard over some of
the richest land in the north, and the fields that once surrounded
it are once more vigorously productive.

At Cramond, on the other hand, the ground is generally fertile,
but the presence of a tenacious clay makes it hard to work. The
main attractions there are the protection afforded by the old fort's
curtain-wall and the quarrying resource so readily available, for,
unusually in this part of the frontier, the defences and internal
buildings were of stone. Another point in its favour is its still-usable
harbour (although this must be the only quayside in the Empire
where you tie your mooring-line to a lion's-head bollard – a
tombstone intended for the fort's graveyard which never quite
made it from ship to shore!) More significantly at both Isca and
Ambona there are active Christian communities; indeed, at
Ambona they meet for worship in the remains of the head-quarters
building, which would of course make an excellent church!

Thinking, too, of where the current crisis in Britannia may
lead, I ask myself: would it all have been different if Aquileia had
gone the other way? What kind of legacy would the 'emperor'
Magnus then have bequeathed? Success would have taken him
to Rome, or perhaps even to Constantinople, and victors do not

Beside the Seaside
A panoramic view of the village of
Cramond (?Ambona), with the ancient
harbour site below and the parish kirk
sitting squarely on top of the Roman
fort's headquarters building.
RCAHMS

necessarily leave richer legacies than victims. Yet, without a
doubt, your father has an enduring memorial, for he had a
dream: a dream of Empire. And by some miracle, in Britannia he
passed on his vision of what might yet come to pass, not just to
those already in power, but to the hill people of the north and
west, furnishing their minds with a memory of *Romanitas* that
will never be totally erased.

Emblem of Mortality
The stone image of a lioness recently
recovered from the foreshore at
Cramond was probably destined to
ennoble a grave in the cemetery
attached to the fort. A symbol of sudden
death, like other funerary emblems, the
carving also represented the survival of
the soul – a doubly appropriate token
for such a striking pointer to our
Roman heritage.
NATIONAL MUSEUMS OF SCOTLAND

As for the immediate future, however, I see no grounds for hope. Armies and emperors will come and go, and the people will be the poorer. But eventually, someone with power, vision, and luck will shepherd each province, diocese, and prefecture back into the one Western fold. He may not be a Roman – more likely an Ostrogoth or a Frank – but to succeed he must be another Magnus, and his legions will be seen as restoring the Light of Rome!

But enough of prophecy, for it is almost daybreak, and the runner has come who shall, God willing, sneak this letter through the siege-lines.

Farewell.

Shortly after this letter was written, Arles fell to the armies of Honorius, and Constantine was executed; of Geraint and Justinianus nothing more is heard. Britain, though now stripped of an imperial defence force, in the sense that the troops that now remained were no longer paid by central government, still considered itself 'Roman', not least because it was still part of the universal Christian Church. Nor was this a one-way view. In AD 429 the bishops of Auxerre and Troyes visited the south of Britain to rescue the British church from the clutches of heresy, and one of them, St Germanus, returning in AD 446-7, became a temporary resistance leader against an invasion of Saxons and Picts. It is possible that this moral support was supplied in lieu of the military aid allegedly sought about this time from Aetius, the Empire's supreme commander in Gaul, by the leaders of the southern communities; such a request (which the roughly contemporary historian Gildas called 'The Groans of the Britons') would not have been thought outrageous by an administration whose hopes of recovering Britain had allowed lists of her long-disbanded garrison to remain on imperial files. Unfortunately, the southern communities in question were already divided by factional strife: Vortigern, traditionally identified as both the son-in law of Magnus Maximus and the person responsible for inviting Saxon mercenaries into Britain, was at feud with Ambrosius Aurelianus (whose family may also have claimed imperial descent). The stage was thus set for Romano-British society to disintegrate into a maze of warring minor states, gradually overwhelmed by external foes. Despite this, throughout southern and western Britain there lingered memories of a Roman past which were nurtured by something more than just the presence of Christian believers and the existence of trade-links with the Late Roman world. Among these memories, the role played by Magnus Maximus is curiously prominent, especially among the traditions of the British tribes of Wales (in whose eyes he achieved heroic status

Birrens Altar Stone
Roman altar dedicated to *Disciplina Augusti* by Antonine troops at Birrens, Dumfries and Galloway. The dedication links two ideas: obedience to the Emperor and military efficiency – doubly appropriate for a garrison stationed near the field-training school at Burnswark.
NATIONAL MUSEUMS OF SCOTLAND

Sub-Roman Scotland
Of the many Latin-inscribed stones associated with Early Christian graves in southern Scotland, one of the most interesting is the Yarrow Stone from Selkirkshire. It commemorates two local Dark Age chieftains, Nudos and Dumnogenos. Its reference to them as the 'most renowned princes' (*insignissimi principes*) echoes not only Church Latin, but also the grandiloquent titles of the Late Empire and perhaps Byzantium.
RCAHMS

as Macsen Wledig). But even in Scotland traces of his influence may have lingered – whether in the belief that the royal house of Strathclyde was descended from Maximus, or in the alleged resettlement of Votadini from around Stirling to west Wales, as a defence against marauding Scots. Elsewhere to the north of the Wall there is little concrete evidence of Roman influence beyond what may be attributed to the activity of the early Christian church. On the other hand, that northern church sprang from a Roman model rooted in the late fourth-century province, and who is to say that its survival long after the legions had departed, is not as valid a token of Maximus' achievements on the frontier as any dynastic legacy?

TIMELINE

Year AD	Event	Emperor
43	Invasion of Britain	Claudius
60–61	Revolt of Boudica	Nero
71–74	Petillius Cerealis governor, campaigns in N. England	Vespasian
74–77	Julius Frontinus governor, campaigns in Wales	Vespasian
77–83	Julius Agricola governor, Scottish campaigns	Vespasian, Titus and Domitian
86–87	Northern conquests given up	Domitian
100–105	Retreat to Tyne-Solway	Nerva and Trajan
122	Hadrian's Wall begun	Hadrian
142–144	Antonine Wall built	Antonius Pius
c. 158	?Re-organisation of frontier	Antonius Pius
c. 163–168	?Antonine Scotland given up	Marcus Aurelius
c. 180–184	Hadrian's Wall attacked	Commodus
197	Govern Albinus makes bid for imperial throne and Wall assailed by northern tribes	Pertinax, Julianus and Severus
208–211	Septimius Severus campaigns against Maeatae and Caledonii dies at York	Septimius Severus
212–215	Caracalla abandons northern outposts in Scotland	Caracalla
287–296	Carausius unsurps power	Constantius Chlorus
305–306	Constantius Chlorus campaigns against Caledonians 'and other Picts' and dies at York	Constantius Chlorus
c. 315	?Successful campaign against Picts	Constantine I
343	?Pictish unrest	Constans
360	Scots and Picts attack frontier areas	Constantius II
364–369	Picts (comprising Verturions and Dicalydones) rebuffed by Count Theodosius	Valentinian I
382–383	Invading Picts and Scots defeated by Magnus Maximus, who usurps power	Theodosius I
396–398	Pictish attack countered by Stilicho	Honorius
407	British usurper Constantine III siezes power	Honorius
409–410	Britain rejects Constantine III and is given control of its own affairs	Honorius
429–446	Last links and appeals for help	Valentinian III

'Roman Scotland' (bracket spanning 71–74 to 212–215)

Flavian (bracket spanning 71–74 to 86–87)

How Do I Find Out More?

Sites To Visit

Visible traces of Roman military structures are to be found in many parts of Scotland south of the Grampians. Unfortunately, it is not always the most important sites that are best preserved, nor are these a wholly representative sample of the various defence systems of which they once formed part. Furthermore, most having been built in such impermanent materials as turf and timber, and rarely of stone, their remains often seem difficult to appreciate on the ground, and even when excavated cannot be presented to the visitor with the structural impact of, say, a chambered tomb or a stone circle. Nevertheless, their regular plan and the knowledge that we possess about their function often help us to see them more clearly in meaningful relationship to an ancient landscape, especially in the case of the larger monuments, like roads and temporary camps, which may even bulk large in the modern countryside.

A number of the sites listed below are opened to the public by Historic Scotland (HS) or other agencies (P), but many are in private ownership and permission should be sought from the owner before making a visit; due care should of course be taken, to avoid both damage to the monument and any personal injury arising from, for example, rough or uneven ground. The sites are grouped alphabetically in local authority areas, with Ordnance Survey grid references indicating their location.

Aberdeenshire

Durno – very large marching-camp (58ha), probably used by the army of Agricola on its way to the battle of *Mons Graupius* in AD 83; no traces of the camp above ground, but the view from within it, looking south towards 528m-high Bennachie (thought by some to be *Graupius* itself), embraces a magnificent possible battlefield.
NJ 699272.

Raedykes – 38ha marching-camp, probably Agricolan, its very irregular defence-circuit is visible on the ground for much of the perimeter.
NO 841902.

Borders

Brownhart Law – fortlet guarding upland sector of Roman road Dere Street, midway on a highly walkable route from Pennymuir (q.v.) across the Border to the complex of Roman works at Chew Green in England.
NT 790096.

Channelkirk – very large and irregularly shaped Severan marching-camp (65ha), adjoining Roman road Dere Street at south end of particularly well-preserved upland sector of several km.
NT 473548.

Eildon Hill – very large (16ha) prehistoric hillfort occupying the northernmost of the three-peaked Eildon Hills; on the summit, surrounded by the scooped platforms of Iron Age timber houses, there is the penannular ditch of a Roman signal-station.
NT 554328.

Lyne – the visible earthworks of an Antonine fort occupy a prominent position in a bend of the Lyne Water; invisible nearby lie the remains of temporary camps and a fortlet, as well as, on the opposite bank, the Flavian fort of Easter Happrew.
NT187405.

Newstead – situated in a classic bridgehead position on the south bank of the Tweed, and at the foot of the imposing Eildon massif, the superimposed remains of at least four forts and their annexes, together with several hundred hectares occupied by large marching-camps of all periods; few visible traces, but as evidence of Roman 'eye' for ground, an unsurpassed location.
NT 571343.

Pennymuir – beside the Roman road Dere Street lie the superimposed remains of two marching-camps, the defence-perimeter of both surviving almost intact; the truncated traces of two more can be made out in pasture to the east. Immediately to the south rises Woden Law, where a native hillfort is enclosed within earthworks once thought to be Roman siege-lines.
NT755140.

Central Scotland

Bar Hill – fort on the Antonine Wall, but detached from the barrier; internal buildings of stone (headquarters, bath-house and latrine); adjacent stretch of the Wall itself, bypassing prehistoric hillfort (HS).
NS 707759.

Bearsden – bathhouse suite of Antonine Wall fort consolidated after excavation (HS).
NS545720.

Braidwood to Carlops – fine upland stretch of Roman road with occasional quarry-pits.
NT 165565 to 192592.

Castle Greg – surprisingly well-preserved early Flavian fortlet, unassociated with road-system and displaying parrot's-beak ditch terminals (P).
NT 050592.

Cramond – site of coastal fort and large extramural settlement of Antonine and Severan date, now overlain by village of Cramond; some internal buildings (headquarters, granary and workshops) consolidated after excavation (P).
NT 189768.

Croy Hill – magnificent upland stretch of the Antonine Wall, the ditch here being rock-cut, and including the sites of a Wall-fort (and fortlet), as well as possible beacon-platforms (HS).
NS 722762 to 741770.

Inveresk — site of coastal cavalry fort and large extramural settlement of Antonine date, now overlain respectively by churchyard and modern Inveresk; remains of hypocausted building in adjacent private garden.
NT 342720.

Kinneil – site of Antonine Wall-fortlet excavated and consolidated (P), with adjacent traces of the barrier overlooking the estuarine waters of the Forth.
NS 977803.

Rough Castle – very well preserved defensive perimeter of Antonine Wall fort (including the famous 'lily-bed' man-traps), with nearby beacon-platforms and magnificent adjoining sectors of the barrier itself (the ditch and counterscarp bank being especially impressive)(HS).
NS 834798 to 856798.

Seabegs Wood – well preserved stretch of the Antonine Wall, the counterscarp bank being particularly remarkable; at the west end the dog-leg change of alignment indicates the presence of a Wall-fortlet (HS&P).
NS 811791 to 815793.

Clydesdale

Bothwellhaugh, Strathclyde Park – Antonine fort and bathhouse, the defences of the former faintly visible, but in a commanding position, the latter excavated and reconstructed (P).
NS 731577.

Cleghorn – marching-camp of c. 18ha and probably Antonine, the north rampart, with two tutulus-guarded gates, preserved in Camp Wood.
NS 910459.

Crawford – small Agricolan and Antonine fort, guarding an important road-junction; its position is indicated by the prominent rectangular platform to the north-west of the medieval motte; the Roman road can be followed for several kilometres to north and south.
NS953214.

Daer to Potrail Water – fine stretch of Roman road leading south-west from Crawford (q.v.), with quarry-pits, stream crossings, and well preserved road-mound; connects with Durisdeer (q.v. Dumfries and Galloway).
NS 915059 to 956163.

Little Clyde – marching-camp of probable Antonine date; sections of rampart and ditch survive (including gate with tutulus), but most significant is the absolute regularity of plan on very awkward terrain.
NS 994159.

Redshaw Burn – Antonine fortlet guarding upland road-sector between Clyde and Annan; road well worth walking, despite enveloping forestry, to connect with White Type watch-tower (q.v. Dumfries and Galloway) on south-east.
NT 030139.

Dumfries and Galloway

Birrens – conspicuous earthworks of large fort occupied in the Flavian, Hadrianic, and Antonine periods. NY 219752.

Burnswark – splendidly preserved and very important complex of structures, adjoining large prehistoric hillfort and comprising temporary camps of various periods as well as long-axis Antonine fortlet, the former holding troops engaged in field-firing exercises. NY 186787.

Drumlanrig – platform of presumed Agricolan and Antonine bridgehead fort above the Nith, conspicuous amidst landscaped policies of major country seat (P). NX 854989.

Durisdeer – well preserved long-axis Antonine fortlet in impressive position guarding upland pass; the Roman road leading from Clydesdale into Nithsdale very well preserved in this sector, connecting with Daer-Potrail Water stretch (q.v. Clydesdale). NX 902048.

Raeburnfoot – small Antonine bridgehead fort enclosed by annexe, the defences of both being exceptionally well-preserved. NY 251990.

White Type – Antonine roadside watch-tower with extensive views from the Devil's Beeftub southward into Annandale; rare example – small, but beautifully preserved. NT 055119 .

Perthshire and Angus

Ardoch – outstandingly important complex, comprising multi-period fort with splendidly preserved defences and annexes, together with several temporary camps of various sizes and dates (P). NN839099.

Black Hill, Meikleour – Flavian watch-tower on isolated hillock guarding north-east approaches to Inchtuthil (q.v.). NO176391.

Fendoch – Flavian glen-blocking fort of earth and timber, its classic site indicated by prominent platform facing the mouth of the Sma Glen, with contemporary watch-tower on high ground 800m to the north-west. NN 919283.

Gask Ridge – series of Flavian watch-towers (some HS) adjoining Roman road between the Earn and the Tay, much of which underlies public highway or forestry track. NN 917185 to NO 020205.

Inchtuthil – Flavian legionary fortress, enclosure and temporary camps, occupying plateau on north bank of the Tay; much of the defence-perimeter of the fortress remains visible in pasture, together with contemporary compound, and superimposed Dark Age burial-mounds. NO125397.

Innerpeffray – in southern fringes of wood, a stretch of the north rampart and ditch of 53ha Severan marching-camp, as well as well-preserved Flavian watch-tower to the north, looking on to westward extension of the Gask Ridge road (q.v.). NN 916184.

Kaims Castle – remains of double-ditched Flavian fortlet with adjacent stretch of Roman causeway, associated with possible Forth-Tay watch-tower system, crowns hillock in loop of modern road north of Ardoch (q.v.). NN 860129.

Kirkbuddo – considerable length of rampart and ditch of 25ha Severan marching-camp. NO 491442.

(above)

Lowland Watch and Ward

At Murder Loch, on the route from
Annandale to lower Nithsdale, a small
roadside post has succumbed to intensive
cultivation, now recognisable only as a
pattern of cropmarks.

RCAHMS

(right)

Dalginross Fort, near Comrie

A classic cropmark representation of a
Roman fort founded in the Agricolan
period and re-occupied in the Antonine.

RCAHMS

Museums

Within the areas identified above, most local authority museums will include displays of Roman material, those at Dumfries, Dundee, Falkirk and Perth being able to draw on a wealth of artefacts from neighbouring sites, while specifically site-related museums, such as Kinneil House and Melrose (for Newstead), are also well worth a visit. Pride of place must go to the Roman collections housed in the new Museum of Scotland, Chambers Street, Edinburgh, and the Hunterian Museum of the University of Glasgow (both of which may be accessed on the Internet). Of further interest is the possibility that the Archaeolink Prehistory Park at Oyne, Aberdeenshire, may soon include among its exhibits a reconstruction of a Roman marching-camp of Stracathro type!

Further Reading

- *Roman Scotland*, David Breeze (Batsford 1996).

- *The Romans in Scotland*, Gordon Maxwell (Mercat Press 1989).

- *Scotland's Roman Remains*, Lawrence Keppie (John Donald 1986).

- *Oxford Illustrated History of Roman Britain*, Peter Salway (Oxford University Press 1993).

- *Roman Britain from the Air*, Sheppard Frere and Kenneth St Joseph (Cambridge University Press 1983).

- *Agricola and the Conquest of the North*, William Hanson (Batsford 1987).

- *A Battle Lost: Romans and Caledonians at Mons Graupius*, Gordon Maxwell (Edinburgh University Press 1990).

- *Rome's North-West Frontier: the Antonine Wall*, William Hanson and Gordon Maxwell (Edinburgh University Press 1983).

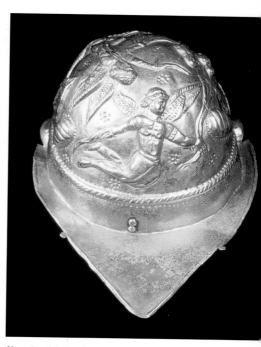

Newstead helmet
An expensive and richly decorated cavalry helmet from Newstead which would not have been exposed to the hazards of the battlefield.
NATIONAL MUSEUMS OF SCOTLAND

Note: Magnus Maximus and Justinianus are real historical figures, though there is no evidence that they were involved jointly in any of the events described in this book. That Vortigern, by tradition a leading figure in fifth-century Britain, was Maximus' son-in-law, is actually recorded on the Pillar of Eliseg, a ninth-century memorial in Powys; the name of Maximus' daughter, however, has been invented. The title of this book refers to Matthew's Gospel, chapter 24, verse 28: 'Wheresoever the carcass is, there will the eagles be gathered together.'

Acknowledgements

I am very grateful to the many friends and colleagues who have helped in the preparation and production of this book: for editorial contributions far beyond the call of duty, to Gordon Barclay and Jackie Henrie; to Hugh Andrew for invaluable advice and encouragement; to Chris Brown and Sylvia Stevenson respectively for the reconstructions and line-drawings that so handsomely amplify the text; to staff of the National Monuments Record Photographic Section, and Drawing Office of the Royal Commission of the Ancient and Historical Monuments of Scotland (RCAHMS), who assembled much of the additional illustrative material, as also to Donald Reid for putting the resultant collection in due order. My thanks are also expressed to the following organisations and individuals for their permission to reproduce specific illustrations: the Royal Commission on the Historical Monuments of England, copyright holder of the illustration on page 17; the Society of Antiquaries of London, copyright holder of the illustrations on pages 19 (top) and 42 (bottom); Lawrence Keppie and the Glasgow Archaeological Society, copyright holder of the illustration on page 44 (bottom right); David Breeze; Angus Lamb; Historic Scotland; the Hunterian Museum, University of Glasgow; National Museums of Scotland; and the RCAHMS.